Also by Grace Young

The Wisdom of the Chinese Kitchen

Also by Alan Richardson

The Four Seasons of Italian Cooking

Opposite page and following spread: Calligraphy for book title and authors' bylines by Cheng Huan Chen.

The Breath of a Wok

Unlocking
the Spirit of
Chinese Wok Cooking
Through Recipes and Lore

Grace Young and Alan Richardson

With Text and Recipes by Grace Young

Simon & Schuster

New York   London   Toronto   Sydney

鑊 Wok, *n.* a boiler or cauldron; an iron pan.

氣 Hay, *n.* breath, energy, spirit.

護氣

作者 楊玉華

攝影者 利雄仁

SIMON & SCHUSTER
Rockefeller Center
1230 Avenue of the Americas
New York, NY 10020

For information regarding special discounts for bulk purchases,
please contact Simon & Schuster Special Sales at
1-800-456-6798 or business@simonandschuster.com.

Designed and produced by Alan Richardson for Plenty Works, Inc., New York, NY
Type consulting by Smythtype, Montclair, NJ
Chinese typography by Birdtrack Press, New Haven, CT
Color prints by Color Resource Center, New York, NY

Manufactured in the United States of America

10   9   8   7   6   5   4   3   2   1

Library of Congress Cataloging-in-Publication Data

Young, Grace.
        The breath of a wok: unlocking the spirit of chinese wok cooking through recipes and lore /
    by Grace Young and Alan Richardson.
        p.   cm.
    Includes bibliographical references and index.
    1. Cookery, Chinese. 2. Wok cookery. 3. Food habits—China. I. Richardson, Alan. II. Title.
TX724.5.C5Y593   2004
641.5951—dc22   2003070403

ISBN 0-7432-3827-3

In memory of my uncle Thomas Jew. His love of family, friends, and the pleasure of cooking lives on. And for Michael.

—GY

In memory of my mother, who gave me a taste for good cooking; and my father, who told me to find myself a good cook. And to Larry, who makes a great gravy.

—AR

感
謝

Acknowledgments

This book would not have been possible without the encouragement and love of my husband, Michael Wiertz, who understood the need for all my wok journeys and good-naturedly accepted that every adventure brought home at least one new wok for my collection. In the midst of all the upheaval that results from creating a book, he was a paragon of calm. For this and much more, I am grateful.

I would like to express my appreciation to my parents, Helen and Delwyn Young, for instilling in me their love and passion for Cantonese cuisine and the unsurpassed brilliance of a stir-fry with *wok hay*. Many thanks to them for their faith in me.

Special thanks to Rosanna and C.Y. Shum; my visit with them in Hong Kong in 2000 indulged me in the fascinating world of Hong Kong–style cooking and in many ways inspired the writing of this book.

From the beginning, Martha Kaplan, my agent and friend, has championed this project and offered wise counsel—usually over a Chinese meal. As the book began to take shape, my dear friend Laura Cerwinske generously did the preliminary editing of my rough drafts, helping me to set the foundation of my story. It was my good fortune to have my uncle Sun Yui Fung give the Chinese titles for each essay and section of the book. He has been a constant advisor from the beginning, patiently researching and consulting on any type of Chinese cultural question that confused me.

I owe a special debt of gratitude to Evie Righter, who came to my rescue on numerous occasions, providing invaluable editorial guidance on the recipes and essays. Her critiques always illuminated the material, offering insights and clarity that eluded me.

In writing this book, Alan and I have had the extraordinary pleasure of meeting many great teachers who generously shared their expertise and friendship. Our profound thanks to the home cooks and chefs who graciously welcomed us into their kitchens.

In the United States: Chef Susanna Foo, Winnie Hon, Chef Henry Hugh, Susan Lin, Julie Tay, Ken Lo, Dr. and Mrs. Kam Toa Miu, Margaret Loo, Bernadette Chan, Chef Ming Tsai, Helen Chen, Chef Danny Chan, Peipei Chang, Jean Yueh, Millie Chan, Florence Lin, Chef Martin Yan, Chef Siu Chah Lung, Ray Lee, Cecilia Chiang, Che Chung Ng, Dickson Hee, Amy Tan, Lou DeMattei, Jin Do Eng, Lijun Wan, Yuhang Wang, Hong Chang Guo, and Yan Zheng Yan.

Heartfelt gratitude and appreciation to the cooks in my family, with special thanks to my auntie and uncle Betty and Roy Lim for hosting our family wok-a-thon party—without their gracious hospitality the event would never have happened. And to all the participants: Bertha Jew; Lillian and William Jew; Frances and Sherman Young; Katherine Jew Lim; Doreen and Mel Song; Sylvia, Fred, and Thomas Chow; Cindy and Zane Matsuzaki; Judy, David, and Timothy Jew.

In Hong Kong and China: Virginia Yee, Tina Yao Lu, Mary Chau, Nevin Lim, Chef Kevin Chuk, Walter Kei, Chef Ip Chi Cheung, Chef Lee Wan Ching, Chef Yip Wing Wah, Chef Poon Chi Cheung, Mr. and Mrs. Yang Lang Ping (Uncle Lang and Auntie Yi), and Liang Nian Xiu.

There are several individuals mentioned in the long list of cooks we interviewed whose contributions extended far beyond our cooking sessions. We are profoundly grateful to Florence Lin, who consulted on numerous culinary questions with exceptional grace and generosity.

Without Millie Chan we would have never had the opportunity to meet Florence Lin. Millie was one of the first cooks we interviewed and from the start of the project she and her husband, Lo-Yi, have been great supporters.

I will always treasure the time spent with my Uncle Lang and Auntie Yi in Foshan, China. When I last saw them over twenty years ago, our relationship was much more formal. I was very touched to be welcomed into their home to spend an afternoon cooking and sharing a meal. I thank them for embracing our project and tirelessly accompanying us to the local markets, *dai pai dong*, and even organizing cooking sessions with their friends.

Thanks also to my cousin and his wife, Mr. and Mrs. Yang Zhi Xiang.

Liang Nian Xiu's hospitality gave us an extraordinary experience during our time in Yangshuo. Beyond our fascinating cooking session with Liang, she also understood our mission and took us on an unforgettable tour of the region that revealed much of the wok culture we sought.

Special thanks to Ken Hom, who found time between his commitments in Europe and Asia for an extensive interview.

Upon arriving in Hong Kong, Walter Chu was instrumental in getting us started with a memorable day-long walk through Kowloon and providing important local information. My interviews with Vivien Cheung, Teddy Leung, Chef Paray Li, Chef Ip Chi Kwong, Chef Ronald Shao, and Chef Cheung Chin Choi also contributed greatly to our understanding of the subtleties of wok cooking. We are also grateful to Nevin Lim—his knowledge of Hong Kong history and Cantonese cuisine was indispensable.

Many individuals helped in our quest to find the talented home cooks and chefs we interviewed. We would like to thank: Ivy Fung, Margaret Sheridan, R. T. Yao, Linda Yao, Tony Yao, Theresa Wang Yao, Mary Yao, Lucy Fong, Susan Yoshimura, Howard Goodman, Teresa Delaney, Nick Malgieri, Marie Lam, Grace Choi, Tammy Shueh, Mimi Chan, Michael Chang and Diana Budiman of the Hong Kong Tourist Association, Sian Griffiths of the Peninsula hotel in Hong Kong, Christina Choy of the Chinese Cuisine Training Institute in Hong Kong, and Gary Goldberg of the New School Culinary Arts program in New York City. From the Shangri-La hotel thanks to Judy Reeves in New York City, Patsy Chan in Kowloon, and Cindi Li in Shanghai.

Special thanks to my cousin Fred Chow, who orchestrated several cooking sessions. Fred put us in touch with Yee Ming Ting in Shanghai, who arranged for Joyce Yang's much needed services as a translator for our interviews in Shanghainese. He is also responsible for the idea of the wok-a-thon.

I am grateful to the following individuals and institutions for their help in researching the history of the wok in America: Professor Priscilla Wegars, Professor Jeffrey Barlow, Maxine Chan, Emma Louie, Lisa See, Roberta Greenwood, David Kerkkonen, Bill G. Quackenbush, Jeannie Woo, Judy Lu, Ralph Eubanks, Joe Evans, Carolyn Micnhimer, David Kessler, California Historical Society, Kam Wah Chung & Co. Museum, Chinese Historical Society of San Francisco, and the Bancroft Library, UC Berkeley.

Many thanks to Professor Mark Swislocki, Alice Lowe, John Stuckey, Professor E. N. Anderson, and Jackie Newman for their assistance in finding historical information on the wok.

As my wok education evolved I discovered I needed to understand technical information. Cen Lian Gen, Robert Wolke, Jim Cassidy of Precision Metal Spinning, Inc., Joseph Yick, Daniel Dechamps, and Chan Kai Yuen are responsible for teaching me about the nature of carbon steel, cast iron, and wok fabrication. Wen Geng Lin, Shelley Smyers, Professor Yih-Shen Hwang, Sui Wan Lok, Kenny Leung, and Tanya Leung provided valuable information on seasoning a wok. I am also grateful to Chef Paul Muller, Chef Che Heng Lee, Judy Wong, Chef Huang Zhen Hua, David Ostwald, and Martha Dahlen for contributing their expertise.

Heartfelt thanks to Tane Chan of The Wok Shop for sharing her vast knowledge and passion for woks. I was charmed by her energy, humor, and devotion as a "wokker."

I offer special thanks to our editor, Sydny Miner, for her superb editing and unwavering support throughout this project. It has also been a pleasure to work with the remarkable team at Simon & Schuster. Many thanks to Victoria Meyer, Aileen Boyle, Tracey Guest, and Chris Wahlers for their support in publicity; Jonathan Brodman, production editor, for his astute handling of the text; Ginger McCrae for her fine copyediting; and Laura Holmes for her assistance. We are especially grateful to Judy Eda for her impeccable proofreading.

We would also like to acknowledge David Sablan Camacho, who generously offered his flat in

Acknowledgments

Hong Kong as a home base during our research and for lending his antique plates for the food photography. Special thanks for sharing his vast knowledge of China and for answering my many questions with patience and good humor.

Heartfelt gratitude to Ray Furse, who consulted on various aspects of the book, generously offering amazing contacts and resources, and sharing his expertise on Chinese culture.

Our deepest thanks to Cheng Huan Chen for the beautiful calligraphy that graces the jacket and title page, and to Dr. Siong Chuan Lee for making this possible. My thanks also to Jeanyee Wong, who provided the calligraphy for the proposal.

As a result of *The Breath of a Wok,* a wok exhibition is planned for New York University in New York City, and for the Portland Classical Chinese Garden in Oregon. My profound thanks to Professor Barbara Kirschenblatt-Gimblett for providing the seed for this idea. I would also like to thank Professor John Kuo Wei Tchen, Carolyn Goldstein, Barbara Haber, Dr. Nancy Jervis, Marsha Matthews, Laura Chen-Schultz, Fannie Chan, Dr. Rubie Watson, Karen Karp, Lesley Wright, Tomas Rojas, Reggie Bardach, Richard Wells, Aaron Paley, Blake Van Roekel, and Franklin Odo.

My friends have been an enormous blessing, offering unflagging support and encouragement through some of the more challenging phases. Heartfelt thanks to Ragnhild Wagenhofer, Michael Zande, J. Robert Purdom, Dr. Joan Golden, Michelle Steffens, Linda Campbell Franklin, Bonnie Slotnick, Andrea DiNoto, Heinrich and Hildegarde Wiertz, Erika and Herri Wiertz, Ulrike Carpus, Janice Easton-Epner, Dr. Kevin Caroll, Marjorie Poore, Alex Fatalevich, Doralece Dullaghan, Kim Park, Andy Clurfeld, Gale Steves, Sunny and Bud Taylor, Amy Besa and Chef Romy Dorotan of Cendrillon restaurant in New York City; and to my godmothers, Anna Kwock and Ronnie Wei Gin.

Special thanks to my cousins Sylvia Chow and Katherine Jew Lim for always looking after me. And to Scott Hunt, whose humor and friendship are precious gifts.

I am forever grateful to Tom Hicks for bequeathing me his well-seasoned flat-bottomed wok.

In closing, my profound thanks to Alan Richardson. With his unerring vision, he has married the text and his elegant photographs to create a book that captures the essence of *wok hay.* It has been an honor and privilege to work with Alan. Many thanks for teaching me the unique beauty of a collaborative effort—I am forever spoiled.

And finally to Henry-san, who sat by my side throughout the writing. You are always in my heart.

—GY

The list of individuals who helped me directly or indirectly with the book is largely synonymous with Grace's, and I want to thank all of those people, too. We realized after each leg of the journey how many people were being so amazingly generous, and we share a deep gratitude to everyone who helped us along the way. But there were a few individuals who gave enormously of their time and knowledge and who did not overlap with Grace's endeavors.

First and foremost, I make few decisions without the input of my partner, Larry Frascella, who is my best friend and bravest advisor. Larry listens to every idea and brings to it the discerning ear of the critic. I value his insight along with his support. As for the rest of my family, a book is a time-consuming commitment, and at times they have taken a backseat to the work process. Thanks to Sarah for making me think, Anna for making me smile, Lawrence for making me laugh, and Laura Mecca for keeping us all together. I want to thank Eleanor, Mai, and the Brown family for all of their patience; and I am grateful to Debby Paull, Kelly Hughes, Robyn Manuel, and Cara Walker for their understanding. Thank you to Antonis Achilleos and Alessandra Mortola, who listen to the difficulties as well as offer constant support and friendship.

The work of crafting a book has many phases, but there were two individuals whose assistance stretched from the beginning to the end of this project. I want to thank Roy Galaday, who was there for me every day from the beginning—when he was hoping that I could somehow ship him off to China with us—to the end, when he was printing the most beautiful rendition possible of every black-and-white image that I managed to bring back. And heartfelt thanks to Cathy Weiner for letting me tap her insightful design and art opinions again and again, and still having the skill to keep it all moving forward.

I am indebted to our editor, Sydny Miner, who through a rare combination of trust and vigilance gave us the freedom to be creative. Martha Kaplan, our agent, came to me by way of Grace and I am very thankful for that. Martha had a thoughtful answer for every dilemma and never steered us wrong.

My dear friend Laura Dwight introduced me to photography many years ago and has given me valuable advice and support on all of my projects, including the making of this book. Early on I went to my design and taste consultants, my friends Anne Disrude and Betty Alfenito, who gave me excellent advice, especially with the recipe design and book layout. My friend Maria McBride has been through the publishing trenches with me and still finds ways to surprise me with her ideas, friendship, and constant championing of our book; thanks. I want to thank Amadeo Lasansky for offering advice whenever it was needed on everything ranging from camera equipment to computers to printing to traveling in China. I want to thank my friend Ming Tsai for giving generously of his time and expertise.

On the production end, I want to single out first Kishore Kinge of Color Resource Center in New York City. Many of the beautiful color images in the book were printed by Kishore; he is a gifted artist. Special thanks to Neil Nanda and Brian Joseph at CRC for their tremendous help with the color images for the book and exhibition.

Laura Smyth of Smythtype in Montclair, NJ, not only did a terrific job consulting on the type design, she was an incredible source of information throughout the production of the book. Thanks to Laura and Elmore Reese for all of their hard work and advice.

I want to thank Chris Frape for putting us in touch with Dennis George Crow, and Dennis for offering his vintage photography resources to the book. Some aspects of the book have required more attention than might be obvious. The Chinese characters for the headlines were put together by Birdtrack Press in New Haven, CT, and I want to thank David Goodrich, who gave much thought, care, and scholarship to the production of that text. At Simon & Schuster, Jonathon Brodman did terrific work on the book; Linda Evans, Linda Dingler, Alyssa Tarragano, and Jackie Seow deserve much credit for their production and art expertise.

Lastly, I want to thank my friend Grace Young. From our earliest musings about the wok, and throughout our collaboration in search of it, she has proven to be a rigorous journalist with the heart of a poet. Grace doesn't surprise me anymore because I have come to expect the exceptional from her.

—AR

Photography Note
The photographs for this book, like the text, were shaped by our journey, and their content evolved as the story unfolded and our knowledge of the wok broadened. All of the photographs, with the few exceptions of the identification shots in the wok-buying guide and the glossary, were taken on location while on the wok trail. The food photographs were taken just as our cooks prepared them. There was no food stylist, although Grace and I both had input on how they were presented, and the dishes we used in the photographs were mostly what we found at the location or were able to pick up along the way. In China our photographic resources were limited and we came to rely on our instincts as street photographers and the use of natural light. Fortunately, the subject took control of the process and the resulting images, though edited to tell our story, are a fair representation of our journey in search of the wok.

—AR

Contents

信

The Breath of a Wok

Introduction

One wok runs to the sky's edge

—Traditional saying

My fascination with the wok began at an early age. From the time I was a child, I was taught to respect *wok hay*—the prized, elusive, seared taste that comes only from stir-frying in a wok. I remember our family dinners in San Francisco's Chinatown as lessons in Chinese culinary appreciation. My father, Baba, knew all the best chefs, and rather than order from the menu, his custom was to stroll into a restaurant's kitchen to discuss with the chef what was best to eat that day. A reserved man, he rarely displayed his emotions, but those visits to the kitchen always charged him with an infectious excitement. "I asked the chef to give us extra *wok hay* tonight," he would tell us,

一
鑊
走
天
涯

When the first dish arrived, usually Baba's favorite— a stir-fry of clams in black bean sauce or a simple stir-fry of ginger and Chinese broccoli—it was wickedly hot, perfumed with an intoxicating aroma. "*Ni dib sung yao wok hay*" (This dish has *wok hay*), Baba would declare, highly pleased. We admired the dish as if we had won a prize. Then, knowing *wok hay* lingers only for a few minutes, we would relish those first irresistible succulent morsels. The taste, the experience of *wok hay*, always conferred a feeling of our good fortune.

Baba liked to describe how the chef had cooked such delicious food: "The powerful flames heat the giant woks until they are nearly red-hot," he'd tell us. "The chef stir-fries the dish in a matter of moments, often manning two woks simultaneously." I wanted so much to see for myself, but it was unthinkable for a little girl to enter a restaurant kitchen. Still, it was easy for me to imagine *wok hay* as the fiery breath of a wok, imparting a special life force or essence from the wok into the food. In my father's dialect, Cantonese, *hay* (more familiar to non-Chinese readers spelled *chi* or *qi*, from the Mandarin pronunciation of the character) is breath—the Chinese concept of vital energy that flows through the body.

On occasion, the restaurant's chef would come out of the kitchen to visit our table. My parents, delighted, showered him with praise, acknowledging his expertise. "The Cantonese chefs are the masters of stir-frying—only they know how to achieve *wok hay*," my father would boast. While the chef would smile humbly, he nevertheless would always nod in agreement. I felt as though I was meeting a celebrity after an outstanding performance.

When I was ten years old my family visited Hong Kong, where my father took every opportunity to point out how the Cantonese excelled in stir-frying. We saw *dai pai dong*, outdoor food stalls where cooks stir-fried in woks alongside their customers. We ate in fine restaurants and were invited to dine in friends' homes. Regardless of the locale, the stir-fries had an intense *wok hay* that was unlike anything I had tasted before. It was in Hong Kong that I realized the connoisseurship of *wok hay*

extended beyond my parents. Aunties, uncles, and family friends were equally discerning and critical, forever discussing the merits of a dish.

When my parents cooked at home, they also aspired to stir-fries with the ineffable *wok hay*. Their efforts began with shopping and selecting only vegetables in season. If an ingredient was not fresh, my parents taught me, no matter how great the technique, it would be impossible to achieve *wok hay*.

When my parents married in 1949, my mother, newly arrived from China, did not know how to cook. I used to wonder if wanting to become assimilated had influenced her decision to adopt some Western customs into her life, such as using modern American cookware. Of course flat-bottomed woks did not exist in America at that time, and from a practical point of view, a skillet attained the heat so necessary for stir-frying far better than a round-bottomed wok on my parents' electric stove. So while my father was adamant in the belief that serious Chinese cooking required a wok, he himself used a skillet. Forced to used a skillet, my father was often dissatisfied with his stir-fries, lamenting that they lacked *wok hay*. One of his favorite dishes, stir-fried butterfly fish and bean sprouts, provided a constant challenge. The cooking of the delicate fish slices requires no more than a minute of heat. I remember watching him furiously trying to turn all the fish slices in the skillet with a spatula before they overcooked. Years later when a chef told me the weakness of stir-frying in a skillet is that you must "chase ingredients around a pan," I had a vivid image of my father's struggles.

While I understood the reasons my parents did not use a wok, I felt drawn to it. Undeterred by my father's warnings that a wok did not work on an American stove, I bought my first wok while I was in college. Unaccustomed to the concept of

Preceding page: There is nothing that compares to the sheen of a hand-pounded wok and ladle.

Opposite: Hand-wrought iron spatulas for sale in the Gao Tian village outdoor market in Guangxi province.

一
鑊
走
天
涯

seasoning a wok, I soon found myself with a slightly rusted cooking utensil, and food stuck to it when I stir-fried. It was years before I purchased my next wok, but ultimately that pan acquired a greasy stickiness. Worse yet, my stir-fries sometimes tasted faintly metallic. I eventually decided that the wok was too troublesome and gave it away.

Often I wondered if my choice of wok had been the problem. In some ways I think it was my fate to walk into the Hung Chong wok store in New York's Chinatown and impulsively purchase a flat-bottomed carbon-steel wok. As an afterthought, I asked the store clerk how to season it. She instructed me to buy some Chinese chives at the produce stand and to wash the wok with soapy water to remove the factory grease. After drying the pan, I was to stir-fry the chives in the wok with oil. The chives, she explained, would absorb the wok's metallic taste.

It made perfect sense, I thought, to season the wok by stir-frying. At the produce stand, the vendor spied the wok handle sticking out of my bag. "Ahh, you must be seasoning your new wok," he said with a smile. It was a revelation. Not only had I unwittingly uncovered an ancient cooking secret, it seemed, but I'd made a culinary soul connection. I later discovered that seasoning a wok with chives is an old culinary ritual practiced by both home cooks and professional chefs. Here I was a Chinese American, in modern-day New York City, and I'd accidentally stumbled upon a valuable piece of traditional Chinese wok lore.

The simple seasoning instructions worked perfectly. The flat-bottomed wok heated up quickly and produced a much higher heat than the round-bottomed woks I had previously tried. In the next weeks, as the pan acquired a patina, the wok gradually developed a nonstick surface. I recognized how easy and efficient cooking in a wok was—and how much more I enjoyed stir-frying. This was the seasoned wok I had always imagined.

Nonetheless, a seasoned wok was only a part of the puzzle—it did not elevate my cooking skills. I was "doing my own thing" with the wok, and I was sometimes pleased with my stir-fries. But I was aware that my cooking lacked technique. I wanted the taste of *wok hay* and to learn the secrets of how experienced cooks stir-fried with a wok. I aspired, as my father had, to excellence.

This compelling desire to know sent me and my collaborator, Alan Richardson, on a journey throughout America, Hong Kong, and mainland China. We sought home cooks, professional chefs, and culinary teachers, asking each their advice on wok cooking. The expertise ranged from that of legendary culinary luminaries such as cooking teacher Florence Lin and famed restaurateur Cecilia Chiang to rice farmer Liang Nian Xiu and my Uncle Lang in Foshan, China. It was my good fortune that each cook demonstrated his or her stir-frying technique by preparing a favorite dish or two.

My wok culinary studies became not only an extraordinary education in the wok but a unique documentation of the wok as a way of life. There were many lessons learned along the way. As each cook stir-fried for me, I wrote detailed notes on the style, material, and size of the wok; the marinade and sauce combinations; the heat levels and cooking times; whether they used a spatula, ladle, or the *pao* action to toss the ingredients in the wok. I observed their movements as if I were watching a dancer's routine. Cooks stir-fry guided by their instincts, monitoring not only visual cues but their sense of smell, taste, touch, and hearing.

While the conditions of a restaurant kitchen are completely different from those of a home, I wanted to see how professionals stir-fry, especially to garner tips on achieving *wok hay*. Traveling to Hong Kong and Guangzhou (Canton), I discovered that the finest Chinese restaurants rely solely on hand-hammered carbon-steel woks. No kitchen would ever attempt to use a skillet or nonstick cookware, especially to achieve *wok hay*. Every chef I met followed the hot wok–cold oil principle for stir-frying. I learned that if oil is added to a wok that has not been pre-heated, any food that is added will stick. The wok must be hot just to the point of smoking before oil is added. It was stunning to witness the ferocious heat of Chinese restaurant stoves. Thirty-five years after my father's restaurant visitations, I was finally allowed in the kitchen. Just as my father had described, superior stir-frying requires high heat and the shortest cooking time.

While my journey began with the focus on stir-frying and my fascination with *wok hay*, cooks showed me numerous other techniques as well. I soon learned the chameleon-like power of the wok as it was used for steaming, pan-frying, deep-frying, poaching, braising, boiling, and smoking. This extraordinary range of techniques far exceeds those that can be used in a pot or skillet. It was staggering to realize that nearly the entire repertoire of Chinese cuisine can be cooked in a wok.

Throughout my wok studies I experimented with countless varieties of woks to determine what styles and materials worked best on the American stove. I tested northern-style, Cantonese-style, and flat-bottomed woks. I tried Chinese cast-iron, enamel-lined Chinese cast-iron, American cast-iron, carbon-steel (hand-hammered, spun, and stamped), stainless-steel with aluminum core, anodized aluminum, five-layer, and even non-stick. I tracked down wok factories, wok artisans, wok stove factories, and specialty wok shops, learning from each the qualities necessary for a durable and superior cooking wok. In order to determine what method produces the best patina on carbon-steel and cast-iron woks, I tested numerous seasoning "recipes" gathered from cooks in China and the West.

Remembering how tentative I once was, it is all the more satisfying that the seasoning, maintaining, and use of a cast-iron or carbon-steel wok is no longer a mystery. But most empowering of all is to stir-fry fully confident that I know how to achieve *wok hay*. Beyond that, my wok is no longer simply a piece of cookware. It embodies all the rich stories and traditions that make Chinese cuisine so remarkable.

In the process of exploring wok traditions I discovered how common my family's choice to forgo the wok is among Chinese Americans. Assimilation and the demands of working life have seriously eroded Chinese culinary culture. When the Chinese came to America in the mid-1800s, they brought with them the traditions of wok cooking. Today the transmission of family recipes and the rituals of wok cooking are no longer an assumed inheritance. It often saddens me to realize generations of Chinese are growing up with no understanding of the wok's long history or of its use.

In China, the wok as a cooking instrument endures because nothing comes close to its versatility and efficiency. In what is left of the rich, old-world cooking culture, the wok is used on a traditional hearth stove, snugly fitted into a hole over the heat chamber. This approach is far different from that of the West, where the wok sits on a metal ring atop a contemporary stove. The old-world method provides a culinary link between the past and present, a glimpse into a vanished era. Today the wok remains the center of family life in much of China. It is the iron thread that connects two thousand years of Chinese culinary history.

In addition to collecting traditional recipes of authentic Chinese wok cooking, my mission with this book became to create both a written and visual document of wok cooking and old-world wok culture. While in Hong Kong I learned the expression "*Yad wok jao tin ngaai*," or "One wok runs to the sky's edge." It has two interpretations: "The wok endures eternally, all the way to the edge of the sky" and "One who uses the wok becomes master of the cooking world."

A Note About the Text

This book is written in my voice, but it is the result of my collaborative partnership with Alan Richardson. Like the Taoist symbol of yin and yang, our respective contributions spilled over into the other's domain, creating an exceptional rapport, a balancing act, that only deepened as the project progressed. Where my voice leaves off, you might very well hear a Richardson whisper.

—GY

Notes *to the Reader*

This book celebrates the Chinese cast-iron and carbon-steel wok. Traditional Cantonese cooks believe that an iron wok imparts *wok hay,* the special taste of the wok, to the food. Throughout this book I have followed the convention established in my last book and used the spelling *wok hay,* even though the standardized Cantonese spelling is *wok hei.* I have taken this liberty because the spelling *hei* can lead to an incorrect pronunciation for the non-Chinese speaker. I feel that *hay* is a closer representation of the Cantonese pronunciation. Chinese terms are rendered in romanized spellings of their Cantonese pronunciations, except for several words already familiar to readers in romanized Mandarin such as: Beijing, Sichuan, and Guangzhou.

If you do not have a traditional wok, all of the recipes are still delicious cooked in a skillet. However, I urge you to experience cooking in a traditional wok, for not only is it easier but the taste is incomparable.

How the Recipes Are Organized

Selection, Seasoning, and Care includes a selection of my favorite seasoning "recipes" with detailed instructions for curing a carbon-steel or Chinese-made cast-iron wok.

The majority of recipes are in The Art of Stir-Frying, organized by food categories—poultry, meat, seafood, rice and noodles, and vegetables. The recipes range in complexity from easy to advanced stir-fries. Here you'll learn the secrets of

how Chinese professional chefs and home cooks stir-fry with *wok hay,* the coveted taste and aroma I call the breath of a wok.

However, no Chinese cook uses the wok solely for stir-frying, for it would be both daunting and inappropriate to prepare a meal of stir-fried dishes only. In keeping with the Chinese principles of yin and yang, a harmonious meal is composed of dishes prepared with a variety of techniques. Eight Treasured Tastes is a tribute to the versatility of the wok. The recipes are organized by the techniques for smoking, pan-frying, braising, boiling, poaching, steaming, and deep-frying. In this section are memorable visits with the legendary Chinese cooking teacher Florence Lin, my family, and Amy Tan, followed by the recipes I learned from them.

The last section, Essentials, includes menu recommendations for family-style meals and for celebrating the Chinese New Year. Recipes that are appropriate for New Year's celebrations are in the Index listed under New Year's Celebrations. If you are unfamiliar with Chinese ingredients, refer to the Glossary, where you will find food identification photographs and information. Sources is a guide to purchasing Chinese ingredients, woks and accessories, and custom-made wok stoves. This section also lists some of my favorite Chinese cultural and culinary contacts.

The Recipes

All of the recipes are adapted from the cooks and chefs whom I interviewed. Please read each recipe before cooking, as well as the sidebars on stir-frying, steaming, and deep-frying if the recipe requires one of those techniques. In Chinese cooking, heat levels are very critical. All the recipes were tested on a KitchenAid residential-style range with gas burners (approximately 14,000 BTUs). If you are cooking on a custom-made wok stove, a professional range, a less powerful gas range, or an electric stove, adjust the heat levels called for, or increase or decrease the cooking times by a few minutes.

General Instructions

• **Ginger** is peeled unless otherwise indicated; I like to remove the peel by scraping it with the edge of a teaspoon. A slice should be about the size of a quarter, ¼ inch thick.

• To make **ginger juice,** grate a small amount of ginger and then squeeze it with your fingers to extract the juice.

• While **peanut oil** has traditionally been the favorite oil in Chinese cooking, the cooks I interviewed used a wide variety of oils. I have called for vegetable oil in the recipes unless the cook specified a particular oil. Curiously, I've seen more and more Chinese markets stock olive oil, especially extra-light olive oil. Whichever oil you choose, be sure that the oil has a high smoke point suitable for stir-frying and deep-frying.

• All **vegetables** should be thoroughly washed in several changes of cold water. Make sure

vegetables are dry by air-drying them in a colander for several hours, or using a salad spinner to remove excess water.

• **Sichuan peppercorns** (see page 226) can be difficult to find in the United States. When a recipe in this book calls for the peppercorns, they may be omitted. If you can obtain the peppercorns, they must be roasted and ground. Stir ¼ cup peppercorns in a dry wok over medium heat 3 to 5 minutes until they are fragrant and just beginning to smoke. Once they're cooled, grind them in a mortar and then store them in a jar.

• **Fresh chilies** are stemmed and unseeded unless otherwise indicated. Always wear gloves when handling chilies.

• **Meat and poultry** should always be trimmed of excess fat.

• **Sesame oil** is Asian style, which is roasted, aromatic, and golden brown in color. Do not use clear cold-pressed sesame oil.

• **Homemade Chicken Broth** (page 195) is a secret to achieving full-flavored dishes; Pacific brand organic chicken broth in a carton, or canned reduced-sodium chicken broth, can be used, but the flavor is inferior to that of homemade.

• When **soy sauce** is called for, I use a thin or light soy sauce such as Kikkoman.

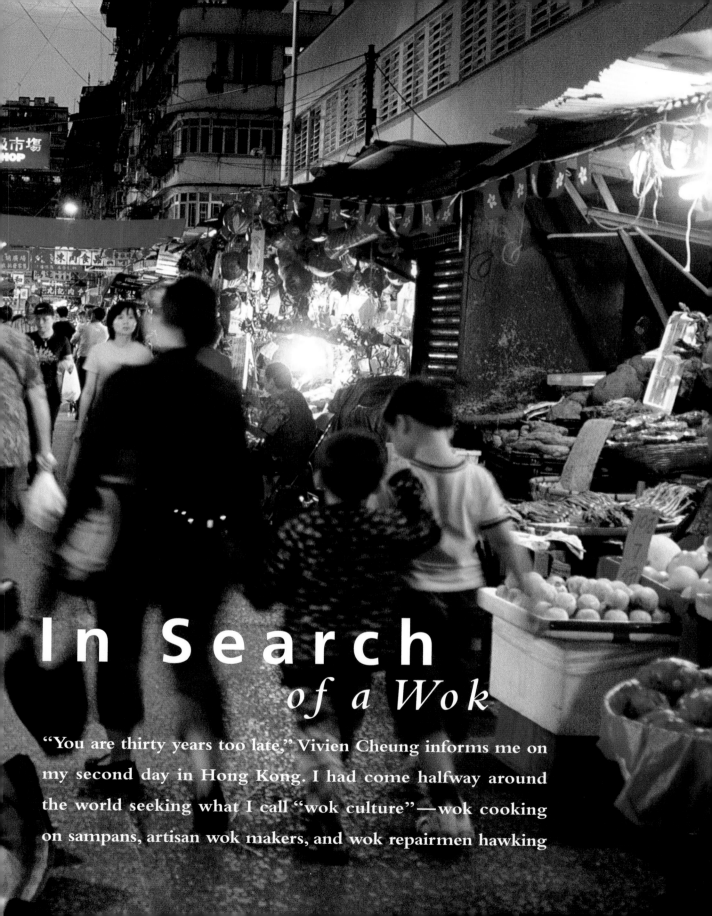

In Search
of a Wok

"You are thirty years too late," Vivien Cheung informs me on my second day in Hong Kong. I had come halfway around the world seeking what I call "wok culture"—wok cooking on sampans, artisan wok makers, and wok repairmen hawking their services on street corners. There was a time when this culture was an important dimension of Hong Kong life, and I remember many of these sights from previous trips. In recent years, however, I'd made no effort to seek them out, assuming them to be integral to Hong Kong's way of life. Never, certainly not in my lifetime, had I expected them to disappear. But they had.

The *dai pai dong*, the famous cooked-food stalls of Hong Kong, have been dwindling in numbers for years. Those I had seen on a visit eighteen months earlier now seemed to be gone. My friend Walter Chu tells me that they fell victim to stricter government bans on street cooking, although a few illegal *dai pai dong* were still operating at night.

That evening I venture over to the Temple Street night market at dusk in search of the *dai pai dong*. I walk down a narrow street filled with produce vendors doing brisk business. In preparation for their evening meal, customers peruse an extraordinary array of fresh vegetables. As night falls a hawker appears and, in no time, sets up a cart with an unusual hat-shaped wok nestled on a portable stove. He begins frying delicious stuffed peppers and eggplant. Suddenly from another direction I smell the appetizing scent of garlic and ginger. Down a side street that had been desolate when I first arrived I spot a row of small fold-up dining tables crowded with customers sitting on stools. Close by, a cook stir-fries razor clams with black bean sauce in a restaurant-sized wok. With great showmanship he jerks the wok a few times, tossing the clams in the air, forcing a blast of flames from his stove. Two older men intently engaged in conversation, oblivious to the cook's activities, share a simple meal of rice and a stir-fry of pork and bean sprouts. At another table a woman feeds her children. It is hard to believe that this lively dining scene is now a rarity in Hong Kong, but my friend Walter tells me that the *dai pai dong* appear and disappear depending on the watchfulness of the local officials.

The next day, walking down famous Nathan Road, I'm thrilled to spot a hawker stir-frying chestnuts, one of my favorite Hong Kong street

foods. He cooks in a mammoth wok over a charcoal-fueled portable stove. Looking into the wok, I'm fascinated to see how the chestnuts are stir-fried in a mixture that resembles fine ebony-colored gravel; the vendor tells me it's sand with a little sugar. I buy a piping-hot bag and devour the treat as I watch him tend his chestnuts and his steady line of eager customers. I can't help wondering if this is the last time I shall see a chestnut hawker in Hong Kong.

Unquestionably, Hong Kong remains a vital Chinese culinary destination, rich in traditional food customs. The chefs and home cooks I interview awe me with their prowess in wok cooking. But unsurpassed as Hong Kong's culinary culture is, it now lacks the old-world wok culture I seek. I am told that the best place to see a wok used on an old-fashioned Chinese hearth stove is a museum in the New Territories. A few ancestral homes still have such stoves, but they are difficult to locate. To find wok cooking on boats, there is only one floating restaurant left in Hong Kong, now a popular tourist attraction. I'm advised to view the historical photographs of Guangzhou's restaurant boats in the Hong Kong Museum of History. I cannot fathom that I must go to a museum to see the wok.

According to Hong Kong heritage researcher Nevin Lim, the wok street culture I seek disappeared in the last few decades as Hong Kong became more Westernized. "Sampan and *dai pai dong* cooking doesn't meet strict hygiene codes," says Lim. "Today there are also government fire and noise regulations that make wok production in Hong Kong impossible. When carbon-steel woks are produced, the heat is extremely intense, and the sound of the hammering is deafening. In addition, the high cost of labor shifted the manufacturing of woks to mainland China, where costs are dramatically lower. As the standard of living has improved, the wok repairmen who used to make house calls also became obsolete. No one repairs a wok when a new one is so cheap," Lim explains.

I suspect the *dai pai dong* street vendors at Temple Street night market and the chestnut hawkers will soon vanish, too. Perhaps their legacy will be

Scenes from Hong Kong. Preceding pages: Temple Street night market. Clockwise from above: Two men engaged in lively conversation at the dai pai dong on Temple Street; stir-fried chestnuts on Nathan Road; a young girl looks out from behind a large wok in the dai pai dong; woks from the famous Chan Chi Kee Cutlery Company.

preserved by a few photographs in a Hong Kong museum. The intent of my trip was to observe the many facets of wok culture, but instead it feels like I'm documenting its last vestiges. It seems all the more important to locate as much traditional wok culture as I can, recording it before it becomes extinct.

On my first morning in Foshan, in Guangdong province, China, my auntie and uncle promise to take me to breakfast at the best *dai pai dong*. I had imagined that this ancient city would offer a more rustic experience of China, but our taxi drive along a big boulevard passing enormous modern buildings, a McDonald's, and a billboard advertising Kentucky Fried Chicken quickly dispels that notion. My heart sinks as the taxi stops in front of a super-modern complex. As we enter the mall, my uncle proudly says this *dai pai dong* has outstanding food. We step off the escalator onto the third floor, where a modern Chinese-style food court is in full swing with a long row of cooks isolated behind a glass wall.

I try to explain to my auntie and uncle that I want to see traditional wok culture. But I can tell they are perplexed by my request. Why would I be interested in seeing "old China" when its modern face is so much more impressive? Foshan, I learn, has transcended its 1,300-year history to become a model of China's economic modernization. *Dai pai dong* have been banned by a government intent on promoting a cosmopolitan image. In answer to my request to see a wok factory, my uncle explains that Guangdong province, like Hong Kong, has grown too prosperous for wok manufacturing.

After days of persistent inquiry, I learn from my cousin of a *dai pai dong* in a nearby town—a night restaurant set up in the parking lot of a supermarket. We arrive late in the evening, just as the last customers are leaving the supermarket. Tables and chairs are set up as diners begin to filter in, and by midnight the *dai pai dong* is bustling. My cousin convinces the owner to take me into the cooking area, which turns out to be the kitchen of a small storefront restaurant by day. The small blackened kitchen has a long commercial stove with several wok stations. The large woks are pitch black and warped by

the extreme heat of the flames. Servers place dishes on the center table. Every minute or so the flames leap up around the wok at one or two stations. The cook gives the contents a final toss and then empties the wok onto the waiting dish. After a quick garnish the plate is rushed out to the tables. This furious pace continues until two in the morning, when the crowd starts to thin and the *dai pai dong* closes up; the scene reverts to a deserted parking lot. As we drive away my cousin points out the telltale signs of *dai pai dong* breaking up along several side streets. Like Temple Street night market, these nightly street gatherings have an energy and warmth made all the more attractive to me because of their chimera-like quality—appearing and disappearing right before my eyes.

My uncle, now enthusiastic about my adventure, calls me the next morning to tell me he has found a wok factory located on the outskirts of Foshan. He and my cousin's wife will take me. As we drive along I learn that my cousin's wife and her girlfriends rarely cook, and that when they do, they prefer nonstick cookware. My uncle regales me with a story about close friends who recently purchased an expensive nonstick wok from Japan. It is obvious that my interest in traditional wok culture remains baffling to them.

We arrive at a large dark factory made of rough-hewn timbers and ragged brick. Outside, a cluster of women hand-polish a large stack of newly pounded woks. The bone-rattling throb of machinery resounds from inside the factory. When I enter, it takes a few moments for my eyes to adjust to the dim light. The massive room reveals a scene that looks to me like something out of a Dickens novel. Individual workers are seated in front of large timber-constructed hammering stations. A heavy metal piston, as large as the worker himself, is poised perilously above a carbon-steel disc that the worker holds under the piston as a thick metal rod is driven forth, all the while keeping his hands and head out of the path of the forceful pounding rod. The piston is powered by a pulley system, and the worker quickly rotates the disc before the metal rod is driven down again.

This process is repeated until all irregularities are pounded out of the metal disc and a perfectly curved new wok results. Each worker stays at his task for long hours, despite the deafening sound of the pistons, producing a new wok every hour and a half. As I walk through the factory, passing a dozen or so of these pounding stations, I am reminded of the wok cooking rhythms—of the actions of spinning and turning, and of the close observation required for the task at hand. As with the wok warrior chefs, the hazards of the work are enormous. At the end of our tour, in a separate area of the factory, two young workers, surrounded by stacks of fresh woks, pound rivets into ear handles. As we prepare to leave, the factory manager presents me with a wok he has carefully chosen from the stacks. We are all—even my uncle and cousin—impressed by the quality of this old-fashioned piece of cookware. I offer it to my uncle as a gift, and he accepts it with a smile.

My next destination lies in the interior of southern China, a city called Yangshuo. My friend David, knowing my mania for Chinese culinary culture, has put me in touch with Liang Nian Xiu, a rice farmer and part-time tour guide. She is a small bundle of energy with a big smile. I like her at once. We stow my gear at the Hong Fu, a beautiful Qing dynasty temple *cum* French inn where I am to lodge, and then head to the market. I am immediately taken by the difference in this rural area. The streets are lined with vegetable and fruit sellers. Each shoulders produce in hand-woven baskets hung from a bamboo yoke. Most vendors squat beside their produce along the sides of the street, but others work the street itself, using the yoke to weave their baskets through the crowd. The produce is fresh and abundant. As we wind our way down one narrow street, the fruit sellers give way to food stalls, and then to cooking stations surrounded by small stools and tables for eating. In the center is a covered area filled with vendors using only woks to stir-fry, braise, steam, and deep-fry food of every variety. Each wok is stationed on top of a small metal drum, and through a side hole I can see burning red-hot coals.

Right: Workers at their pounding stations in a wok factory in Foshan, Guangdong province, China. These woks are shaped by hand, but the pounding is done by heavy machinery rather than a wok artisan's hammer. Far right: A young worker attaches ear-shaped handles to Cantonese-style woks. In the foreground is a stack of northern-style woks.

踏
破
鐵
鞋

I stop to watch a woman making cakes from green dough. She presses them into a mold before placing them in a bamboo steamer set in a wok. As she works, her partner lifts the wok off the burner and, using a pair of tongs, removes a whitened honeycomb-shaped piece of charcoal from the drum. Immediately she replaces the spent fuel with another piece, which is pitch black. This simple heating source is used to power the woks. I expect the air to be foul and choking. Instead it is filled with the wonderful aromas of food cooking.

In the central area, on a table covered with a brightly patterned oilcloth, there is a row of spicy condiments in colorful bowls. One diner sits on a stool eating a bowl of noodles. I try not to stare, but I am so drawn to this scene, wanting to know what each bowl, each plate, each wok contains. Next to the noodle stand I see *joong* (Chinese-style tamales) heating on a steamer; beyond that, bean sprouts are being stir-fried with scallions, batter is being poured into a wok filled with hot fat for frying, and a large fowl is being lowered into a bath of boiling herbs.

Beside me, there is a large wok covered with a thin wooden lid. On top of the lid are stacks of bamboo steamers catching the steam as it pours through holes in the surface of the wood. Food is being prepared all around me. Bowls of soup with bits of thinly sliced meat cook in a hot broth. Crispy fritters and pancakes frying in oil are strained out. Eggs steep in a soy sauce marinade. Thin rice pancakes brown in a large wok. Sitting at the little stools, the customers hold rice bowls up to their lips, using chopsticks or a Chinese spoon to eat. Many diners are alone; others sit in groups of two and three enjoying a meal together. It seems I have found the wok culture I seek. But to do it I have had to travel back in time to a place not yet transformed by Western-style development. I feel ecstatic and exhausted. And tomorrow Liang Xiu is going to cook for me.

The next morning as I float down the Dragon River on a bamboo raft, I watch Liang Xiu pedal her bike along the small trails that run through the golden rice fields. We are on our way to her home

In the Yangshuo dai pai dong. Opposite: Shallow bamboo trays are set over woks for steaming. Right: Condiments are laid out on a long table for diners to add to their food. Far right: Snails cooked in a spicy sauce with red peppers are served up from a wok sitting on a charcoal burner.

The trip to Liang Nian Xiu's village follows the Dragon River in Guangxi province. Farmers in this picturesque region surrounded by limestone formations use traditional yoke baskets to carry their produce to market.

in the village of Moon Hill. Small mountains that look like brush strokes surround the glowing rice fields, and clumps of bamboo and acacia dot the landscape. We arrive first at Liang Xiu's mother's birthplace, a "minority" village. As we make our way through the stone alleys of the nearly deserted village, Liang Xiu tells me how the villagers overthrew the landlord during the time of the Cultural Revolution. Now the few remaining villagers use the old kitchen of the landlord's house. Liang Xiu takes me into the main house. The kitchen is just inside the central courtyard. She grins because she knows I have been looking for an example of a large communal-type wok. There are two in this kitchen, and they are huge—at least forty-two inches in diameter—and sit on an immense hearth stove. Large enough to cook the food for the entire village, they were used for everything. Today the village women boil soybeans in them for making tofu. They are also used for fermenting sweet potatoes or rice when making wine. Liang Xiu tells me that in

villages, a wok this size can be used to feed the animals, even to boil water for washing clothes or bathing. I try to lift one of the massive woks, but it is far too heavy for me. Liang Xiu gives me a hand, but only her side lifts off the stove.

Liang Xiu has one other surprise for me before we reach her home. We head for the village blacksmith whose hammering I can hear from the end of the street. Upon entering the metal shop, I see the blacksmith, Mr. Wan, is holding a piece of rough-cut iron in a coal forge. He uses a fan to increase the heat of the fire. As he holds the metal in the flames it begins to glow red and then white. He pulls the metal from the fire, tosses it onto an anvil, and pounds it with his hammer. I suddenly realize that he is making a wok for me. The blacksmith tells me that wok making is not his full-time occupation, but if someone in the village wants a wok or needs to have one repaired, they come to him. The shop looks like something out of the American Wild West, with metal parts scattered about. A few extra

This communal wok in Dragon village is 3½ feet in diameter and 15 inches deep. The traditional stove supporting it is built of brick and covered with cement. Opposite: An elderly woman sorts sundried soybeans, which will be used for making tofu in the communal wok.

discs have already been cut for woks. The wok-making work is slow and loud, and the blacksmith asks us if we want to come back later. The wok will be ready in two hours. I am hungry and excited about cooking with Liang Xiu, so we head for her home.

Liang Xiu's outdoor kitchen opens onto a garden in back where we are surrounded by her fruit trees and chickens. She plans to cook three dishes for me: two vegetable stir-fries and a special egg dish for which she has bought fresh pork, snow peas, corn on the cob, beans, and tomatoes. Liang Xiu removes the pork from the screened safe where she stores most of her staples and utensils. She chops it together with garlic, scallions, cilantro, chilies, and shiitake mushrooms, perfuming the air with the wonderful smell of fresh herbs. She removes several chicken and duck eggs from the safe, cracks them into a bowl, and, using a pair of bamboo chopsticks, beats them with salt. They turn a dark, rich, almost amber color. Liang Xiu pushes a couple of rice stalks through the stoke hole and into the burning chamber of her traditional hearth stove. The flames

leap into the air, and she pours a small amount of oil into the wok. She gives it a quick swirl and adds a spoonful of the beaten eggs. They sputter and fry, and while the egg is still loose, she drops a spoonful of pork mixture into its center. Using a spatula, she folds the egg over the pork mixture once and then again, to form a fat cigar. Liang Xiu pushes the "omelet" higher up the side of the wok, where it continues to cook at a lower heat. The moment the center of the wok is empty, she spoons in more egg and repeats the process. When the new omelet is ready to be pushed up the side of the wok, she removes the first one to a side dish. After a few omelets, the fire dies down and Liang Xiu increases the heat by adding a new rice stalk to the fire. Once all of the egg and pork has been used, Liang Xiu returns the entire batch of little omelets to the wok and adds the mushroom soaking liquid. By now the fire is low. Liang Xiu places a lid on the wok and allows the omelets to braise over this low heat for a few minutes. When she removes the lid, steam rushes out and she places the juicy omelets on

In Gao Tian village, Guangxi province. Opposite: Taut arms wield the blacksmith tools as Mr. Wan pounds an iron wok. Right: A street hawker serves up a bowl of steaming food straight from the wok. Far right: A portable wok and charcoal burner positioned on the back of a bicycle hold a bamboo steamer filled with fresh buns.

踏
破
鐵
鞋

a platter, tops them with cilantro, and brings them directly to the table. A little spicy and so tender, the omelets are unbelievably delicious.

As I watch Liang Xiu cook, I realize that this stove is the very type I was told to find in a museum. The brick stove with stoke hole and fire chamber has been in existence since the Han dynasty, its fuel efficiency dictated by centuries of shortages and need. In fact, the entire workplace is a marvel of efficiency. The brick retains the heat from the burning chamber, allowing Liang Xiu to cook over high heat or low heat when the fire subsides. The 2½-foot-high stove is the perfect height for stir-frying; Liang Xiu is petite and yet she can fully extend her arm while she stirs the wok.

After lunch, we return to Mr. Wan. He presents me with a very rustic wok, crafted from a sheet of recycled metal. It is nearly flat and about 15 inches in diameter, with a carefully repaired hole in the center and a welded seam on one end. It is clear that this wok is made for rugged use. Liang Xiu and I decide that it is perfect for frying potstickers.

I leave rural Yangshuo for cosmopolitan Shanghai, where I am excited to find that *dai pai dong* and street cooking thrive. Even more amazing,

it had never occurred to me that woks were still being handmade in such a modern city. In a residential neighborhood far from the skyscrapers and big boulevards, past open markets bustling with shoppers, I hear the unmistakable sound of metal being hammered. I follow the sound to a small outdoor area where two men sit crouched, working alternately at heating pairs of carbon-steel discs on a forced-air charcoal burner and then carefully hammering them into woks.

Cen Lian Gen, a boyish-looking man, is shy to answer my questions at first. Through an interpreter I ask about his woks and their quality. He stops his work and brings me into his "shop." I step into a tiny room with a wall of cubbyholes filled with woks. Stacks of woks make it hard to move around what little floor space remains. The woks are beautiful, with rich, dull, pebbled finishes and exquisite crafting. They are like nothing I have ever seen before. In Shanghainese Cen explains that his father started the business more than seventy years ago, and that he and his brother, Cen Rong Gen, have continued producing the famous hand-hammered carbon-steel woks, which they call fire-iron woks. Each one requires at least five hours to produce.

Far left: Liang Nian Xiu's sweet and potent rice wine is made by fermenting rice in a wok. Left: A wall of personal mementos in Liang Xiu's home in Moon Hill village, Guangxi province. Opposite: Liang Xiu's outdoor kitchen is equipped with a traditional hearth stove. She uses dried rice stalks as fuel in the stove.

Tongs are used to hold paired discs of forge-heated metal during the first stages of pounding a wok; after separating the roughly formed discs, Cen Lian Gen puts the finishing touches on them. He estimates that it takes at least five hours to complete a single hand-hammered wok.

踏
破
鐵
鞋

"A hand-hammered wok is better than a factory-made wok. Hand-hammering changes the structure of the metal, giving it greater strength and durability," Cen tells me. Although the brothers sell to individual customers, the biggest demand for their woks comes from Shanghai's most famous restaurants.

Cen and his brother work without a staff. Once they retire, the business will end. Again I feel a disappointment that yet another wok tradition is destined to vanish. I ask Cen if it bothers him that Chinese home cooks no longer rely solely on the traditional wok. Cen shrugs his shoulders. "Today many home cooks are switching to modern cookware. People are too busy and they have less time to cook. But I don't worry about the fate of the wok. A good restaurant will always use a traditional carbon-steel fire-iron wok. Everyone has a different style. Today in China many people eat Western foods, but there are also those who want real Chinese food. For authentic Chinese food, serious cooks will always use a traditional carbon-steel fire-iron wok."

The Chinese have an old saying: "Falling leaves return to their roots," or "*Lok yip gwai gan.*" The expression is intended for overseas Chinese like myself, encouraging a return to China. To understand the wok, I had to return. Watching Liang Xiu cook on her hearth stove helped me to appreciate the wok's brilliance. In rural China the wok is used very much the same way it was in olden days—a testament to its intelligent design. Even today it is the focal point of village life.

China's modernization has come quickly. It is inevitable that much of the wok culture I found throughout China will cease to exist. I can imagine someday towns and cities in China will replace *dai pai dong* with modern food courts, and the art of making woks by hand will eventually disappear. But I cannot imagine farmers like Liang Nian Xiu relinquishing their traditional fuel-efficient stoves and woks. And it is inconceivable that Chinese restaurant chefs will ever forsake the wok. It is the most treasured tool of their trade—no pan compares. While I lament the general loss of wok culture, the simple farmer and the gourmet chef, at two ends of the culinary spectrum, continue the vibrant tradition of wok cooking. The carbon-steel fire-iron wok, as Cen Lian Gen so wisely observed, will always be used by serious cooks of Chinese cuisine.

Far left: Cen Lian Gen explains that his Shanghainese-style wok with its two ear handles is similar to a Cantonese-style wok but deeper. Left and opposite: Shanghai still thrives with authentic street food and wok culture. But with China's rapid modernization comes the threat that many of these traditions will soon disappear.

Selection,
Seasoning,
and Care

For more than 2,000 years, the wok has been the essential tool of the Chinese kitchen. The ritual of preparing it for use remains unchanged. The wok is said to last for eternity when one cares for it with honor in daily life.

Reverence *for a Wok*

鑊
之
傳
統

All afternoon, throughout the restaurant's lunch service, I watched the young master chef stir-fry nonstop. My parents had brought me to a popular new restaurant located—to my surprise—in a mall in Richmond, California. The chef executed dish after dish with impressive precision. But all the exuberance he exhibited while cooking disappeared the moment I began my interview. I struggled to coax him to elaborate on the advantages of wok cooking, but his answers were brief and matter-of-fact. He didn't seem to know what to make of me or my questions. Why, after all, would a Chinese woman not understand the importance of the wok?

Eventually, I framed my question differently: Why did he cook in a wok and not a skillet? He smiled. As he watched me scribbling away in my notebook, he said: Imagine if you were asked to write Chinese calligraphy with a pen rather than a calligraphy brush. Certainly every character can be written with a pen, but the writing lacks grace and beauty. With a brush the writer becomes an artist able to control the thinness and thickness of the stroke as well as the lightness and darkness of the ink. A calligraphy brush allows artistic expression that isn't possible with a pen. Now I understood the Chinese chef's experience with the skillet.

Without exception, every chef I interviewed declared that he had greater cooking control with a wok. One described stir-frying in a skillet as "chasing ingredients around a pan." In a skillet everything is spread out. The spatula lifts only the small amount of food it can hold. Each time the spatula lifts that food, it shifts to the opposite side of the pan. In a wok, on the other hand, the concave shape makes stirring easier, as each motion of the spatula draws ingredients in the wok partially up the sides of the pan, allowing them to tumble back into the well.

The concentration of heat in the well not only conserves fuel but sears the ingredients quickly and imparts a delicious smoky aroma, quite different from that of a skillet. Another chef explained that a skillet, especially an expensive one, is thicker than a wok. It therefore requires a longer time to heat. The rapidity with which a traditional cast-iron or carbon-steel wok heats up has no equal. The wok utilizes the heat that spreads to its sloping sides, in contrast to a skillet, whose sides are not a cooking surface. One chef pointed out that when stir-frying, much more oil is necessary to coat a 14-inch skillet than the small amount needed for the well of a 14-inch wok. In addition, once a traditional iron wok becomes seasoned, it requires less oil for cooking and only improves with age.

Home cooks extol the practical advantages of the wok's beautiful design: the sloping sides prevent food from spilling out, and during deep-frying the wok's depth and sloping sides allow for more food to be fried at once. The broad surface of the well enables liquids to reduce quickly. Its depth accommodates a stack of bamboo steamers. The slope provides enough space in which to fit a large fish, whether it is being steamed, poached, or fried. The round domed lid, another clever element, offers more flexibility than the flat or slightly rounded Western-style lid.

Indeed, the wok is the only pan ideally suited for stir-frying, pan-frying, braising, poaching, boiling, deep-frying, steaming, smoking foods, and even cooking rice. For me, however, the attraction is more than its versatility. When I cook with the wok, I feel a connection in my soul to the long lineage of Chinese cooks before me. I like the idea of cooking in the same type of pan that was used thousands of years ago—when Chinese cooking was still in its infancy. The thought that home cooks, not only in China but on every continent,

have woks similar to mine fills me with the pleasure of sustaining a long tradition. I often remind myself that in the humblest homes in China, the wok is sometimes the only cooking pan in the kitchen.

I find it inspiring to look to the past for instruction—to cook in the same type of pan that master cooks of China used during the Han dynasty. I'm awed by the discovery that the wok is as practical today as it was 2,000 years ago. During the Cultural Revolution, when the practice of classical Chinese arts was forbidden (even in the cooking of former imperial dishes), no one ever considered banning the wok.

I love the wok's humility. The cast-iron or carbon-steel 14-inch wok that I use is a fraction of the price of a professional-style sauté pan. There is

no reason to aspire to a more expensive or fancy wok. There is no difference between the wok a master chef buys for his home kitchen and the one a novice buys. In cooking, it is each cook's culinary expertise and wisdom, not the cost of the wok, that make the cooking distinct.

The very best endorsement of a wok, though, is to venture into the kitchen of any Chinese restaurant. You will never find a skillet. After all, why chase after food in a pan?

Preceding pages and above:
The finest chefs in China look for hand-hammered woks. Sitting in a wok artisan's work yard, these woks have a beautiful sheen and make a fine advertising display hanging outside his shop.

Acquiring a **Virtuous Wok**

For years I've frequented large food markets in Chinatowns, invariably drawn to the section where all manner of woks are stacked, some on dusty shelves, others in towers on the floor. I especially love to survey the giant *Guangdong wok*, or Cantonese-style woks, used by restaurants, surrounded by all of the different sizes in descending order. The utterly utilitarian presentation of the merchandise conjures images for me of ancient wok markets in China.

I used to ask why some woks that I assumed were all made of carbon steel looked so different from each other. In reply, clerks would mutter in Cantonese, *saang teet*, or *suk teet*. The translation of *saang teet* is "raw iron" and *suk teet* is "cooked iron," but what did that mean? Even my Chinese language teacher, Mr. Wen, could not translate, although he had a definite opinion on which was the superior wok: "A *saang teet* wok is best for stir-frying with *wok hay*," he said emphatically. After much research my Uncle Sam, who is a physicist, explained that *saang teet* is cast iron and *suk teet* is carbon steel. At last the mystery was beginning to unfold. The pans that didn't quite look like carbon-steel woks to me were, in fact, made of cast iron, *saang teet*. But because they were made in China, they bore little resemblance to American cast-iron cookware. Chinese cast-iron woks are nearly as light and thin as carbon-steel woks and, consequently, extremely delicate. If smacked against a counter, they shatter.

The earliest Chinese woks date back to the Han dynasty (206 B.C.–A.D. 220). According to University of California, Riverside, anthropology professor Eugene Anderson, author of *The Food of China*, they were probably made of cast iron in what is now referred to as the Cantonese style with a round bottom and two small ear-shaped handles. So vital were they to the Chinese way of life that miniature pottery models of them were found in Han tombs, for use by the dead in the afterlife.

Intrigued by the idea that the original wok was cast iron and Cantonese style, I decided that I had to go to China, where the wok is still used as it was in earlier times. Throughout my travels I met many cooks, but it was my visits with those working on a traditional hearth stove and a Cantonese-style wok that taught me how unsurpassed the wok is as a cooking instrument. A hearth stove has a large lipped hole to support the wok. The fire beneath the wok is so well insulated that when stir-frying the wok sizzles loudly throughout the cooking—the addition of wet ingredients or a large quantity of food does not lower its temperature. When I do this on my Western gas stove, the wok's heat drops dramatically. On a hearth stove the wok is so secure in the hole that there is no need for a cook to hold it when cooking. Both hands are free to stir with a spatula, reach for ingredients, or stoke the fire with rice stalks.

The flared Cantonese-style wok bowl provides ample room to stir ingredients with a spatula, ensuring that everything cooks evenly. Washing the wok is simply a matter of running two or three cups of tap water directly into it and swishing the water around with a bamboo brush. The only time a cook actually touches the wok with his hands is to lift it out of the stove by its two small ear-shaped handles to discard the water. He returns the wok to the stove to dry, where it remains when not in use. On a hearth stove, the Cantonese-style wok is not only ingeniously fuel efficient but makes work optimally efficient for a cook.

As I travel back to Hong Kong I can't help

These hand-hammered woks stored on dusty shelves owe their distinguished shape to the bronze ting, *an ancient cooking vessel with three legs.*

thinking that these are modern times and traditional hearth stoves are a rarity. I recall an afternoon I had spent with Tane Chan, owner of The Wok Shop in San Francisco's Chinatown. "I can almost bet which customers will buy the northern-style wok," says Chan, who has been selling woks since 1968. "Men love it. The moment they pick it up by that long metal handle they start flipping it, imitating the *pao* motion they've seen chefs demonstrate on *The Iron Chef*. The northern-style wok requires arm strength, perfect for men who like to flex their muscles," says Chan with a smile. The northern-style wok that she calls the pow wok or Peking pan is also a favorite of cooks from Beijing, Sichuan, and Wuhan. All favor the round bowl shape and the wok's long handle, ideal for the *pao* motion.

For customers who cook on an electric range, Chan advises against both the northern-style and Cantonese-style wok. "A round bottom is ineffective on an electric or ceramic stove top," she explains. "The round bottom requires a gas flame, but most residential gas ranges are not powerful enough to adequately heat a round-bottomed wok." Consequently, Chan generally recommends her best-selling wok: a Westernized 14-inch flat-bottomed carbon-steel wok with a long wood handle and a small helper handle also made of wood. "Cooks in the West prefer a wok that's more like a pot. A flat-bottomed wok has all the same attributes of a traditional wok, but with a few adaptations that make it better for a Western stove: the small flat bottom sits securely on the range and closer to the heat source; and the wood handle is more comfortable to grasp than the non–heat resistant metal or ear-shaped handles."

Chan's words ring in my ears as I arrive back in Hong Kong on my way to meet Chef Kevin Chuk of the Chinese Cuisine Training Institute. Chef Chuk, a native of Sichuan province, is adamant that nothing compares to the practicality of a lightweight northern-style carbon-steel wok. His style of stir-frying relies on holding the wok by its long metal handle and using the *pao* action to keep the food moving in the rounded bowl-shaped wok; he

rarely uses a ladle. Chef Chuk makes it look effortless, but it is unquestionably a much more physically demanding style of stir-frying. I can imagine that with an inexperienced cook, half the food would end up on the floor. "The northern-style wok is best for cooking small dishes," Chef Chuk explains. "I find it more comfortable. However, if you're unaccustomed to using it, it's easy to develop calluses on the hand." Fellow Instructor Chef Cheung Chin Choi adds that it is equally challenging for northern-trained chefs to use a Cantonese-style wok. "It's rare that a chef uses both styles with the same ease," says Chef Cheung. "I'm accustomed to the Cantonese-style wok. When I cook with a northern-style wok it is very awkward and extremely tiring."

The next day I catch the Star Ferry to Kowloon, where I'm invited by Chef Ip Chi Cheung at the Shang Palace restaurant in the Shangri-La hotel. I have come to see the Cantonese-style, *Guangdong,* wok used in a professional Cantonese kitchen. I arrive during lunch rush hour. Five or six stainless-steel stoves in a row run the length of the room. Like traditional hearth stoves, each stove contains a large round hole exclusively to hold one wok. These stoves are fueled by compressed gas that provides well over 150,000 BTUs of power. The chefs here work at a furious pace, each with a 19-inch carbon-steel wok. One chef adds a dash of rice wine to a stir-fry of bok choy, grasping the wok by one of its ear-shaped handles in a *pao* motion that releases a sudden burst of furious flames. Another chef expertly deep-fries spring rolls. Next to him, a young chef pan-fries a noodle cake, swirling the wok with one hand for even browning. He gives the wok a gentle *pao,* and the cake flips over. On the stove beside him, Napa cabbage braises with Chinese mushrooms, and in the last station chicken stock simmers in a mammoth 28-inch wok.

Chef Ip tells me that the Cantonese-style carbon-steel wok used by home cooks is also ideal for a professional kitchen, but in a larger size and preferably hand-hammered, which makes it more durable. A Cantonese-style cast-iron wok is too fragile for the rough work environment of a

professional kitchen. In fact, cast-iron woks are not even manufactured for restaurant use. "We prefer the 19-inch Cantonese-style wok to stir-fry, pan-fry, braise, boil, poach, steam, and deep-fry. For great quantities such as banquet-style food the Cantonese have woks as big as 48 inches. You can't find northern-style woks larger than 18 inches. The *pao* action would be impossible in such a wok, because it would be too heavy to lift with its long metal handle. A 19-inch Cantonese-style wok is more practical—we can easily lift the wok to *pao*, and because the wok is so spacious, if we don't want to *pao*, there's room to stir-fry with a ladle," Chef Ip explains.

I leave Kowloon much wiser about the use of Cantonese and northern-style woks. I live in America, though, where stoves are not nearly as powerful as those found in Hong Kong and mainland China. I recall that Chinese cooking teachers who live in the West, such as Ken Hom, Florence Lin, and Jean Yueh, have all expressed to me their preference for a Westernized flat-bottomed wok. "Although these design changes seem to go against the purpose of the traditional rounded shape, living outside a traditional Chinese kitchen requires adjustment," explains Hom.

I like having the same wok that Chinese cooks used 2,000 years ago. The brilliant design of a traditional round-bottomed wok concentrates the heat in the well and makes stirring easier. But I must admit when I cook with the traditional wok, I realize it was never intended for a Western stove. It is not nearly as stable or comfortable on my gas stove as it is on a Chinese hearth stove. The metal ear-shaped handles make it clumsy to lift with one hand, especially with pot holders. At home, I have a traditional Cantonese-style cast-iron wok, but I cook mainly with my flat-bottomed carbon-steel woks. Owning both styles reflects the duality of being Chinese American; I am compelled to embrace my heritage even as I live an American life.

Wok Buying *Guide*

Considerations When Choosing a Wok

Carbon Steel Versus Cast Iron

Carbon steel and cast iron produce the best woks, especially for stir-frying. In all my travels and research, I never came across a chef or home cook who owned both a cast-iron and a carbon-steel wok. Obviously there are two different philosophies on which material is superior for wok cooking.

The great advantage of carbon steel is that it heats and cools down quickly, preventing overcooking once the wok is removed from the heat. Heavy-gauge (14) carbon steel conducts heat evenly; light-gauge (18) sells for half the price of the heavier-gauge woks but tends to have hot spots, is less durable, and is also more likely to warp. Because the gauge is seldom indicated on the wok, you can test by gently pressing in on the sides of the wok with two hands to see if the pressure will flex the metal. If the pan cannot be flexed, it is most likely heavy gauge.

Carbon-steel woks are either hand hammered or factory made. The hand-hammered examples have a slightly rougher, nubbier surface and are well regarded by restaurant chefs and home cooks for their durability. They are available only with round bottoms. Factory-produced woks have a smoother surface and are either spun, stamped, or machine pounded. They are available with flat or round bottoms. Spun woks are also extremely durable. They can be identified by the faint concentric circular pattern on the sides of the wok. Surprisingly, there is not a dramatic difference in price between hand-hammered and factory-spun woks. Stamped woks are the least expensive and also the least durable. They have a totally smooth surface, and many are made with light-gauge carbon steel.

Cast-iron woks are slower to heat than carbon-steel woks, but because cast iron retains heat well, it is excellent for stir-frying, braising, and slow cooking. Unlike carbon-steel pans, cast-iron pans do not respond quickly to heat adjustments. Less experienced stir-fry cooks often find that once the wok is removed from the heat, the food must be immediately transferred to a platter or it will continue to cook in the hot wok.

Cast-iron woks manufactured in China are preferable to cast-iron woks made in America: they are much thinner and lighter in weight. Consequently they heat more quickly and are easier to lift. The average weight of a 14-inch wok is 3 to 4 pounds, compared to about 9 pounds for an American-made 12-inch cast-iron wok. A Chinese-made cast-iron wok is fragile. If it is smacked against a hard surface, the wok will shatter. The cast-iron handles can have sharp edges from the manufacturing process. These can be smoothed out with sandpaper.

Flat Bottomed Versus Round Bottomed

The flat-bottomed wok is essential for cooking on a residential range because it sits directly on the burner, in close proximity to the heat. I feel that it is the only wok that is effective on an electric range, and it works equally well on a gas range. While you may be able to cook with a round-bottomed wok on an electric range, the wok will never become as hot as a flat-bottomed wok.

The classic round-bottomed wok is ideal for stir-frying with ease and requires the least amount of oil. It works best on a custom-made wok stove, but it can be used on a gas range if it is stabilized; it is difficult to heat properly on an electric range. If the wok is unsupported when you are cooking, it is very dangerous, especially if you are deep-frying. There are several ways to stabilize a round-bottomed wok on a gas stove:

• Inexpensive aluminum wok rings, also known as fire rings, can be purchased as an accessory where most woks are sold. They are a recent invention, and in many cases, either because the ring is too high or does not fit on a gas burner properly, they prevent the wok from heating properly. The ring can be notched or cut back with wire cutters or tin snips so that the bottom of the wok will sit closer to the burner. Be advised that a cut wok ring may permanently scratch the stove surface.

• Some gas stoves have wok stands or rack accessories. Many are set too high and prevent the wok from sitting close enough to the burner to attain sufficient heat.

• The grids on some gas stoves, when turned over, work well to hold the wok securely.

The Following Woks Are Not Recommended
• Stainless-steel woks. A stainless-steel wok is excellent for steaming but not for stir-frying. The heat is uneven, and the pan tends to require more oil to prevent sticking.

• Nonstick woks. In her classic book *The Modern Art of Chinese Cooking,* author Barbara Tropp compares stir-frying in Teflon to "trying to boil an egg in a steamer; the nature of the cooking vessel is inimical to the task." Food writer and retired chemistry professor Robert Wolke adds, "Nonstick cookware is indeed horrible for stir-frying, because when the juices coagulate from the heat, they don't stick to the pan and brown there, producing all those wonderful browned flavors. Instead, they stick to the pieces of food and remain there as a coating, less accessible to the hot metal." According to Wolke this is also true of the newer reinforced nonstick pans. Each year new styles of nonstick woks enter the market. Regardless of the new technology, I prefer the traditional carbon-steel or cast-iron wok used by chefs and home cooks. Once seasoned, these pans have a natural nonstick surface that is unsurpassed.

• Electric woks. These are highly unsuitable because of their nonstick surfaces and their heat, which cycles on and off and makes a proper stir-fry impossible.

• Five-layer woks. This relatively new wok has an aluminum core with stainless steel interior and exterior layers. The pan can be five to ten times the price of a traditional carbon-steel or cast-iron wok. It is slower to heat than an iron wok and not nearly as efficient for stir-frying.

Equipment Choices

American and Chinese specialty cookware stores carry a vast selection of woks that vary in material, shape, fabrication, and size. To help narrow down the options, I address below the woks and accessories that I recommend. To begin with, for a residential-style range purchase a 14-inch wok with a depth of 4 inches to prevent spattering. A larger wok can be used on a custom-made wok stove or on a professional range.

Carbon-Steel Cantonese-Style Wok
round bottomed with two metal ear handles

This is the wok favored by southern Chinese home cooks and restaurant chefs. It is available from 10 to 48 inches in diameter.

Carbon-steel Cantonese-style woks; the 14-inch wok is the most popular for home use.

With its flared open shape, it is sufficiently wide for stir-frying with a metal spatula. It is excellent on a custom-made wok stove, or when stabilized with a wok ring on a gas range or a professional range. It is not suited for an electric range. If you have an electric stove, a modernized version of this style is available with a flat bottom and two wooden spool ear handles.

Cast-Iron Cantonese-Style Wok
round bottomed with two metal ear handles

This is the traditional Chinese wok that was used before the invention of carbon steel. Made in China, this cast iron is thinner and lighter in weight than American cast iron. Many old-fashioned Cantonese home cooks insist that a Chinese-made cast-iron wok is the only way to achieve stir-fries with *wok hay*. The design is the same as the carbon-steel Cantonese-style wok. However, restaurant-sized woks are not made

Cast-iron Cantonese-style wok; Chinese chives are traditionally used to season a cast-iron wok.

Carbon-steel Westernized wok; a spatula with a deep shovel-like shape and slightly rounded corners works best for a Westernized wok or a Cantonese-style wok.

Carbon-Steel Westernized Wok
flat bottomed with a long wooden handle and a helper handle

Equally suited for the beginner and advanced cook, this is the wok of choice for any residential range. It incorporates the best features of the Cantonese- and northern-style wok: the flared bowl is sufficiently wide for stir-frying with a metal spatula; the long handle approximates that of a saucepan. The two heat-resistant wood handles make lifting the wok when it is filled with food easier. The diameter of the flat bottom should be no more than 5 or 6 inches before it curves up the sides. If the flat bottom is wider than 6 inches, the pan no longer has a wok shape. The pan should be as level as possible. This wok is available in sizes up to 14 inches.

from cast iron, as it is too fragile. This wok is excellent on a custom-made wok stove, or when stabilized with a wok ring on a gas range or a professional range. It is not suited for an electric range. When purchasing a cast-iron wok examine it carefully for cracks. Some people check the wok by tapping the outside of it, listening for a clear bell-like tone. A cracked wok or a wok with an uneven thickness is said to have a dull sound and is ill suited for cooking. A modernized version is available with black enamel on the outside, which makes the wok more durable, but I have had unsatisfactory results cooking with it; stir-fries tend to stick. I also don't like American cast-iron woks, which are heavy and unwieldy, and take too long to heat.

Carbon-Steel Northern-Style Wok
round bottomed with a long hollow metal handle

Also known as a *pao* wok or Peking pan, this wok is the favorite of home cooks and restaurant chefs in northern China. If you're even thinking about purchasing a northern-style wok, it presupposes a certain level of expertise. The *pao* wok is intended for very skilled cooks accustomed to using a Chinese ladle and the *pao* action for tossing food when stir-frying. Although the hollow metal handle is heat resistant, if the wok is placed over heat for a long time, the metal handle will get hot. The small round deep bowl shape is dramatically less flared than the Cantonese-style wok, making it not only suited for the *pao* action but good for braises because of its depth. This wok is excellent on a custom-made wok stove, or when stabilized with a wok ring on a gas range or a professional range. It is not suited for an electric range. For the *pao* action it is preferable to have a smaller wok; the 12-inch wok is the best size for a residential gas stove. A modernized version is available with a long wooden handle.

Hand-hammered carbon-steel northern-style wok; the ladle's shape matches the deep curve of this kind of wok.

Ladle
The Chinese metal ladle is the utensil of choice for stir-frying with a northern-style wok. The ladle fits the curvature of the deep bowl-shaped wok better than a spatula. The ladle is used facing down in a quick back-and-forth motion. The best size for home cooking is 14 inches long.

Spatula
When stir-frying with a Westernized wok with a flat bottom or a Cantonese-style wok, I use a Chinese metal spatula. It has a shovel-like shape and a slightly rounded lip designed to fit the contour of a flared-shaped wok. The recessed rim holds more food than a Western-style flat metal spatula. The best size for home cooking is 14 inches long.

Wok Lid
Wok lids are made of aluminum and must be an inch smaller than the diameter of the wok; a 14-inch wok requires a 13-inch lid. Purchase your lid with your wok so that you can see exactly how it fits; it will seldom be tight fitting, but choose the one that comes closest. There are two styles: I prefer the domed lid to the flat type because less condensation drips down onto the food, especially when steaming.

A dome-shaped lid sits on Margaret Loo's carbon-steel wok as she preps her ingredients for a recipe. This lid shape is best because it reduces the amount of condensation that drips onto the food.

Opening *a Wok*

開
鑊

A new wok represents the beginning of countless culinary possibilities. The ritual of seasoning initiates the wok's culinary life. The Cantonese describe this process as "opening the wok," or *hoi wok*. For an experienced Chinese cook, seasoning a wok is the most ordinary of culinary tasks. There is nothing complicated or difficult about the process. With age and care a cast-iron or carbon-steel wok will develop a patina that seals it, protecting it from rust and creating a non-stick surface that is ideal for cooking.

When I began asking traditional Chinese cooks about the wok seasoning process, their explanations were vague. They weren't deliberately withholding information, but I was reminded of the many aspects of Chinese culture that have an elusive mystique, that are better understood when experienced rather than explained. Thus, I met with numerous Chinese home cooks, cooking teachers, master chefs, and cookbook authors to learn their techniques. Each time I brought a new wok for the expert to season.

Some cooks spent as long as forty-five minutes seasoning the wok; others required only four. Some worked intuitively, knowing purely by sense when the seasoning process was complete; others had a specific test for judging completion. I was perplexed by these great disparities.

In the West, the most common approach to seasoning a wok requires alternating applications of cooking oil and heat. The cooks I met with were divided between using this technique and applying an old-fashioned method requiring Chinese chives and pork fat. I found many variations on both techniques, as well as a myriad of other methods. Oddly, most cooks knew only one—the method they used when they first seasoned their woks, some as long as fifty years ago.

Even though seasoning a wok with Chinese chives is a common practice among traditional cooks, I had never read about it in any Chinese cookbook. My introduction to the "recipe" came from a fateful encounter with a clerk at the Hung Chong wok shop in New York's Chinatown who, upon selling me a new carbon-steel wok, told me to stir-fry Chinese chives in oil in the new wok. I later learned that not only the home cook but even Chef Huang Zhen Hua, one of China's premier chefs and a specialist in classical imperial dishes, also seasons by stir-frying Chinese chives in oil. Countless other chefs in Hong Kong and China taught me more seasoning "recipes," calling for stir-frying chives with fatty pork, insisting that pork fat was superior to oil for this process.

While every cook's method differed slightly from that of the others, each explained the use of chives and pork fat nearly identically: the combination of Chinese chives and pork fat is best for "washing," or *sai wok*, the metal and ultimately for seasoning it. Despite their unanimity, no one gave me a clear understanding why this technique works. Chef Huang offered that the chives' long fibers make them ideal for the scrubbing action, although scallions can substitute. "The chives remove the metal flavor from the wok, and the pork fat prevents food from sticking to the pan," says Chef Paray Li of The Peninsula in Hong Kong. Another cook theorized about the inexpensiveness of Chinese chives and pork fat in China, thereby suggesting that economics dictates their use. In America, where chives are higher in price, he finds it permissible to use other produce as long as it's a green vegetable. I was not convinced. When my

Mr. Wen demonstrates an unusual technique for seasoning a cast-iron wok that involves rubbing it first with Chinese chives and then a light coating of lard.

Chinese language teacher, Mr. Wen, described the custom in his Cantonese village of rubbing a new cast-iron wok with Chinese chives and then allowing the chive juice to "marinate" in the pan before rubbing it with pork fat or lard, I was certain that something unusual in chives made them uniquely suited for seasoning a wok.

A close examination of the vegetable offered me no clues. Chinese chives resemble hearty Western chives except for the hard stem end, about an inch of white that turns into a flat, dark green leaf approximately ¼ inch wide. Chinese chives are sold in Asian produce markets in small to medium bunches ranging from 10 to 16 inches in length.

In the reference book *Vegetables as Medicine* I discovered that the chives contain sulphide. Speculating that sulphide might disinfect the wok, I asked my local pharmacist. He confirmed sulphide's antibacterial properties. I remembered that the Chinese are fond of cooking chives in soups because they believe chives clear the body of certain toxins. Could the chives have a cleansing effect on the wok, too? I consulted with Dr. Kam Toa Miu, a Chinese herbalist. He told me that Chinese chives are the only vegetable used as a medicinal herb. They have the unique ability to be both cleansing and restorative to the body. According to Dr. Miu, in addition to their antibacterial qualities, the chives are particularly good for removing toxins from the liver.

I posed the same question to my friend Shelley Smyers, a chemist. She confirmed the antiseptic and antifungal properties of foods found in the garlic/onion/chive family and explained that these can be traced to the chives' relatively high sulfur/sulfide content. My Uncle Sam, who is a physics professor, recommended a chemistry professor I might query. Professor Yih-Shen Hwang actually studied

Many traditional recipes for seasoning a wok require the use of Chinese chives, called gao choy *in Cantonese. These long flat chives are sold in bunches in Asian markets and should not be confused with flowering garlic chives or yellow chives.*

Chinese chives (*Allium tuberosum*) for their chemical composition. He conducted this research at ISK Mountain View Research Center in Sunnyvale, California, during the 1990s. He wrote:

The sulfur-containing compounds in Chinese chives have long been known to be antibacterial. Recent literature reports that S-methyl methanethiosulfinate and S-methyl 2-propene-1-thiosulfinate, in particular, showed significant antibacterial activities against E. coli. The quantities of the active components in the plant are invariably minute and, therefore, may or may not be enough to do the antiseptic job in a wok. We do know that the plant in small amounts may or may not kill the bugs in the wok. The subsequent heat can definitely kill off most of the pathogens. The cause and effect relationship (which kills the bug, chive or fire or both or alone?) should be further researched.

As a budding food anthropologist I was thrilled with the impressive chemical breakdown and vindicated by scientific confirmation of the antibacterial properties of the chives. But Dr. Hwang's caution that the presence of sulfur was too minute to be of consequence was disheartening. Though disappointed, I wasn't surprised at the futility of trying to force an old Chinese custom to make scientific sense.

A week later, Julie Tay, founder and director of Wossing Center for Chinese in New York City, invited me for a chive-and-pork wok-seasoning session using her family's favored method. Analyzing the process from the cultural perspective, Tay offered what became my favorite interpretation, describing the use of chives and pork fat as symbolic as well as functional. Superstition and symbolism are powerful forces in Chinese culture, especially in the kitchen. Tay explained that the Cantonese word for chives, *gao choy*, reminds the Chinese of the expression *ceung gao*, which means "long life." With this understanding, the seasoning of a wok with chives becomes a ritual in hopes that the wok will be everlasting. Scallions and cilantro are often used for

Chinese festive occasions because their greenness is a symbol of life. Tay speculates that the green chives also symbolize vitality.

Likewise, pork and its fat is regarded by the ever-imaginative Chinese as an auspicious ingredient, one central to the Chinese sense of well-being. A popular food offering in rituals, it is favored on a practical level for its greasiness, which is ideal for seasoning a carbon-steel or cast-iron wok.

My cooking sessions with countless Chinese cooks and chefs introduced me to numerous other folk seasoning recipes. Several home cooks informed me that bean sauce, *meen si*, can be substituted for chives in a cast-iron wok. Like the chives, bean sauce is also said to "wash" the wok's metal. Another method came from my friend Shelley's mother, who was raised in the village of Toisan in southern China. She seasons her wok by cooking a piece of pork on the bone in boiling water. Other cooks told me to rub oil into the wok with a chunk of ginger. The ginger blackens and is said to remove toxins from the wok. Chef Ip Chi Kwong, of the Shang Palace restaurant in Shanghai, likes to first pan-fry tofu in a little oil, which he says absorbs the metal flavor from the wok. Then he adds Chinese chives and stir-fries both ingredients together. Chef Danny Chan showed me an altogether unique method: he boils water in a new wok with a little distilled vinegar. This is how he seasoned his wok at home thirty years ago, as well as every wok for his restaurant kitchen. Several restaurant chefs told me they season by using high heat to burn their woks, but only in kitchens equipped with a powerful exhaust system. Restaurant chef and owner Ming Tsai seasons his restaurant woks at the Blue Ginger on high heat with salt.

Tane Chan, owner of The Wok Shop in San Francisco, taught me an intriguing seasoning "recipe." In her oven oil method for a carbon-steel wok (page 51), Chan lightly coats the wok with oil and then bakes the wok about twenty minutes. After the wok cools, she removes as much of the oil coating as possible with a stainless-steel scrubber. She then repeats the process several more times. The resulting wok can have an amazing lacquer-like patina.

In my quest I imagined discovering the definitive seasoning method. Instead I came to understand that seasoning, like cooking, is very personal; there are many ways to achieve the same desired result. Reviewing the different seasoning methods I've learned, I think many of them, despite their contradictory styles, work just as long as you reinforce the seasoning by cooking frequently with your wok. It is equally important not to rush the seasoning process.

Cooks unaccustomed to seasoning a wok often doubt they've done it correctly. Jean Yueh, who has taught Chinese cooking for years, says she's received countless calls from panicked students alarmed to see discoloration or a dark ring form on the bottom of their carbon-steel woks after seasoning—just as it's supposed to. "I assure my students, no matter how you season a wok, eventually all woks get seasoned," says Yueh. "It is more important to understand that beyond the initial seasoning, it is constant use that best develops the wok's patina."

This advice was reiterated when I met Helen Chen, president of Joyce Chen Inc., for a seasoning session. After applying five or six layers of oil to a new carbon-steel wok over medium heat, Chen predicted food stir-fried in the newly seasoned wok might still stick. "It is only by cooking that a wok truly gets seasoned. Each time you cook, the seasoning is renewed," says Chen.

My personal choice for seasoning a new wok is any of the Chinese chive and pork stir-fry methods. While I love the patina the oven oil method for a carbon-steel wok can produce, seasoning by cooking food seems the most natural. I believe this technique goes to the heart of Chinese cooking—a combination of fact, fable, and superstition. I remain convinced that it is Chinese alchemy at work. The technique is simple and effective, and I hope it will be passed on to future generations. There is beauty in having a wok that is anointed with auspicious ingredients to ensure its long life. Respect ritually paid to a family's primary cooking pan creates harmony in the kitchen.

Basic Steps to Seasoning a Wok

The First Washing

Before proceeding to season the wok, no matter whether it looks clean, vigorously wash both sides of the wok with hot soapy water, using a stainless-steel scouring pad. Typically, carbon-steel woks are coated on both sides with a film of machine oil or grease that prevents the pan from rusting before its first use. Chinese-made cast-iron woks do not have an oil coating, but residual metal powder must be removed. Many experts advise that this first washing is the only time a wok should be cleaned with liquid dishwashing detergent. Following this thorough washing, dry the wok with paper towels. Do not be alarmed if the paper towels turn a dark gray color—this is residual oil or metal dust that has yet to be removed.

In addition to using dishwashing soap, you may also use Chinese chives, scallions, or ginger to "wash" the wok, removing its metallic taste. These cleansing agents are a secondary washing and are incorporated into the following seasoning processes.

Heating

Most methods begin the seasoning of a new wok with heating. Heat opens the pan's metal pores, thereby allowing better absorption of oil or pork fat to seal and temper the metal for cooking. Heating the pan will produce smoke, so be sure to open windows and turn on the exhaust fan. Paper towels are best for wiping away excess oil or pork fat and removing any residual machine oil. Old kitchen towels or rags can also be used, but be certain they are lint free. Be careful when wiping the wok, as the hot oil and pan can cause burns. If the wok is set over a flame, be cautious about the possibility of starting a grease fire. One cook I met wisely holds the paper towels with tongs. You may wish to throw out the hot oil-soaked paper towels in a garbage bag lined with newspapers. The newspapers will both absorb the oil and temper the heat so as not to melt the plastic liner.

Seasoning

Some of the following seasoning "recipes" are specifically for carbon-steel while others are only for Chinese-made cast-iron woks. Chinese cooks approach seasoning a cast-iron wok differently from how a Western cook seasons a cast-iron skillet.

Cooking in a Newly Seasoned Wok

A good method for quickly developing a patina in a newly seasoned wok is stir-frying; don't skimp on the oil. Deep-frying is even better. A new wok can be said to "drink" oil, and cooking fatty foods greatly accelerates the seasoning process, as compared to braising or stewing. Even in America, where cast-iron skillets are popular, food authority Colman Andrews says that after seasoning a cast-iron skillet it is wise to "cook bacon or fry chicken—something good and greasy—in it the first five or six times you use it." Be careful to avoid cooking tomatoes or any dish that contains vinegar in the wok until the seasoning is set. Highly acidic foods stress the wok's finish and easily destroy a new patina and, depending on the amount of acid and the length of time they are left in the pan, can even pit the wok's surface. Similarly, steaming, boiling, and poaching should also be avoided until the wok is well seasoned.

Ideally the wok should be used daily, or at least several times a week. A wok that is used only occasionally takes a long time to develop a patina. Even with constant use, it can take months for a cast-iron wok to blacken. The patina on a carbon-steel wok evolves even more slowly. Years may pass before the patina ultimately develops a color ranging from a deep rich brown to ebony.

Recipes for **Seasoning a Wok**

開
鑊

Wen Geng Lin's Chinese Chive Rub
Chinese Cast-Iron Wok

My Chinese language teacher, Mr. Wen, has always cooked in a classic Chinese-made cast-iron wok. This method for seasoning a wok is favored by his native village in Guangdong province, China. The wok's interior surface is cleaned by being vigorously scrubbed with Chinese chives, whose "juice" removes any rust before lard is rubbed in. See Julie Tay's Chinese Chive and Pork Fat Stir-Fry (opposite) for information on Chinese chives.

1 bunch Chinese chives (about 14 ounces)
¼ cup lard

1. Wash the inside and outside of the wok with hot water, using a stainless-steel scrubber and liquid dishwashing soap to remove any residual metal dust. Rinse with hot water. Bring 1 quart of water to a boil in the wok over high heat. Carefully pour out the water and dry the wok with paper towels. The towels will be gray.

2. Grab a small handful of the unwashed chives and fold them in half in your hand. Rub the chives over the wok's entire interior surface, scouring it as you would a dirty pot. The chives will begin to blacken. Rotate the bundle of chives in your hand to reveal the fresh portion and continue rubbing. When the entire handful has blackened, set those chives aside (do not discard) and use a fresh handful. Continue rubbing the wok until all of the chives have been used and are totally blackened.

3. Spread the reserved blackened chives across the entire surface of the wok and allow to rest 30 minutes so that the chive juices will penetrate the cast iron. Discard the chives. Wipe the interior of the wok thoroughly with clean paper towels. The paper towels will be gray.

4. Using fresh paper towels, spread the lard over the entire interior surface of the wok and allow to rest

30 minutes so that the fat will penetrate the cast iron. Wipe the outside of the wok with paper towels to remove any lard that may drip once the pan is heated.

5. Open the window and turn the exhaust fan on high. Heat the wok over medium heat. Start rotating the wok slowly from side to side until the lard is liquefied, 1 to 2 minutes. The wok will smoke. Remove from the heat. Cool 15 minutes. Wipe the wok with clean paper towels to remove excess fat. Carefully pour 1 quart of water into the wok and bring to a boil over high heat. Pour the water out. Dry over low heat 1 to 2 minutes. The wok is seasoned and ready for cooking.

Hung Chong Chinese Chive and Oil Stir-Fry
Carbon-Steel Wok

The first time I seasoned a wok without problems, I used this recipe, which I learned at the Hung Chong wok shop in New York's Chinatown. Make sure the chives are very dry after washing to prevent the oil from spattering. One bunch of scallions cut into 3-inch pieces and ½ cup of sliced ginger can be substituted for the chives in this recipe. Scallions and ginger are said to remove the wok's metallic taste. Smell the wok after seasoning—the metal will have a strong fragrance from the aromatics.

½ bunch Chinese chives (about 7 ounces)
2 tablespoons vegetable oil

1. Wash the inside and outside of the wok with hot water, using a stainless-steel scrubber and liquid dishwashing soap. Rinse with hot water. Dry the wok with paper towels, then place over low heat 1 to 2 minutes until the pan is totally dry. Cut the chives into 2-inch pieces.

2. Open the window and turn the exhaust fan on high. Heat the wok over high heat until a bead of water vaporizes within 1 to 2 seconds of contact. Swirl in the oil and add the chives. Reduce the heat to medium and stir-fry 5 minutes, using a spatula to push the mixture up the sides of the wok to the edge. If the mixture becomes dry, add an additional tablespoon of oil. Remove from the heat. Cool. Discard the chives.

3. Wash the wok with hot water and a soft sponge. Dry over low heat 1 to 2 minutes. The wok is seasoned and ready for cooking.

Julie Tay's Chinese Chive and Pork Fat Stir-Fry

Chinese Cast-Iron Wok

In Singapore Julie Tay learned to season a wok using Chinese chives and pork fat. Chives come in three varieties: Chinese chives, flowering garlic chives, and yellow chives. Chinese chives, called gao choy, *look like hearty Western chives or very young scallions, but the bunches are much bigger. They are dark green with an inch of white at the stem end. This vegetable is sold in medium bunches ranging from 10 to 16 inches in length. Western chives cannot be substituted.*

½ bunch Chinese chives (about 7 ounces)
8 ounces pork fat, cut into ½-inch cubes

1. Wash the inside and outside of the wok with hot water only (no dishwashing soap), using a stainless-steel scrubber to remove any residual metal dust. Rinse with hot water. Dry the wok with paper towels. Cut the chives into 2-inch pieces.

2. Open the window and turn the exhaust fan on high. Heat the wok over high heat until a bead of water vaporizes within 1 to 2 seconds of contact. Add the pork fat and reduce the heat to low. Stir slowly with a metal spatula, allowing the fat to liquefy. As the fat cooks, bring the fat cubes to the sides of the pan and up to the edge to "wash" the entire interior surface with the pork fat. When the fat turns golden and is no longer releasing liquid fat, increase the heat to high and add the chives. Stir-fry 10 to 15 minutes, spreading the chive–pork fat mixture with a spatula over the entire surface of the wok; do not neglect the upper edges.

3. Carefully add 1 cup of water—the fat may spatter. Cook 5 minutes, continuing to spread the wet mixture along the sides with the spatula. Carefully pour the mixture into a disposable can and cool before discarding.

4. Wash the wok with cold water. Dry with clean paper towels. Dry over low heat 1 to 2 minutes. The wok is seasoned and ready for cooking.

Although Julie Tay's method for seasoning a cast-iron wok is called a stir-fry, the pork fat in fact cooks on low heat. Tay uses a spatula and chopsticks to baste the sides with the mixture rather than tossing it.

Recipes for Seasoning a Wok

Basic Oil Method

Carbon-Steel Wok

Some cooks follow this method to season a carbon-steel wok, using only two applications of oil. The process takes less than 5 minutes. Often after you wipe the wok the paper towel will still be gray. Many cooks are not bothered by this and feel the wok is seasoned and ready to cook in. Even with additional applications of oil this process takes no more than 15 or 20 minutes. It is critical with the oil technique to rotate the wok from side to side over the heat. Never allow the pan to rest on the bottom, where heat is naturally concentrated.

1 to 4 teaspoons vegetable oil

1. Wash the inside and outside of the wok with hot water, using a stainless-steel scrubber and liquid dishwashing soap. Rinse with hot water. If there are still sticky spots, rub the surface with a tablespoon of salt, using the abrasive side of a sponge made for nonstick cookware, until the surface is smooth. Rinse with hot water. Dry the wok with paper towels. Dry over low heat 1 to 2 minutes. If the wok has a wooden or plastic handle, wrap it in aluminum foil to prevent the handle from burning.

2. Open the window and turn the exhaust fan on high. Heat the wok over high heat. After about 5 seconds, the wok will begin to smoke. Continue heating the wok, rotating it from side to side about 1 minute. A yellow or blue ring will form around the interior base of the wok. Remove from the heat and cool 30 seconds.

3. Pour ½ teaspoon oil into the wok. Using a double-folded paper towel, wipe the inside of the wok, spreading oil over the entire surface. Put the wok over low heat, rotating it slowly from side to side 30 seconds, never resting the pan on the bottom. Remove from the heat and cool 30 seconds.

4. Repeat step 3. The paper towel will probably be a little gray from any remaining factory oil. Cool the wok. Using clean paper towels, wipe away any excess oil. Wash the wok with hot water. Dry over low heat 1 to 2 minutes. The wok is seasoned and ready for cooking.

5. If desired, repeat step 3 several more times or until a paper towel is no longer gray colored after the wok is wiped. This is the best indication that the wok is seasoned and all of the machine oil has been removed.

Cooking teacher Ken Lo, of New York City, compares a newly seasoned flat-bottomed wok, in his left hand, with the patina of a well-used one.

Tane Chan's Oven Oil Method

Carbon-Steel Wok

I learned this method from Tane Chan, owner of The Wok Shop in San Francisco's Chinatown. Unlike all of the other seasoning recipes, this unusual baking technique can give a wok a lacquer-like finish. Each time the wok is removed from the oven, after it cools, scrub the wok as if you had made a mistake and are trying to remove the oil coating to restore the original metal. If the wok has a wood or plastic handle, remove it before following this recipe. If the handle cannot be removed, wrap the wood handle with a wet washcloth. Then wrap the washcloth with heavy-duty aluminum foil. Be careful, as the handle will get very hot and steamy. Check the handle from time to time to make sure the washcloth has not dried out. I do not recommend placing a plastic handle in a 450°F oven, even when wrapped with a wet washcloth and foil.

2 to 3 teaspoons vegetable oil

1. Preheat the oven to 450°F. Wash the inside and outside of the wok with hot water, using a stainless-steel scrubber and liquid dishwashing soap. Rinse with hot water. Dry the wok with paper towels. Dry over low heat 1 to 2 minutes. If the wok has a wooden handle, follow the directions in the headnote. Open the window and turn the exhaust fan on high.

2. Using a paper towel, spread ½ teaspoon oil over the entire inside surface. Put the wok in the oven 20 minutes. Remove from the oven with pot holders and cool until warm to the touch, about 5 minutes. Scrub the inside of the wok with hot water only (no detergent) 2 or 3 minutes, using a stainless-steel scrubber. Dry over low heat 1 to 2 minutes.

3. Repeat step 2 three or four more times. When the wok becomes bronze colored, remove from the oven and cool 5 minutes. Wash the wok with hot water and scrub it with a stainless-steel scrubber. Dry over low heat 1 to 2 minutes. Do not coat with oil again. The wok is seasoned and ready for cooking.

Western-Style Oven Oil Method

Chinese Cast-Iron Wok

This method is only for a Chinese-made cast-iron wok without black plastic handles. Chinese cast-iron woks are extremely porous and easy to season by baking in the oven. I coat only the inside of the wok, but some cooks recommend putting a light coating of oil on the outside as well. The wok is placed upside down on a sheet of aluminum foil in the oven so that any excess oil drips out of the wok and does not solidify in its well. Use pot holders when handling the wok, as it will be very hot.

1 teaspoon vegetable oil

1. Preheat the oven to 300°F. Wash the inside and outside of the wok with hot water, using a stainless-steel scrubber and liquid dishwashing soap. Rinse with hot water. Dry the wok with paper towels. The towels will be gray. Dry over low heat 1 to 2 minutes.

2. Heat the wok over high heat until a bead of water vaporizes within 1 to 2 seconds of contact. Remove from the heat. Using a double-folded paper towel, spread the oil over the entire inside surface. Carefully put the wok upside down on a sheet of aluminum foil on a rack in the oven. Bake 40 minutes. Turn off the oven and cool the wok in the oven 2 hours.

3. The surface of the wok will be slightly sticky to the touch. Wash the inside of the wok with hot water only (no detergent), scrubbing it with the abrasive side of a sponge made for nonstick cookware. Dry over low heat 1 to 2 minutes. Cool. The wok is seasoned and ready for cooking. If desired, repeat steps 2 and 3 once more.

The **Face** *of a Wok*

The first thing I noticed on the open shelf in my friend's kitchen was the handsome wok with the beautiful handles. I asked to examine it. My friend confided this carbon-steel wok was his prize. But as I peered into the pan, I discovered the interior surface was coated in rust! Any food cooked in this rusted pan would be inedible. I was horrified. In response to my expression my friend confessed that he had recently made the mistake of cooking sauerbraten in the wok, and the vinegar had totally stripped the wok of its patina.

Maybe I should stop asking to see people's woks, for they tell me more than I probably should know about a cook. The appearance of the patina is a clear indication of a cook's expertise. The wok's "face" reveals whether a cook is a novice or an experienced chef. It tells whether the wok has been cared for or neglected. A wok used daily has a rich patina and a sheen like radiant skin. Its surface is smooth and silky. Rarely used woks have a dull metallic finish that's often marred with rust. Sometimes the surface will be rough and tacky.

The cooks I interviewed used woks that ranged in age from five to fifty years. Many of these pans were culinary works of art. A well-seasoned cast-iron wok is ebony black, like a cast-iron skillet. But a well-seasoned carbon-steel wok may range in color from a rich mahogany tea color to totally black. A new cast-iron wok takes about a year to blacken, depending on how often it is used. A new carbon-steel wok takes longer. My friend Tom Hicks said that after seven months of use his carbon-steel wok's bottom was black and the sides were medium amber-brown. Often the face of a carbon-steel wok will develop the brown hues mottled with warm, golden tones reminiscent of an old European landscape painting.

The most extraordinary wok I have ever seen is Chef Danny Chan's home wok. The interior of the wok was a delicate teak tone reminiscent of the color often found in Chinese silk scroll paintings. I was captivated by its unusual color; it was the first time I ever saw a well-seasoned, old carbon-steel wok that wasn't black. Though he was amused by my interest in the color, Chef Chan's genuine pride was in the smoothness of the wok's surface. Brushing his hand over the interior, he described it in Cantonese as being *ping waat*, flat smooth, the rare polished texture and nonstick surface that results from years of cooking.

The character evident in a wok's patina is a testament to the culinary journey a cook has taken. It reveals how long the cook has owned the wok and how it's been used. Many cooks have a shared history with their woks that spans a lifetime if not more. Some cooks have received their woks as wedding presents; others have had their woks since college days. My friend Judy Wong feels honored to have inherited her mother's twenty-year-old wok. "My mom used to cook everything in that wok, from frying dessert cookies and shrimp chips to poaching whole fish and stir-frying lobster for New Year's dinner," Judy recalls.

The silky interior surface of a well-used wok is the result of pampering the pan. Very particular chefs insist on washing their wok themselves, protecting it from family members or roommates whose careless handling might destroy the pan's seasoning. I must confess I am so attached to my cast-iron and carbon-steel woks that, except for my husband, I allow no one else to clean them.

The Chinese call an old wok "a thousand-year-old wok." "A well-seasoned wok provides flavor," says Chinese cooking authority Ken Hom. It is the cook's most treasured pan. No cook would willingly part with a well-seasoned wok in favor of a new one. My friend Sui Wan Lok still laments the loss of her twenty-year-old Chinese-made

cast-iron wok, accidentally broken while being washed. I have several woks ranging in age from two to ten years old, still youngsters. I look forward to their accompanying me into old age as I watch their "faces" acquire ancient beauty.

Cleaning the Wok After Cooking

The Chinese are fastidious about keeping a wok pristine. All cooks agree that if the wok is not clean, food cannot taste right and is likely to stick in the pan. A cast-iron or carbon-steel wok must always be hand-washed. Cleaning a wok in the dishwasher inevitably results in badly rusted pans. The easiest way for the home cook to wash a wok after cooking is simply with water.

Most of the time when I use my wok I also cook a pot of rice for the meal. As is the Chinese custom, I rinse the raw rice grains in several changes of cold water until the water runs clear before I cook it. Years ago a Chinese friend taught me to save about 4 cups of this rinsing water for cleaning the wok: I pour the cloudy rice water into the wok and let it stand 5 or 10 minutes. By cleanup time, the wok has soaked long enough to make removal of any food particles with a soft sponge easy; the rice water contains just enough starch to remove the wok's greasiness without having to use soap. If I haven't cooked rice, I simply soak the dirty wok in plain water. I also scrub the outside of the wok with a sponge and rinse it with water to remove surface impurities.

Some home cooks insist a wok must be washed immediately after cooking, just as restaurant chefs do. I believe the practice of adding cold water to a scorching hot wok is not advisable, because the dramatic change in temperature eventually warps the bottom of the pan. This is not a concern for restaurants where woks are routinely replaced—but a

As is customary in restaurant kitchens, Chef Ming Tsai gives one of his woks a vigorous scrubbing after a stir-fry.

wok for the home cook is meant to last for years. Besides, why sacrifice serving piping-hot food or a stir-fry with *wok hay* for the sake of washing out a pan? Cleaning the wok can wait until after the meal is finished.

Many cooks recommend washing the wok only in water and never using detergent, which is said to strip the seasoning from the wok, causing food to stick and leaving a taste that cannot be rinsed away. In my experience, if the wok becomes extremely greasy, a minute amount of mild liquid dishwashing soap can be applied with a sponge. I have never had problems with sticking or with tasting soap in my food. However, I use soap rarely and *never* use any kind of abrasive powder cleanser.

I prefer to clean my carbon-steel wok with a sponge recommended for cleaning a nonstick pan. I typically use the soft side for cleaning the interior and the rough side for cleaning sticky spots and the outside surface, where clinging bits of food must be thoroughly scrubbed off. Some cooks prefer a soft natural-bristle brush. The traditional wok-scrubbing tool is a hard bamboo brush, which I do not recommend for home cooks. Unless the wok is used constantly, the patina on a home carbon-steel wok tends to be thin and delicate; the hard bamboo brush scratches it off. In addition, food particles easily lodge in the brush, making it difficult to clean. The bamboo brush is excellent

How to Combat Grease Buildup in the Kitchen

Over time, stir-frying and deep-frying cause grease to build up on the exhaust hood, backsplash, and kitchen cabinets around the stove. To clean, dissolve ¼ cup baking soda in a quart of hot water. Use a dishcloth or sponge to wash soiled surfaces. Rinse with hot water. After the surfaces dry, wipe any resulting white residue that remains from the baking soda.

for restaurant woks that have thick patinas.

After I clean a wok, I touch the bottom surface to make sure it is smooth and silky. Sometimes the wok appears clean, but if there are even minute food particles, food will stick when you cook. If there is residual food or sticky spots on a carbon-steel or cast-iron wok, I rub a tablespoon of salt lightly onto the spot with a damp sponge. I rinse the salt off to prevent rusting and pitting, then thoroughly dry the wok over low heat. If the wok has any white spots or streaks, the salt has not been completely removed. Rinse and dry the pan again.

Maintenance of woks for restaurant cooking is different. At Blue Ginger restaurant in Wellesley, Massachusetts, Chef Ming Tsai's 16-inch northern-style carbon-steel woks are cleaned once a day over blazing-hot 80,000-BTU burners until they're charcoal white. Salt is added and scrubbed with a bamboo brush until the salt turns black. According to Ming Tsai, the salt takes away any grit. The woks are then wiped with a dry cloth before being rubbed down with a cloth soaked in canola oil. Ming Tsai does not recall where he learned this method, but this is also how he seasons new woks. Over the course of a day the woks are simply washed with water and a wok brush immediately after each use.

Cast-iron woks have sturdy patinas that can withstand the abrasive power of a rough pad, but although the patina is more resilient, Chinese-made cast-iron woks are fragile and can shatter. When handling the wok be careful not to smack it against a hard surface because it will break. Scrub the inside and outside of the cast-iron wok with a stainless-steel pad and rinse under cold water. (My friend Sui Wan Lok likes washing the stainless-steel pad in a secure compartment of the dishwasher.)

Once the wok is cleaned and rinsed, dry it over low heat 2 to 3 minutes or until all of the visible water drops are evaporated. Towel drying alone is not as effective as this method. Never dry a wok on a dish rack; it will rust. Some cooks rub ¼ to ½ teaspoon of peanut or other cooking oil into a newly seasoned wok with a paper towel once it is dry, but *only* for the first week or two. According to Chinese food expert Florence Lin, the oil rubbed on a wok becomes rancid and the flavor stays in the pan. In addition, the oil will attract dust and become tacky.

Store the wok in a dry area, either by hanging it from a pot rack or placing it in a drawer or on a shelf where the patina is protected from scratching. Humid weather, especially at the seashore, will make a wok more susceptible to rust. If a wok is used only occasionally, Chef Martin Yan recommends storing it in a large paper bag to help protect it from humidity and dust.

How to Clean a Rusted or Sticky Wok

For woks with rust or severe stickiness, my cousin Cindy's husband, Zane, taught me this excellent cleaning technique, which is most effective on a gas stove. Heat 1 cup of salt in the wok over high heat about 1 minute. Reduce the heat to low and, using a metal spatula, push the salt onto the problem areas. (Hot salt can be very dangerous; handle it with care.) Heat the salt 5 minutes. Cool the wok until the salt is just warm, about 5 minutes. Scrub the warm salt with a soft, clean double-folded rag on any problem spots. Wipe the wok clean. Heat the wok over high heat until the wok just begins to smoke. Using a paper towel, smear ½ teaspoon oil over the inside surface. Allow the wok to cool, then rinse under hot water, washing lightly with the soft side of a sponge. Dry the pan over low heat 2 to 3 minutes to make sure the pan is totally dry. If the problem is severe, choose one of the seasoning recipes and reseason the wok.

Clockwise from above: Cookbook author Millie Chan describes the tough nonstick surface that develops on her well-seasoned woks; bamboo brushes for washing a wok; a young woman in the Yangshuo dai pai dong *scrubs her wok*; Chef Ip Chi Cheung pounds the dents out of a wok warped by the intense heat of a Hong Kong restaurant stove.

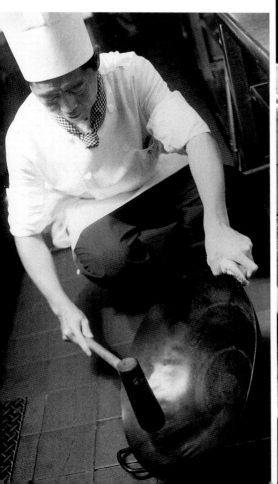

The Art of
Stir-Frying

For the Chinese a stir-fry is a revered dish—
the quintessential balance of flavor, texture,
and unique seared aroma. Differences in
technique separate accomplished home
cooks and master chefs, but all agree that
the wok is the best pan for stir-frying.

Wok Hay *The Breath of a Wok*

鑊
氣

My father taught me early in life that there is nothing quite as delicious as the rich, concentrated flavors of a Cantonese stir-fry, in which morsels of meat are cooked just quickly enough to ensure their juicy succulence and vegetables are rendered crisp and refreshing. It is a far cry from the oily, overcooked, heavily sauced renditions to which most Americans are accustomed.

In Hong Kong and Guangzhou, the stir-fry is a culinary art form. Nowhere else in the world are stir-fries scrutinized by both professional chefs and ordinary people with identical criteria: Does the stir-fry possess the prized, sublime taste of *wok hay*? Discerning Cantonese consider a stir-fry without *wok hay* to be like bad wine, dead and flat.

I think of *wok hay* as the breath of a wok—when a wok breathes energy into a stir-fry, giving foods a unique concentrated flavor and aroma. Of course, the Cantonese definition of *wok hay* varies from cook to cook. Many chefs will immediately talk about controlling the *fo hao*, fire power, for only the correct intense heat combined with a short cooking time elicits the *heung mei*, the fragrant aroma that characterizes *wok hay*. "A wok must be very hot for stir-fries to have the grilled, smoky flavor that is so distinctive of *wok hay*," says Chinese cooking authority Ken Hom. "A well-seasoned carbon-steel wok is also essential for creating *wok hay*—the blacker the pan, the more intense the *wok hay* flavor."

Some cooks define *wok hay* as the "taste of the wok." Other cooks describe *wok hay* in near poetic terms. My friend Vivien Cheung says, "*Wok hay* is both elusive and real." She speculates that it has to do with the design of the wok. "I imagine the wok to be like a volcano. Stir-frying on high heat incorporates hot air and motion, releasing a prized essence into the food. In a skillet that essence is all dissipated." Hong Kong heritage researcher Nevin

Lim thinks *wok hay* is a harmony of taste. "When the Cantonese stir-fry garlic and spinach, they use the garlic to remove the raw taste of spinach. With good *wok hay* you will not taste the harsh flavor of garlic. Instead, the two ingredients combine to create a harmony of taste," says Lim.

In Hong Kong, where people tend to be very superstitious, *wok hay* is so coveted that "when a customer is served a stir-fry void of *wok hay*, it is often interpreted as an ominous sign of bad luck," says Chief Instructor Chef Ronald Shao, of the Chinese Cuisine Training Institute in Hong Kong. No investments or wagers should be made on such an inauspicious day. My own family is no exception in their reverence for *wok hay*. My eighty-nine-year-old father has celebrated his birthday with dinner at Lichee Garden restaurant in San Francisco for over twenty years because of his admiration for Chef Siu Chah Lung's stir-fries. Baba relishes the intensity of *wok hay* in every stir-fry—for him it is an auspicious symbol of vitality and life. According to Chef Siu, "*Wok hay* makes the food powerful and strong."

The concept of *wok hay* is so ingrained in my own knowledge of food that I assumed the term was known by all Chinese. But *wok hay* is a strictly Cantonese expression. The cooking vessel that the Cantonese call a *wok* is, in fact, called *guo* in Mandarin. Neither the word nor the characters are the same. I showed the *wok hay* characters to countless people during my travels throughout China. The *wok* character refers to the pan; the

Preceding pages and opposite: Whether cooking Liang Nian Xiu's Moon Hill Corn and Beans (page 132) on a traditional hearth stove or stir-frying shredded vegetables over a metal drum filled with charcoal, the same principles of high heat and fast cooking create the coveted taste of wok hay.

hay character (known as *chi* or *qi* in Mandarin) means "energy" or "breath." Culinary professionals were often familiar with the expression, but the average non-Cantonese person had no idea how to read the *wok* character, and those who could often looked at me in bafflement, wondering what wok energy or breath could possibly mean. I even searched for *wok hay* in a Chinese dictionary, but because it is so particular to the Cantonese dialect, it was not there.

"In China, only the Cantonese stress the importance of *wok hay* in a stir-fry," says legendary Chinese food expert Florence Lin. "The Cantonese superiority at stir-frying is well known." Lin, a native of Ningbo, near Shanghai, explains that when cooks of her region stir-fry, it is often done slowly in a medium-hot wok to accentuate texture instead of *wok hay*. It was Lin who first explained to me that Cantonese weather—hot and humid throughout the year—prompted the Cantonese style of stir-frying. "In the summer months when temperatures can climb to well over a hundred degrees Fahrenheit, no one wants to stand in front of a stove longer than necessary." She points out that in northern China, where there is a cold season, one finds more braises and slow-cooking stews. In the old days in Guangzhou, without refrigeration a stew could easily spoil from the afternoon until evening.

In addition, Lin explains, because Guangzhou's growing season was longer, chefs had a richer selection of fresh produce, and proximity to the water provided a wealth of seafood. Cantonese chefs discovered that their style of stir-frying imparted a distinct wok flavor or *wok hay* while retaining the integrity of the ingredients.

Walking through the open-air markets of Guangzhou, I am always astounded by the quality of local produce. Fruits and vegetables have the sheen and fragrance found only in just-harvested crops. I watch a fishmonger net a swimming rock cod from a tank and place it on his cutting board, where he calmly fillets the live fish for a waiting customer. When ingredients are stir-fried at their peak flavor and texture, they deliver a true experience of *wok hay*.

Even though my stove at home cannot produce the fierce heat of a restaurant stove, I have nevertheless found ways to achieve *wok hay*. For example, I seek the freshest possible seasonal vegetables, such as Chinese broccoli in the winter or asparagus in the spring. I know if the produce is not at its peak ripeness, my stir-fry will have neither depth of flavor nor *wok hay*.

Standing at the stove, I reach for my well-seasoned flat-bottomed carbon-steel wok, which sits closer to the flame. I cut my ingredients into uniform, small sizes, to ensure even cooking. I begin to heat the wok.

Many chefs taught me that *wok hay* is achieved only by adding cold oil to a hot wok. Heating the wok to the point of faint smoking before adding oil prevents food from sticking to the pan. If the wok is hot, the cold oil will dance or ripple on the sur-

Baba brings Mama's Noodles with Mushrooms and Ham (page 123) to the table. He is adamant that the wok hay *of the stir-fry should be savored immediately, before the intense flavor and aroma have time to dissipate.*

face. More important, "The cold oil functions to cool down the wok slightly and thus makes food more tender," says Chef Poon Chi Cheung of the Spring Moon restaurant in Hong Kong. According to Chef Poon, if the oil is heated in a cold wok, *wok hay* will not be achieved; ingredients will stick and burn, while remaining raw inside. Chef Martin Yan compares the stir-fry technique of hot wok–cold oil to working with a barbecue grill. "If food is put on a cold grill, it's guaranteed to stick."

Chinese cooking authority Ken Hom believes that properly heating the wok is critical for achieving *wok hay*. "Cooks who are unaccustomed to stir-frying never get the wok hot enough. It's the biggest obstacle to overcome," explains Hom.

When I stir-fry, I judge the heat by placing the palm of my hand about 2 inches above the wok's surface until I feel a warmth similar to that of a hot radiator. At this point the wok also gives off a wisp of smoke, and a bead of water will evaporate within 1 to 2 seconds of contact. I swirl in the oil while rotating the wok to spread the oil across the bottom. When the wok is hot enough, the aromatics I add will sizzle. "We cook by sound," says Chef Ming Tsai. "If the wok is hot enough, you will have a sizzling sound at all times."

Once the stir-frying begins, my challenge is to protect the wok's heat from dropping too drastically and sacrificing the *wok hay*. When a wok is not scorching hot, food cannot be seared and a stir-fry becomes watery. A wet or soggy ingredient can also lower the heat in the wok to a degree that makes the quick searing action of the stir-fry impossible to achieve. I always wash greens and then dry them thoroughly in a salad spinner. I remember my mother washing her vegetables early in the morning, so that they could drain in the open air until dry to the touch.

While I admire restaurant chefs' expertise, some of their techniques do not make sense for the home cook. For example, restaurant chefs frequently oil-blanch ingredients for a stir-fry. This means that the ingredients are deep-fried for a few seconds before they are used in a stir-fry. At home

oil blanching is unnecessary and impractical. Without it, stir-fries taste even lighter and fresher than those cooked in restaurants.

When Chinese chefs stir-fry they use a cooking technique called *pao*, which requires jerking the wok in a small circular motion to toss the food, ensuring that everything cooks evenly. This, too, is impractical at home because it cools down the wok. I like to alternate between jerking the wok back and forth on the burner and using a metal spatula to keep the ingredients in constant motion.

On a home range, too much food in the wok reduces the temperature, changing any quick stir-fry into a slow braise. I never stir-fry more than 12 ounces of meat or a pound of chicken in a 14-inch wok. Any more than this and meat turns foamy gray within seconds, releasing its juices, crowding the wok, and making it impossible to sear. I also spread the meat around the wok to prevent any pieces from clumping together and losing contact with the wok's hot surface. I resist the temptation to touch the meat for 20 seconds to 1 minute. This is critical because it allows the meat to sear, intensifying the flavors so distinctive to *wok hay*. After that I stir-fry the meat with a spatula 10 to 15 seconds, spread it again in the wok, allow it to sear for 30 seconds, and then stir-fry it again.

I stir-fry no more than 3 to 4 cups of vegetables at a time; with larger quantities vegetables on the bottom scorch while those on the top remain uncooked, again forcing the wok's temperature to drop. Vegetables can be briskly stirred with a spatula the moment they are added to a wok. With good *wok hay*, vegetables have a crisp texture the Cantonese call *song*, highly valued in Chinese cooking.

A stir-fry's *wok hay* must be relished the moment it is cooked, before the elusive vital essence dissipates (similar in a way to a soufflé). I always serve my stir-fries immediately. A classic Cantonese stir-fry confers a special eating experience, and like my father and countless Chinese I covet a stir-fry that possesses the rarified taste of *wok hay*—cherishing the sublime pleasure such a culinary wonder offers.

Tips for Stir-Frying with *Wok Hay*

• The best wok for a residential Western-style stove is a 14-inch flat-bottomed carbon-steel wok. If using a wok with metal handles, be sure to use pot holders when touching the handles.

• Make sure the ingredients are thoroughly prepped and uniformly sliced to ensure even cooking.

• Make sure vegetables are dry, to prevent stir-fries from becoming soggy. Allow vegetables to air-dry in a colander for several hours, or use a salad spinner to remove excess water.

• Measure and group all ingredients in order of their use in the recipe beside the stove for easy access.

• The wok must be hot before the oil is added. A carbon-steel or Chinese-made cast-iron wok must be heated on high heat until a faint wisp of smoke rises from the pan. Another test is to flick a bead of water into the pan; if it vaporizes within a second or two, the pan is hot enough.

• When using a powerful stove, I heat the wok until a faint wisp of smoke rises. I quickly turn off the heat, swirl in the oil, and then return the heat to high. This prevents the oil from smoking.

• Add the oil by swirling it into the wok down the sides and then rotate the pan, allowing the oil to spread across the bottom.

• Whether stir-frying raw meat or poultry, spread the meat evenly in the wok, let it cook undisturbed 20 seconds to 1 minute, allowing the meat to sear. Then stir-fry the meat with a spatula 10 to 15 seconds, spread the meat again in the wok and let it sear for 30 seconds more, and then continue stir-frying.

• Do not stir-fry more than 12 ounces of meat, 16 ounces (1 pound) of chicken, or 4 cups of vegetables in a 14-inch wok. Too many ingredients in a wok lowers the wok's temperature, causing ingredients to steam rather than stir-fry.

• Alternate between jerking the wok back and forth on the burner and using a metal spatula to keep the ingredients in constant motion.

• Swirl sauce mixtures or any liquids into the wok down the sides to prevent the temperature of the wok from dropping.

Fueled by compressed gas, Hong Kong wok stoves like this one at Spring Moon restaurant are far more powerful than their American counterparts.

Stir-Frying

Poultry

Chicken with Sichuan Peppercorns CCTI

Instructor Chef Kevin Chuk, of the Chinese Cuisine Training Institute in Hong Kong, stir-fries this dish using a northern-style wok. I have adapted Chef Chuk's recipe by making it medium hot, but for more heat increase the chili oil. Sichuan peppercorns add a wonderful aromatic taste. (photo page 66)

12 ounces skinless, boneless chicken thigh, cut
    into ½-inch cubes
3 teaspoons Shao Hsing rice wine or dry sherry
1 teaspoon cornstarch
¾ teaspoon salt
¼ teaspoon ground white pepper
1 teaspoon black soy sauce
1 tablespoon Chinkiang or balsamic vinegar
2 teaspoons sesame oil
1 teaspoon sugar
¼ teaspoon chili oil
2 tablespoons Homemade Chicken Broth
    (page 195)
1 tablespoon vegetable oil
8 small dried red chilies
1 teaspoon thinly sliced ginger
1 small garlic clove, thinly sliced
¼ teaspoon roasted and ground Sichuan
    peppercorns (see page 9)
1 scallion, chopped

1. In a medium bowl combine the chicken, 1 teaspoon of the rice wine, the cornstarch, ¼ teaspoon of the salt, and the white pepper. In a small bowl combine the black soy sauce, vinegar, sesame oil, sugar, chili oil, broth, the remaining 2 teaspoons rice wine, and the remaining ½ teaspoon salt.

2. Heat a 14-inch flat-bottomed wok over high heat until a bead of water vaporizes within 1 to 2 seconds of contact. Swirl in the vegetable oil, add

the dried chilies, and carefully add the chicken, spreading it evenly in the wok. Cook undisturbed 1 minute, letting the chicken begin to brown. Then, using a metal spatula, stir-fry 1 to 2 minutes or until the chicken is browned on all sides but not cooked through. Transfer to a plate and set aside.

3. Add the ginger, garlic, ground Sichuan peppercorns, and scallion and stir-fry in the dry wok 15 seconds. Return the chicken to the wok. Stir the sauce mixture and swirl it into the wok. Stir-fry 30 seconds or until the chicken is just cooked through and the sauce is slightly thickened. Discard the chilies. *Serves 4 as part of a multicourse meal.*

Stir-Fried Chicken and Shallots

Fermented black beans (see page 221) and minced garlic and ginger create a perfect balance of flavors in this simple but highly seasoned stir-fry. Shallots vary in size, but no matter how big they are, cut them into smaller pieces about the size of a small garlic clove, so that they need only a few minutes to cook.

1 pound skinless, boneless chicken thigh, cut into
    1-inch cubes
2½ teaspoons soy sauce
1 teaspoon Shao Hsing rice wine or dry sherry
½ teaspoon sugar
¼ teaspoon salt
⅛ teaspoon ground white pepper
1 tablespoon cornstarch
1 tablespoon fermented black beans, rinsed
1 teaspoon minced garlic
1 teaspoon minced ginger
1 tablespoon vegetable oil
4 small whole shallots, peeled (about ½ cup)
⅓ cup Homemade Chicken Broth (page 195)
1 scallion, chopped

1. In a medium bowl combine the chicken, 1½ teaspoons of the soy sauce, the rice wine, ¼ teaspoon of the sugar, the salt, and pepper. Sprinkle the cornstarch over the chicken mixture and toss well to combine. The chicken will be a little dry and

Preceding pages:
Left: Chicken with Sichuan Peppercorns CCTI
Right: Freshness of ingredients is vital to a good stir-fry. Live chickens arrive at a Chinese market on the back of a motorcycle.

sticky to the touch. In a small bowl, using a fork, mash the black beans, garlic, ginger, and the remaining 1 teaspoon soy sauce and ¼ teaspoon sugar.

2. Heat a 14-inch flat-bottomed wok over high heat until a bead of water vaporizes within 1 to 2 seconds of contact. Swirl in the oil and carefully add the chicken, spreading it evenly in the wok. Cook undisturbed 1 minute, letting the chicken begin to brown. Then, using a metal spatula, stir-fry 1 to 2 minutes or until the chicken is browned on all sides but not cooked through. Add the black bean mixture, shallots, and broth and stir-fry 1 to 2 minutes or until the chicken is cooked through and the sauce is just thickened. Stir in the scallion. *Serves 4 as part of a multicourse meal.*

Uncle Sherman's Home-Style Chicken and Vegetables

Here is one of Auntie Frances and Uncle Sherman's scrumptious stir-fries. They vary the vegetables according to what is in season, adding dried shiitake mushrooms when the selection of produce is limited. The wonderful garlicky ginger bean sauce is equally delicious with beef or pork.

12 ounces skinless, boneless chicken breast, cut into ¼-inch-thick bite-sized slices
6 slices ginger
1½ teaspoons plus 1 tablespoon minced garlic
1½ teaspoons cornstarch
2 teaspoons soy sauce
1 teaspoon plus 2 tablespoons vegetable oil
¾ teaspoon salt
3 teaspoons bean sauce
1 cup small broccoli florets
1 cup small cauliflower florets
4 cups bok choy, cut into 1-inch pieces
10 small button mushrooms, quartered
Cilantro sprigs, optional

1. In a medium bowl combine the chicken, 2 slices of the ginger, the 1½ teaspoons garlic, 1 teaspoon of

Uncle Sherman and Auntie Frances assemble a platter of Uncle Sherman's Home-Style Chicken and Vegetables for The Family Wok-a-thon party (page 166). The author watches from over their shoulders.

the cornstarch, 1 teaspoon of the soy sauce, the 1 teaspoon oil, and ¼ teaspoon of the salt. Set aside. In a small bowl combine the remaining ½ teaspoon cornstarch and 1 teaspoon soy sauce with 1 tablespoon cold water. Set aside.

2. Heat a 14-inch flat-bottomed wok over high heat until a bead of water vaporizes within 1 to 2 seconds of contact. Swirl in 1 tablespoon of the oil. Carefully add the chicken, spreading it evenly in the wok. Cook undisturbed 1 minute, letting the chicken begin to brown. Add 1 teaspoon of the bean sauce. Then, using a metal spatula, stir-fry 1 to 2 minutes or until the chicken is browned on all sides but not cooked through. Transfer to a plate.

3. Swirl the remaining 1 tablespoon oil into the wok. Add the remaining 4 slices ginger, 1 tablespoon minced garlic, broccoli, and cauliflower and stir-fry 30 seconds. Add the remaining 2 teaspoons bean sauce and ½ teaspoon salt with ¼ cup cold water and stir-fry 1 minute. Add the bok choy and mushrooms with 2 tablespoons cold water and stir-fry 1 minute. Return the chicken to the wok. Stir the cornstarch mixture, swirl it into the wok, and bring to a boil, stirring constantly, until the sauce has thickened and the chicken is cooked through, about 1 minute. Garnish with the cilantro if desired. *Serves 4 as part of a multicourse meal.*

Mrs. Miu's Stir-Fried Chicken with Cashews

When Mrs. Kam Toa Miu prepares this dish she adds the roasted cashews just before serving so that the nuts remain crisp. In addition to celery, one medium sliced red pepper can be added.

1 pound skinless, boneless chicken thigh or
    breast, cut into 1-inch cubes
1¼ teaspoons Shao Hsing rice wine or dry sherry
1 teaspoon plus 1 tablespoon vegetable oil
1½ teaspoons cornstarch
1¼ teaspoons soy sauce
1 teaspoon ginger juice (see page 9)
¾ teaspoon sugar
¾ teaspoon salt
⅓ cup raw cashews
2 teaspoons thinly sliced ginger
2 cups diced celery
¼ cup Homemade Chicken Broth (page 195)

1. Preheat the oven to 375°F. In a medium bowl combine the chicken, rice wine, the 1 teaspoon oil, the cornstarch, soy sauce, ginger juice, sugar, and salt. Scatter the cashews on a baking pan and roast 7 to 10 minutes or until golden brown. Set aside.

2. Heat a 14-inch flat-bottomed wok over high heat until a bead of water vaporizes within 1 to 2 seconds of contact. Swirl the remaining 1 tablespoon oil into the wok, add the ginger slices, and stir-fry 10 seconds. Carefully add the chicken mixture, spreading it evenly in the wok. Cook undisturbed 1 minute, letting the chicken begin to brown. Then, using a metal spatula, stir-fry 1 to 2 minutes or until the chicken is lightly browned.

3. Add the celery and stir-fry 1 minute. Swirl in the broth and stir-fry 1 minute or until the chicken is just cooked through and the sauce is slightly thickened. Transfer to a platter and sprinkle with the cashews. *Serves 4 as part of a multicourse meal.*

Mrs. Miu's Chicken with Pickled Ginger, Pineapple, and Green Pepper

Mrs. Kam Toa Miu is a naturally innovative home cook. She is not fond of the tough skin on green pepper, so she removes it with a vegetable peeler. This is easier to do on peppers that don't have a lot of crevices. When I tasted the pepper, I loved the unexpected velvety texture. Mrs. Miu makes her own pickled ginger, which makes this dish even better, but jarred pickled ginger available in special Asian grocery stores is also excellent.

12 ounces skinless, boneless chicken thigh
1 teaspoon Shao Hsing rice wine or dry sherry
1½ teaspoons cornstarch
1 teaspoon soy sauce
½ teaspoon ginger juice (see page 9)
½ teaspoon sugar
½ teaspoon salt
¼ teaspoon ground white pepper
1 tablespoon vegetable oil
1 medium green bell pepper, peeled and
    julienned
One 8¼-ounce can pineapple chunks
    in juice, drained
1 tablespoon pickled ginger slices

1. Cut the chicken into ¼-inch-thick slices, then stack the slices and cut into matchsticks. In a medium bowl combine the chicken, rice wine, cornstarch, soy sauce, ginger juice, sugar, salt, and pepper.

2. Heat a 14-inch flat-bottomed wok over high heat until a bead of water vaporizes within 1 to 2 seconds of contact. Swirl in the oil and carefully add the chicken mixture, spreading it evenly in the wok. Cook undisturbed 30 seconds, letting the chicken begin to brown. Then, using a metal spatula, stir-fry 1 minute or until the chicken is lightly browned but not cooked through. Add the bell pepper, pineapple, and pickled ginger and stir-fry 1 to 2 minutes or until the chicken is cooked through. *Serves 4 as part of a multicourse meal.*

Kung Pao Chicken

The secret of making Kung Pao Chicken is to first season the oil with ginger, garlic, and dried chilies. Make sure to open the window and turn on your exhaust fan when cooking the chilies, as the aroma can be very strong. I use the whole dried red chilies that are 3 to 4 inches in length. The heat often varies, depending on the freshness of the chilies.

1 pound skinless, boneless chicken thigh or
    breast, cut into ¾-inch cubes
4 teaspoons soy sauce
1 teaspoon plus 1 tablespoon Shao Hsing rice
    wine or dry sherry
2 teaspoons cornstarch
½ teaspoon sugar
2 tablespoons Homemade Chicken Broth
    (page 195)
2 teaspoons Chinkiang or balsamic vinegar
¾ cup shelled, raw peanuts
2 tablespoons vegetable oil
2 tablespoons minced garlic
2 tablespoons minced ginger
2 dried red chilies, split lengthwise
2 large red bell peppers, cut into 1-inch cubes
1 teaspoon salt
¼ cup minced scallions

1. Preheat the oven to 375°F. In a medium bowl combine the chicken, 2 teaspoons of the soy sauce, the 1 teaspoon rice wine, the cornstarch, and sugar. In a small bowl combine the broth, vinegar, and the remaining 1 tablespoon rice wine and 2 teaspoons soy sauce. Set aside. Scatter the peanuts on a baking pan and roast 7 to 10 minutes or until golden brown. Set aside to cool.

2. Heat a 14-inch flat-bottomed wok over high heat until a bead of water vaporizes within 1 to 2 seconds of contact. Swirl in 1 tablespoon of the oil, add the garlic, ginger, and dried chilies, and stir-fry 20 seconds. Carefully add the chicken mixture, spreading it evenly evenly in the wok. Cook undisturbed 1 minute, letting the chicken begin to brown. Then, using a metal spatula, stir-fry 1 minute, or until the chicken is browned on all sides but not cooked through. Transfer to a plate.

3. Swirl the remaining 1 tablespoon oil into the wok over high heat. Add the bell peppers and stir-fry 1 minute or until slightly softened. Return the chicken to the wok. Stir the broth mixture, swirl it into the wok, and stir-fry 1 minute or until the chicken is just cooked through. Add the peanuts, salt, and scallions and stir-fry 30 seconds or until the scallions are bright green. Discard the chilies before serving. *Serves 4 as part of a multicourse meal.*

Tina Yao Lu's Chicken with Spinach

I was so surprised by the ingredients in this stir-fry, which I first tasted in Shanghai at my Auntie Linda's home, prepared by her daughter Tina. The juicy chicken is served with an unexpected delicate sauce reminiscent of creamed spinach, yet it has definite Chinese flavors.

12 ounces spinach, stems removed
12 ounces skinless, boneless chicken breast, cut
    into ¾-inch cubes
1½ teaspoons soy sauce
¾ teaspoon Shao Hsing rice wine or dry sherry
4 teaspoons cornstarch
1 teaspoon salt
½ teaspoon sugar
2 tablespoons vegetable oil
1 tablespoon finely minced garlic
2 cups sliced button mushrooms
1 cup Homemade Chicken Broth (page 195)
⅛ teaspoon ground white pepper

Preceding pages:
Left: The Graham Street outdoor market in Hong Kong, famous for tremendous variety, has fresh eggs and poultry of every type.
Right: Black chickens, used exclusively for restorative herbal soups.

1. In a 14-inch flat-bottomed wok bring 1½ quarts water to a boil over high heat and add the spinach. Cook until just limp, about 30 seconds. Drain in a colander and rinse under cold water. Squeeze the spinach with both hands to remove excess water. The spinach should be as dry as possible. Put on a cutting board and chop finely. Set aside. Rinse the wok and dry it thoroughly.

2. In a medium bowl combine the chicken, soy sauce, rice wine, 2 teaspoons of the cornstarch, ½ teaspoon of the salt, and the sugar. In a small bowl combine the remaining 2 teaspoons cornstarch with 1 tablespoon cold water. Set aside.

3. Heat the wok over high heat until a bead of water vaporizes within 1 to 2 seconds of contact. Swirl in 1 tablespoon of the oil, add the garlic, and stir-fry 20 seconds. Carefully add the chicken mixture, spreading it evenly in the wok. Cook undisturbed 1 minute, letting the chicken begin to brown. Then, using a metal spatula, stir-fry 1 minute or until the chicken is lightly browned on all sides but not cooked through. Transfer to a plate.

4. Swirl the remaining 1 tablespoon oil into the wok. Add the mushrooms and stir-fry 30 seconds or until they begin to soften. Return the chicken to the wok. Add the broth, pepper, the remaining ½ teaspoon salt, and the spinach and bring to a boil. Stir the cornstarch mixture, swirl it into the wok, and stir-fry 1 minute or until the chicken is just cooked through and the sauce is slightly thickened. *Serves 4 as part of a multicourse meal.*

Chicken with Garlic and Sugar Snaps

This is a classic Cantonese stir-fry. The chicken is marinated in a mixture of soy sauce, cornstarch, rice wine, sugar, and salt. The marinade not only tenderizes the chicken but enriches the broth to create a lightly thickened sauce at the end of the stir-fry. Sesame oil is drizzled just before serving to keep the flavor fresh.

1 pound skinless, boneless chicken thigh, cut into
    ¼-inch-thick bite-sized slices
2 teaspoons soy sauce
1 teaspoon cornstarch
1 teaspoon Shao Hsing rice wine or dry sherry
¼ teaspoon sugar
½ teaspoon salt
¼ cup Homemade Chicken Broth (page 195)
2 tablespoons vegetable oil
2 tablespoons minced garlic
1 cup sugar snap peas, strings removed
    (about 3 ounces)
½ cup canned baby corn, halved lengthwise
    and rinsed
½ cup thinly sliced carrots
½ cup canned sliced bamboo shoots, rinsed
1 teaspoon sesame oil

1. In a medium bowl combine the chicken, 1½ teaspoons of the soy sauce, the cornstarch, rice wine, sugar, and ¼ teaspoon of the salt. Set aside. In a small bowl combine the broth and the remaining ½ teaspoon soy sauce and ¼ teaspoon salt. Set aside.

2. Heat a 14-inch flat-bottomed wok over high heat until a bead of water vaporizes within 1 to 2 seconds of contact. Swirl in 1 tablespoon of the vegetable oil, add the garlic, and carefully add the chicken, spreading it evenly in the wok. Cook undisturbed 1 minute, letting the chicken begin to brown. Then, using a metal spatula, stir-fry 1 to 2 minutes or until the chicken is browned on all sides but not cooked through. Transfer to a plate.

3. Swirl the remaining 1 tablespoon vegetable oil into the wok and add the sugar snaps, corn, carrots, and bamboo shoots. Stir-fry 1 minute or until the vegetables begin to soften. Return the chicken to the wok. Stir the sauce mixture and swirl it into the wok. Stir-fry 1 minute or until the chicken is cooked through and the sauce is just thickened. Drizzle with the sesame oil. *Serves 4 as part of a multicourse meal.*

Sweet and Sour Chicken

This is a home-style sweet and sour chicken—very different from the sweet and sour dishes served in restaurants. The chicken is not deep-fried and the sauce tastes much lighter and fresher. If desired, a cup of fresh cubed pineapple can be added in the last minute of cooking.

12 ounces skinless, boneless chicken breast, cut into 1-inch cubes
2 garlic cloves, thinly sliced
4 teaspoons soy sauce
1 teaspoon Shao Hsing rice wine or dry sherry
3 teaspoons cornstarch
½ teaspoon plus 1 tablespoon sugar
½ teaspoon salt
⅛ teaspoon ground white pepper
⅓ cup Homemade Chicken Broth (page 195)
2 teaspoons black soy sauce
2 teaspoons sesame oil
2 tablespoons rice vinegar
2 tablespoons ketchup
1 tablespoon plus 2 teaspoons vegetable oil
1 green bell pepper, cut into 1-inch cubes
1 red bell pepper, cut into 1-inch cubes
3 scallions, cut into 2-inch pieces

1. In a medium bowl combine the chicken, garlic, 2 teaspoons of the soy sauce, the rice wine, 1½ teaspoons of the cornstarch, the ½ teaspoon sugar, ¼ teaspoon of the salt, and the pepper. Set aside. In a small bowl combine the broth, black soy sauce, sesame oil, rice vinegar, ketchup, and the remaining 1 tablespoon sugar, 2 teaspoons soy sauce, 1½ teaspoons cornstarch, and ¼ teaspoon salt. Set the sauce aside.

2. Heat a 14-inch flat-bottomed wok over high heat until a bead of water vaporizes within 1 to 2 seconds of contact. Swirl in the 1 tablespoon vegetable oil and carefully add the chicken, spreading it evenly in the wok. Cook undisturbed 1 minute, letting the chicken begin to brown. Then, using a metal spatula, stir-fry 1 minute or until the chicken is browned on all sides but not cooked through. Transfer to a plate.

3. Swirl the remaining 2 teaspoons vegetable oil into the wok, add the peppers and scallions, and stir-fry 30 seconds. Stir the sauce and swirl it into the wok. Return the chicken to the wok and stir-fry 1 to 2 minutes or until the chicken is just cooked through and the sauce has slightly thickened. ***Serves 4 as part of a multicourse meal.***

Ray Lee's Chicken and Choy Sum

A former restaurant chef, Ray Lee, like many traditional Cantonese cooks, insists on adding a little chicken skin to his stir-fry to enrich the taste. Lee blanches the choy sum (see page 220) in chicken broth to flavor the vegetables. If you don't have black soy sauce, regular soy sauce can be used, but the taste is not as robust.

12 ounces boneless chicken breast with skin
2 teaspoons Shao Hsing rice wine or dry sherry
2¾ teaspoons cornstarch
2 teaspoons plus 2 tablespoons vegetable oil
1 teaspoon soy sauce
1½ teaspoons black soy sauce
2 tablespoons egg white, beaten
6 ounces choy sum
1 cup Homemade Chicken Broth (page 195)
7 slices ginger
4 small garlic cloves, smashed
1 tablespoon oyster sauce
¼ teaspoon salt

1. Remove the skin from the chicken and set aside a 2-inch-square piece. Cut the chicken into ¼-inch-thick bite-sized slices. In a bowl combine the chicken, rice wine, 2 teaspoons of the cornstarch, the 2 teaspoons oil, the soy sauce, 1 teaspoon of the black soy sauce, and the egg white. Marinate uncovered in the refrigerator 1½ hours. Remove from the refrigerator and set at room temperature 30 minutes.

2. Trim the tops and stems of the choy sum by ¼ inch. Bring ½ cup of the broth to a boil over high heat in a medium saucepan with 3 slices of the ginger and 1 garlic clove. Add the choy sum, cover, reduce the heat to medium, and blanch 1 minute. Drain the choy sum in a colander and discard the broth, ginger, and garlic. In a small bowl combine the oyster sauce, salt, and the remaining ½ cup broth, ¾ teaspoon cornstarch, and ½ teaspoon black soy sauce.

3. Heat a 14-inch flat-bottomed wok over high heat until a bead of water vaporizes within 1 to 2 seconds of contact. Swirl in 1 tablespoon of the oil and the remaining 4 slices ginger and 3 garlic cloves. Carefully add the chicken, spreading it evenly in the wok. Cook undisturbed 1 minute, letting the chicken begin to brown. Then, using a metal spatula, stir-fry 2 to 3 minutes or until the chicken is lightly browned on all sides and is just cooked through. Transfer to a platter. Rinse the wok and dry it thoroughly.

4. Swirl the remaining 1 tablespoon oil into the wok. Add the reserved chicken skin and stir-fry 30 seconds. Add the blanched choy sum and stir-fry 10 seconds. Stir the oyster sauce mixture, swirl it into the wok, and bring to a boil, stirring constantly, until the sauce has thickened, about 1 minute. Spoon the vegetables and sauce over the chicken, discarding the browned chicken skin. *Serves 4 as part of a multicourse meal.*

Ray Lee's Chicken and Choy Sum

Susanna Foo's Mango Chicken

This is my version of the extraordinary mango chicken I tasted at Susanna Foo's restaurant in Philadelphia. Chef Foo's secret for making this chicken extra succulent is to marinate it in vodka, egg white, cornstarch, and oil. She prefers the flavor of vodka rather than rice wine for cooking. Chef Foo recommends stir-frying this dish with corn oil.

1 pound skinless, boneless chicken breast, cut
    into 1-inch cubes
1 tablespoon vodka or dry vermouth
1 large egg white, beaten
1 tablespoon plus 1 teaspoon cornstarch
¾ teaspoon salt
4 tablespoons corn oil
½ cup minced onion
1½ teaspoons minced garlic
½ cup dry white wine
2 tablespoons oyster sauce
1 tablespoon soy sauce
1 cup Homemade Chicken Broth (page 195)
4 stalks Shanghai bok choy, trimmed
3 tablespoons finely shredded ginger
¼ cup julienned red bell pepper
6 asparagus, sliced diagonally into 1-inch pieces
1 large ripe mango, peeled and cut into
    ¾-inch cubes
¾ cup Candied Walnuts (page 215)

1. In a medium bowl combine the chicken and vodka. Add the egg white, 1 tablespoon of the cornstarch, and ½ teaspoon of the salt and mix well. Stir in 1 tablespoon of the oil. Marinate uncovered 30 minutes in the refrigerator.

2. In a small bowl combine the remaining 1 teaspoon cornstarch with 1 tablespoon cold water. Set aside. Heat 1 tablespoon of the oil in a medium saucepan over high heat until hot but not smoking. Add the onion and cook, stirring, until golden, 2 to 3 minutes. Add the garlic and cook another minute. Add the wine, oyster sauce, and soy sauce. Cook, stirring, 2 minutes. Add the broth and bring to a boil. Stir the cornstarch mixture, add to the saucepan, and stir until slightly thickened. Reduce the heat to low and simmer, uncovered, 30 to 40 minutes or until reduced to about 1 cup. Strain the sauce and set aside.

3. In a medium saucepan bring 3 cups water and the remaining ¼ teaspoon salt to a boil over high heat. Add the Shanghai bok choy and blanch 20 seconds or just until bright green. Drain well and set aside.

4. Heat a 14-inch flat-bottomed wok over high heat until a bead of water vaporizes within 1 to 2 seconds of contact. Swirl 1 tablespoon of the oil into the wok and carefully add the chicken mixture, spreading it evenly in the wok. Cook undisturbed 1 minute, letting the chicken begin to brown. Then, using a metal spatula, stir-fry 1 minute or until the chicken is lightly browned but not cooked through. Transfer to a plate and set aside.

5. Swirl the remaining 1 tablespoon oil into the wok, add the shredded ginger, and stir-fry 1 minute. Add the bell pepper and asparagus and stir-fry 5 seconds. Swirl in the reduced sauce. Return the chicken to the wok and stir-fry 1 to 2 minutes or until the chicken is just cooked through. Add the mango and stir-fry 30 seconds or until just heated through. Transfer to a platter and garnish with the bok choy. Top with the walnuts. ***Serves 4 as part of a multicourse meal.***

It is rare to find women chefs in Chinese restaurant kitchens, but Susanna Foo had the strength and prowess to break through physical and cultural stereotypes. She recalls being told that a woman couldn't lift the heavy woks or handle the 10- to 12-hour workdays in the blazing heat. She gracefully presides over her award-winning restaurant, Susanna Foo, in Philadelphia. Here she presents her famous Mango Chicken.

Stir-Frying
Meat

Stir-Fried Pork with Scallions

This recipe exemplifies the simplicity of a stir-fry. For busy nights when I'm in a rush, this is the perfect meal for two with steamed rice. The preparation and cooking time are minimal. This is also an excellent dish for novice cooks to practice the technique of stir-frying. To elevate this dish, I substitute Chinese chives for the scallions.

12 ounces lean pork butt, cut into ¼-inch-thick
    bite-sized slices
1½ teaspoons Shao Hsing rice wine or dry sherry
2 teaspoons soy sauce
1½ teaspoons sesame oil
2 teaspoons cornstarch
¼ teaspoon ground white pepper
1 tablespoon vegetable oil
3 slices ginger
6 scallions, halved lengthwise and cut into
    2-inch pieces
½ teaspoon salt
½ teaspoon sugar

1. In a medium bowl combine the pork, rice wine, soy sauce, sesame oil, cornstarch, and pepper.

2. Heat a 14-inch flat-bottomed wok over high heat until a bead of water vaporizes within 1 to 2 seconds of contact. Swirl in the vegetable oil and ginger and carefully add the pork, spreading it evenly in the wok. Cook undisturbed 1 minute, letting the pork begin to brown. Then, using a metal spatula, stir-fry 1 minute, or until the pork is browned but still slightly rare.

3. Add the scallions, salt, and sugar and stir-fry 1 to 2 minutes or until the pork is just cooked and the scallions are bright green. ***Serves 4 as part of a multicourse meal.***

Chiu Chow–Style Pork Spring Moon

Chiu Chow–Style Pork Spring Moon

This is my version of a dish I tasted at the Spring Moon restaurant in Hong Kong. When the eggs are swirled in, it is important not to cook them over direct heat or they will be dry.

One 1.76-ounce package cellophane noodles
½ cup Homemade Chicken Broth (page 195)
2 teaspoons Shao Hsing rice wine or dry sherry
1 teaspoon soy sauce
¾ teaspoon salt
2 cups mung bean sprouts
2 large eggs
⅛ teaspoon ground white pepper
1 tablespoon vegetable oil
1 teaspoon minced ginger
4 ounces ground pork (about ½ cup)

1. In a medium bowl, soak the cellophane noodles in cold water to cover 15 minutes or until softened. Drain thoroughly. In a 14-inch flat-bottomed wok combine the broth, 1 teaspoon of the rice wine, the soy sauce, ¼ teaspoon of the salt, the bean sprouts, and the cellophane noodles. Bring to a boil over medium heat and cook, stirring, 2 to 3 minutes or until the noodles and bean sprouts are just cooked through. Transfer to a plate. Rinse the wok and dry it thoroughly. In a small bowl beat the eggs with ¼ teaspoon of the salt and the pepper.

2. Heat the wok over high heat until a bead of water vaporizes within 1 to 2 seconds of contact. Swirl in the oil, add the ginger, and stir-fry 10 seconds. Add the pork, spreading it evenly in the wok. Cook undisturbed 20 seconds, letting the pork begin to brown. Add the remaining 1 teaspoon rice wine. Then, using a metal spatula, stir-fry the pork, breaking it up, until no longer pink, about 30 seconds. Add the bean sprout mixture and the remaining ¼ teaspoon salt, and stir-fry 15 seconds. Swirl in the eggs and stir-fry 15 seconds. Remove from the heat and continue to stir-fry until the eggs are just set and the pork is cooked through, about 30 seconds. ***Serves 4 as part of a multicourse meal.***

Helen Chen's Pork and Cucumber

Helen Chen, who runs the cookware company started by her legendary mother, Joyce Chen, taught me this dish. The Chinese love to stir-fry cucumbers, but the peel is sometimes tough. Chen's solution is to call for English cucumbers, which are perfect for absorbing the pungent flavors of the fermented black beans (see page 221).

12 ounces lean pork butt, cut into ¼-inch-thick
   bite-sized slices
1½ teaspoons Shao Hsing rice wine or dry sherry
2 teaspoons cornstarch
½ teaspoon soy sauce
¾ teaspoon sesame oil
1 teaspoon salt
1 tablespoon fermented black beans, rinsed
2 tablespoons canola oil
2 tablespoons thinly sliced garlic
½ English cucumber, unpeeled, halved lengthwise
   and cut into ¼-inch-thick slices
1 medium red bell pepper, cut into ¼-inch-wide
   strips
3 tablespoons Homemade Chicken Broth
   (page 195)
¼ teaspoon sugar

1. In a shallow bowl combine the pork, rice wine, cornstarch, soy sauce, sesame oil, and ½ teaspoon of the salt. In a small bowl mash the black beans.

2. Heat a 14-inch flat-bottomed wok over high heat until a bead of water vaporizes within 1 to 2 seconds of contact. Swirl in 1 tablespoon of the canola oil and add the garlic and pork, spreading it evenly in the wok. Cook undisturbed 20 seconds, letting the pork begin to brown. Add the mashed beans and, using a metal spatula, stir-fry the pork until it is browned but still slightly rare, 1 to 2 minutes. Transfer to a plate. Swirl in the remaining 1 tablespoon canola oil, add the cucumber and bell pepper, and stir-fry 2 to 3 minutes or until the vegetables are just limp. Stir in the pork, broth, sugar, and the remaining ½ teaspoon salt, and stir-fry 1 minute or until the pork is cooked. *Serves 4 as part of a multicourse meal.*

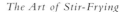

The Art of Stir-Frying

Virginia Yee's Moo Shoo Pork with Mandarin Pancakes

In Hong Kong, I had the honor of learning from Virginia Yee how to make Moo Shoo Pork and Mandarin Pancakes. These two recipes are for a more advanced wok cook. At first they may seem very labor intensive, but the results are well worth the effort. The taste of tender homemade pancakes is incomparable, especially when served with the flavorful pork mixture.

⅓ cup cloud ears
5 dried shiitake mushrooms
One 1.76-ounce package cellophane noodles
8 ounces lean pork butt
3 teaspoons soy sauce
2½ teaspoons Shao Hsing rice wine or dry sherry
2 teaspoons cornstarch
¾ teaspoon sugar
⅛ teaspoon ground white pepper
½ teaspoon salt
2 tablespoons vegetable oil
2 slices ginger
2 scallions, cut into 2-inch pieces and shredded
1½ cups shredded Napa cabbage
½ cup canned shredded bamboo shoots, rinsed
1 tablespoon sesame oil

1. Put the cloud ears in a medium bowl with enough cold water to cover, set aside 30 minutes or until softened. Drain thoroughly. Remove the hard spots from the cloud ears and cut into fine shreds. In a separate medium bowl soak the mushrooms in ½ cup cold water 30 minutes or until softened. Drain and squeeze dry, reserving ¼ cup soaking liquid. Cut off and discard the stems and thinly slice the caps. Set aside. In another bowl soak the cellophane noodles in cold water to cover, 15 minutes or until softened. Drain thoroughly and cut the noodles roughly into 3-inch pieces.

2. Cut the pork into 2-inch-wide strips. Cut the strips into ¼-inch-thick slices, then stack the slices and cut into 2-inch-long matchsticks. Put the pork in a shallow bowl and add 1 teaspoon of the soy sauce, ½ teaspoon of the rice wine, 1 teaspoon of

the cornstarch, ¼ teaspoon of the sugar, and the pepper. Stir to combine. In a small bowl combine the salt and the remaining 2 teaspoons soy sauce, 2 teaspoons rice wine, 1 teaspoon cornstarch, ½ teaspoon sugar, and the reserved mushroom soaking liquid. Set aside.

3. Heat a 14-inch flat-bottomed wok over high heat until a bead of water vaporizes within 1 to 2 seconds of contact. Swirl in the vegetable oil, add the ginger, and stir-fry 10 seconds. Discard the ginger. Add the scallions and mushrooms and stir-fry 1 minute. Push the scallion mixture to the side and add the pork, spreading it evenly in the wok. Cook undisturbed 20 seconds, letting the pork begin to brown. Then, using a metal spatula, stir-fry, separating the pork until it is no longer pink, 1 to 2 minutes.

4. Add the cloud ears, cabbage, and bamboo shoots and stir-fry 1 to 2 minutes or until the cabbage is tender. Add the cellophane noodles and stir-fry just to combine. Stir the cornstarch mixture, swirl it into the wok, and bring to a boil, stirring constantly, until the sauce has thickened and the cellophane noodles are just cooked through, about 1 minute. Stir in the sesame oil. *Serve as a filling with Mandarin Pancakes. Serves 4 as part of a multicourse meal.*

Mandarin Pancakes

Mandarin pancakes are rolled out in pairs and then cooked in a dry wok. After cooking, the hot pancakes must be slapped down several times on a cutting board. This action eventually creates a tiny opening along the edge; the pancakes can be carefully peeled apart only when they are piping hot. Once the pancakes have cooled, they are impossible to separate. If the wok has hot spots, the pancakes are also difficult to separate. The pancakes can be made ahead, wrapped in foil, and refrigerated. When ready to serve, bring water to a boil in a steamer. Stack the pancakes on a heatproof plate and put in the steamer. Cover and steam 5 minutes or until piping hot. The pancakes can be kept in the steamer over low heat for up to an hour; replenish the water as needed. The pancakes can also be wrapped in freezer wrap, put in a plastic bag, and frozen for up to 2 months. To defrost, place in the refrigerator overnight, then heat in a steamer.

2 cups all-purpose flour, plus additional
    for kneading
1 tablespoon sesame oil

1. Put the 2 cups flour in a medium bowl and make a well. Pour ¾ cup boiling water into the well, immediately stirring with a wooden spoon until the mixture begins to pull away from the sides of the bowl. If some flour remains, add more boiling water by the teaspoonful. Lightly dust your hands with flour and knead the mixture for a few seconds at a time, as the mixture will be very hot, to form a dough. Turn onto a work surface lightly dusted with flour, and knead with lightly floured hands 5 minutes, adding more flour if necessary, until smooth and elastic. Cover with a slightly damp cloth and allow to rest 30 minutes.

2. Knead the rested dough for a few minutes on a lightly floured surface. The dough should be smooth, elastic, and not sticky. Divide the dough in half. As you work, always cover any dough not being worked with a slightly damp cloth. Roll one-half of the dough into an even rope about 12 inches long. Cut the rope into 12 equal pieces and roll each piece into a ball. Pat each ball into a 2-inch round, a scant ¼ inch thick. Lightly dust the rounds with flour.

3. Using a pastry brush, spread a thin film of sesame oil evenly over the tops of all the rounds. Sandwich the rounds in pairs, with the oiled sides touching, to form 6 rounds. Lightly dust both sides of each round with flour. Using a floured rolling pin, roll each round into a 7- to 8-inch circle, about a scant 1/16 inch thick. Lightly cover with a dry cloth. Repeat with the remaining dough.

4. Heat a dry 14-inch flat-bottomed wok over medium-low heat. The wok must be hot but not scorching. Add one pancake and cook until it puffs from the steam that builds in the center and the bottom is a little dry with tiny, pale brown spots, 30 seconds to 1 minute. If the pancake has large brown spots, the wok is too hot and the pancake will become dry and hard. Turn the pancake over and cook another 20 to 30 seconds. The first pancake may take longer. A pancake is cooked when the dough is dry to the touch but still supple.

5. Slap the pancake down on a cutting board several times. If you examine the pancake carefully you'll find a ¼- to ½-inch opening along the edge. Peel the pancake apart carefully, as it will be *very* hot. Put the pancakes browned side down on a cutting board and cover them with a slightly damp cloth. Continue cooking the pancakes in the same manner. ***Makes 24 pancakes.***

Virginia Yee shows the two rounds of dough that get sandwiched together to make the Mandarin Pancakes for her Moo Shoo Pork.

Walter Kei, Hong Kong culinary writer and author, uses a traditional cast-iron wok to prepare this easy Shanghainese-style stir-fry.

Walter Kei's Shanghai-Style Pork and Bean Sprouts

Walter Kei taught me this simple peppery Shanghainese-style stir-fry. Many traditional cooks prefer the "head and tail" of the bean sprout to be removed. In Hong Kong, produce vendors sell trimmed sprouts, called "silver sprouts." Interestingly, Kei uses Bertolli Classico Olive Oil for this stir-fry.

8 ounces lean pork butt
2 teaspoons grated garlic
4 teaspoons Shao Hsing rice wine or dry sherry
1½ teaspoons cornstarch
½ teaspoon soy sauce
½ teaspoon sesame oil
½ teaspoon sugar
1 teaspoon salt
½ teaspoon ground white pepper
2 tablespoons olive oil
1 pound mung bean sprouts

1. Slice the pork into ¼-inch-thick slices, then stack the slices and cut into 2-inch-long matchsticks. Put the matchsticks in a shallow bowl and add the garlic, 2 teaspoons of the rice wine, the cornstarch, soy sauce, sesame oil, sugar, ½ teaspoon of the salt, and ¼ teaspoon of the pepper. Stir to combine.

2. Heat a 14-inch flat-bottomed wok over high heat until a bead of water vaporizes within 1 to 2 seconds of contact. Swirl in the olive oil and add the pork, spreading it evenly in the wok. Cook undisturbed 20 seconds, letting the pork begin to brown. Then, using a metal spatula, stir-fry the pork until it is no longer pink, about 1 minute. Add the bean sprouts, the remaining 2 teaspoons rice wine, ½ teaspoon salt, and ¼ teaspoon pepper and stir-fry 1 to 2 minutes or until the pork and bean sprouts are just cooked through. *Serves 4 as part of a multicourse meal.*

Walter Kei's Chili Pork

Walter Kei's father used to prepare this spicy pork dish with baby corn. The substitution of peppers and XO sauce are Kei's innovative twist. The spice level of this dish is mild. Boneless pork belly is a popular item sold in Chinese butcher shops.

12 ounces boneless pork belly, cut in half
1½ teaspoons sugar
¾ teaspoon salt
1 tablespoon XO sauce (page 214) or store-bought
¼ teaspoon sesame oil
1½ teaspoons chili bean sauce
¼ teaspoon chili oil
3 slices ginger
3 scallions, cut into 2-inch pieces
3 tablespoons Shao Hsing rice wine or dry sherry
2 tablespoons olive oil
1 tablespoon minced garlic
½ medium red bell pepper, cut into 1-inch cubes
½ medium yellow bell pepper, cut into 1-inch cubes
½ medium green bell pepper, cut into 1-inch cubes
One 8-ounce can sliced bamboo shoots, rinsed and drained

1. Put the pork in a dish and sprinkle with ½ teaspoon of the sugar and ½ teaspoon of the salt. Set aside 30 minutes. In a small bowl combine the XO sauce, sesame oil, chili bean sauce, and chili oil.

2. In a 14-inch flat-bottomed wok bring 2 cups water to a boil over high heat. Add the ginger slices and scallions and boil 1 minute. Add 1 tablespoon of the rice wine and boil 1 minute. Add the pork, cover, and reduce the heat to low. Simmer 8 minutes. Pour out the water and seasonings. Rinse the pork in cold water, put it on a cutting board, and cut into ¼-inch-thick bite-sized slices. The pork should still be slightly pink. Rinse the wok and dry it thoroughly.

3. Heat the wok over high heat until a bead of water vaporizes within 1 to 2 seconds of contact. Swirl in the olive oil and garlic and stir-fry 15 seconds. Add the pork, swirl in the sauce mixture, and stir-fry 30 seconds. Cover, reduce the heat to medium, and cook 1 minute. Increase the heat to high, add the peppers and bamboo shoots, and stir-fry 1 minute. Add the remaining 1 teaspoon sugar and ¼ teaspoon salt and stir-fry 1 minute. Add the remaining 2 tablespoons rice wine and continue to stir-fry 1 minute. *Serves 4 as part of a multicourse meal.*

Stir-Fried Pork and Chilies CCTI

Instructor Chef Kevin Chuk of the Chinese Cuisine Training Institute in Hong Kong uses a special type of preserved chili from Sichuan province for this recipe. I was surprised that even without that ingredient I was able to adapt the recipe with equally fiery results. When Chef Chuk slices the pork into matchsticks, it is nearly as delicate as strands of vermicelli. Such knife skills are hard to replicate. This recipe can be made by just cutting the pork into thin slices. (photo page 92)

⅓ cup cloud ears
12 ounces lean pork butt
2¼ teaspoons cornstarch
3½ teaspoons Shao Hsing rice wine or dry sherry
1½ teaspoons plus 1 tablespoon vegetable oil
2¾ teaspoons soy sauce
½ teaspoon salt
¼ cup Homemade Chicken Broth (page 195)
2 teaspoons Chinkiang or balsamic vinegar
1 teaspoon sugar
2 teaspoons sesame oil
1 tablespoon thinly sliced garlic
1 tablespoon thinly sliced ginger
1 tablespoon plus 1 teaspoon chili bean sauce
½ cup canned shredded bamboo shoots, rinsed

1. Put the cloud ears in a medium bowl with enough cold water to cover. Let stand 30 minutes or until softened. Drain thoroughly. Finely shred the cloud ears and set aside. Cut the pork into 2-inch-wide strips. Cut the strips into ¼-inch-thick slices, then stack the slices and cut into 2-inch-long matchsticks. Put the matchsticks in a shallow bowl and add 1½ teaspoons of the cornstarch, 1½ teaspoons of the rice wine, the 1½ teaspoons vegetable oil, ¾ teaspoon of the soy sauce, and ¼ teaspoon of the salt. In a small bowl combine the broth, vinegar, sugar, sesame oil, and the remaining 2 teaspoons soy sauce, 2 teaspoons rice wine, ¾ teaspoon cornstarch, and ¼ teaspoon salt.

2. Heat a 14-inch flat-bottomed wok over high heat until a bead of water vaporizes within 1 to 2 seconds of contact. Swirl in the remaining 1 tablespoon vegetable oil, add the garlic and ginger, and stir-fry 10 seconds or until fragrant. Carefully add the pork, spreading it evenly in the wok. Cook undisturbed 20 seconds, letting the pork begin to brown. Add the chili bean sauce and, using a metal spatula, stir-fry the pork until it is browned but still slightly rare, about 1 minute. Add the bamboo shoots and cloud ears. Stir the cornstarch mixture, swirl into the wok, and bring to a boil, stirring constantly, until the pork is just cooked and the sauce is thickened slightly, 1 to 2 minutes. *Serves 4 as part of a multicourse meal.*

Stir-Fried Pork, Mushrooms, and Carrots

Chinese gourmets judge a stir-fry not only by the combination of flavors but by how finely the ingredients have been sliced to ensure that each bite contains an array of different textures and flavors.

6 dried shiitake mushrooms
8 ounces lean pork butt
1 teaspoon Shao Hsing rice wine or dry sherry
1½ teaspoons cornstarch
½ teaspoon soy sauce
½ teaspoon sesame oil
1¼ teaspoons salt
½ teaspoon sugar
2 tablespoons vegetable oil
1½ teaspoons minced garlic
2 cups shredded Napa cabbage
2 cups julienned celery
1 cup julienned carrots
½ cup canned shredded bamboo shoots, rinsed
½ cup thinly sliced scallions
¼ teaspoon ground white pepper

1. In a medium bowl soak the mushrooms in ½ cup cold water 30 minutes or until softened. Drain and squeeze dry. Cut off and discard the stems and thinly slice the caps. Set aside. Cut the pork into 2-inch-wide strips, then into ¼-inch-thick slices. Stack the slices, then cut into 2-inch-long matchsticks. Put the matchsticks in a shallow bowl and add the rice wine, cornstarch, soy sauce, sesame oil, ¼ teaspoon of the salt, and ¼ teaspoon of the sugar.

2. Heat a 14-inch flat-bottomed wok over high heat until a bead of water vaporizes within 1 to 2 seconds of contact. Swirl in 1 tablespoon of the vegetable oil and add the pork, spreading it evenly in the wok. Cook undisturbed 20 seconds, letting the pork begin to brown. Then, using a metal spatula, stir-fry, separating the pieces until the pork is browned but still slightly rare, about 1 minute. Transfer to a plate.

3. Swirl the remaining 1 tablespoon vegetable oil into the wok, add the garlic, and stir-fry 5 seconds or until the garlic is fragrant. Add the cabbage, celery, carrots, bamboo shoots, scallions, and sliced mushrooms and stir-fry 2 to 3 minutes or until the cabbage and celery are just limp. Stir in the pork, pepper, and the remaining 1 teaspoon salt and ¼ teaspoon sugar, and stir-fry 1 minute or until the pork is cooked through. *Serves 4 as part of a multicourse meal.*

Martin Yan's Genghis Khan Beef

I will never forget watching Chef Martin Yan stir-fry. He used a northern-style wok, and each time he threw the wok in the pao *action, the flames jetted up. Just as the stir-frying was complete he gave a final* pao, *throwing the ingredients into the air and impressively catching them with his ladle. This beef has dramatic flavor, as memorable as Chef Yan's performance.*

1 tablespoon black soy sauce
1 tablespoon soy sauce
2½ teaspoons cornstarch
12 ounces lean flank steak, cut into ½-inch cubes
10 scallions
2 tablespoons hoisin sauce
1 teaspoon sesame oil
1 teaspoon chili sambal
1 tablespoon plus 1½ teaspoons vegetable oil
3 tablespoons thinly sliced garlic
6 fresh red Thai chilies, stemmed

Chef Martin Yan demonstrates his mastery of stir-frying. With effortless ease he utilizes the pao *action to toss the ingredients of his Genghis Khan Beef.*

1. In a medium bowl combine the black soy sauce, soy sauce, and cornstarch. Add the beef and stir to coat. Let stand 20 minutes. Cut the white part of the scallions into 3-inch pieces. Sliver enough of the green part of the scallions to measure ¼ cup as a garnish. In a small bowl combine the hoisin sauce, sesame oil, and chili sambal.

2. Heat a 14-inch flat-bottomed wok over high heat until a bead of water vaporizes within 1 to 2 seconds of contact. Swirl in the 1 tablespoon vegetable oil and add the beef, spreading it evenly in the wok. Cook undisturbed 30 seconds, letting the beef begin to brown. Then, using a metal spatula, stir-fry 1 to 2 minutes or until the beef is browned and barely pink in the center. Transfer to a plate.

3. Swirl the remaining 1½ teaspoons vegetable oil into the wok. Add the garlic and chilies and stir-fry until fragrant, about 15 seconds. Add the white parts of the scallions and stir-fry 1 minute. Return the beef to the wok. Add the hoisin sauce mixture and stir-fry about 30 seconds. Garnish with the slivered scallions. *Serves 4 as part of a multicourse meal.*

Chef Kevin Chuk works with a northern-style wok on a professional wok stove at the Chinese Cuisine Training Institute in Hong Kong. Opposite: Stir-Fried Pork and Chilies CCTI (page 90)

Bernadette Chan's Stir-Fried Beef and Tofu

Bernadette Chan's beef and tofu is a classic Cantonese comfort food dish, perfect for a weeknight meal. The sauce is intensely flavored and delicious served over rice. Try to remove as much moisture as possible from the tofu to prevent the oil from spattering during the pan-frying. I find it easiest to use bamboo chopsticks for turning the tofu pieces as they brown.

3 squares firm tofu (about 11 ounces), rinsed
1 tablespoon plus 2 teaspoons vegetable oil
8 ounces lean flank steak
2 teaspoons soy sauce
2 teaspoons Shao Hsing rice wine or dry sherry
2½ teaspoons cornstarch
½ teaspoon sugar
¼ teaspoon salt
2 tablespoons oyster sauce
2 scallions, cut into 2-inch pieces
1 tablespoon finely shredded ginger

1. Lightly pat dry the tofu squares with a paper towel. Cut each square into 1-inch cubes. Heat a 14-inch flat-bottomed wok over high heat until a bead of water vaporizes within 1 to 2 seconds of contact. Swirl in the 1 tablespoon oil, add the tofu, and pan-fry until light golden, about 3 minutes, turning midway through cooking. Transfer to a plate.

2. Cut the beef with the grain into 2-inch-wide strips. Cut each strip across the grain into ¼-inch-thick slices. Put the beef in a shallow bowl and add the soy sauce, rice wine, 1½ teaspoons of the cornstarch, the sugar, and salt. Set aside no more than 10 minutes. In a small bowl combine the remaining 1 teaspoon cornstarch and the oyster sauce with ⅓ cup cold water.

3. Heat the unwashed wok over high heat until hot and a faint wisp of smoke rises from the pan. Swirl in the remaining 2 teaspoons oil, the scallions, and ginger and carefully add the beef, spreading it evenly in the wok. Cook undisturbed 30 seconds, letting the beef begin to brown. Then, using a metal spatula, stir-fry 1 minute until the beef is lightly browned but not cooked through. Add the tofu and stir-fry 30 seconds. Stir the cornstarch mixture, swirl it into the wok, and bring to a boil, stir-frying 1 to 2 minutes until the sauce has thickened. *Serves 4 as part of a multicourse meal.*

Jean Yueh's Beef with Onions and Peppers

According to Chinese cookbook author and teacher Jean Yueh, this is a simple Shanghai-style family dish, normally made with only onions and beef. Shanghainese cooking is known for its use of soy sauce and sugar. Here the sweetness comes mainly from the onions and peppers. Yueh recommends partially freezing the beef to make it easier to cut into matchsticks or shreds.

12 ounces lean flank steak
4 teaspoons plus 2½ tablespoons soy sauce
2 tablespoons dry sherry
½ teaspoon freshly ground black pepper
3 teaspoons cornstarch
3 tablespoons vegetable oil
1 teaspoon sugar
2 medium onions, cut into ¼-inch-thick
    half-moon slices
½ medium green bell pepper, julienned
½ medium red bell pepper, julienned

1. Cut the beef with the grain into 2-inch-wide strips. Cut each strip across the grain into ¼-inch-thick slices, then stack the beef slices and cut into 2-inch-long matchsticks. Put the beef in a shallow bowl and add 4 teaspoons of the soy sauce, 1 tablespoon of the sherry, the pepper, and 2 teaspoons of the cornstarch. Stir to combine. Add 1 tablespoon of the oil and mix thoroughly.

2. In a small bowl combine the remaining 2½ tablespoons soy sauce, 1 tablespoon sherry, the sugar, and the remaining 1 teaspoon cornstarch. Stir to combine and set aside. Put the onions in a large bowl and separate the slices.

3. Heat a 14-inch flat-bottomed wok over high heat until a bead of water vaporizes within 1 to 2 seconds of contact. Swirl in 1 tablespoon of the oil and add the beef, spreading it evenly in the wok. Cook undisturbed 20 seconds, letting the beef begin to brown. Then, using a metal spatula, stir-fry, separating the beef matchsticks until the beef changes color, about 2 minutes. Transfer beef to a plate.

4. Swirl the remaining 1 tablespoon oil into the wok, add the onions, and cook about 2 minutes. Add the green and red peppers and stir-fry 1 to 2 minutes. Return the browned beef to the wok. Stir the sauce and swirl it into the wok. Stir-fry about 30 seconds or until the sauce is slightly thickened. *Serves 4 as part of a multicourse meal.*

Cousin Zane's Sichuan Beef

When my cousin Cindy's husband, Zane, a professional chef, stir-fries beef, he prefers a cut called flatiron (available in San Francisco's Chinatown), which is so tender it does not need to be marinated. If he uses flank steak, he marinates it and adds cornstarch. Zane drains the beef after stir-frying. He feels the meat juices cloud the flavors of the sauce.

8 ounces lean flank steak
2 tablespoons Shao Hsing rice wine or dry sherry
1½ teaspoons plus 1 tablespoon soy sauce
5 slices ginger, smashed
2½ teaspoons cornstarch
2 tablespoons ketchup
2 tablespoons hoisin sauce
2 teaspoons chili bean sauce
½ teaspoon sesame oil
1 tablespoon vegetable oil
1 medium green bell pepper, slivered
1 small onion, thinly sliced
1 cup Homemade Chicken Broth (page 195)
2 scallions, cut into 1-inch pieces

1. Cut the beef with the grain into 2-inch-wide strips. Cut each strip across the grain into ¼-inch-thick slices. Put the beef in a shallow bowl and add

Cousin Zane, a professional chef experienced at wok cooking, shows his wife, Cindy, how he tosses ingredients using the pao *action.*

the rice wine, 1½ teaspoons of the soy sauce, and 2 slices of the ginger. Set aside 30 minutes. Drain the beef. Stir 1 teaspoon of the cornstarch into the beef mixture and mix well.

2. In a small bowl combine the ketchup, hoisin sauce, chili bean sauce, sesame oil, and the remaining 1 tablespoon soy sauce. In a separate small bowl combine the remaining 1½ teaspoons cornstarch with 1 tablespoon cold water. Set aside.

3. Heat a 14-inch flat-bottomed wok over high heat until a bead of water vaporizes within 1 to 2 seconds of contact. Swirl in the vegetable oil and the remaining 3 slices ginger and stir-fry 30 seconds. Carefully add the beef, spreading it evenly in the wok. Cook undisturbed 1 minute, letting the beef begin to brown. Then, using a metal spatula, stir-fry 30 seconds or until the beef is lightly browned but not cooked through. Transfer to a colander set over a plate and let drain.

4. Without adding additional oil to the wok, add the pepper and onion and stir-fry 1 minute or until the vegetables begin to sear. Swirl in the broth and bring to a boil over high heat. Stir the ketchup mixture, swirl it into the wok, and return to a boil. Stir the cornstarch mixture, swirl it into the wok, and bring to a boil, stirring constantly, until the sauce has thickened. Add the beef and stir-fry until it is just cooked through, about 30 seconds. Garnish with the scallions. *Serves 4 as part of a multicourse meal.*

The **Wok Warriors**

大師父將軍

It is the heat that will wear you down. Stir-frying is tough physical work. Just standing in front of a restaurant wok stove, feeling 100,000 to 200,000 BTUs of heat, is sufficient to melt away any soul. But no wok chef is ever allowed to stand still. The toughest part of the day is the dinner shift. It has a frenetic, grueling pace. "In Cantonese we say *bat ting*, never stopping. You must be fast. If you slow down for a moment, you cannot do it," says Chef Danny Chan.

In Hong Kong and mainland China it is the chef working in an outdoor kitchen who exemplifies the harsher aspects of the wok warrior's life. I watch Chef Lee Wan Ching, a delicately framed man not much bigger than I am, expertly wield hot oil for deep-frying and stir-frying in nothing more than shorts, a loose T-shirt, and flip-flops at the Yee Hen restaurant on Lantau Island, Hong Kong. When I question the safety of working without protective chef-wear, Lee smiles, acknowledging the dangers. "You must have total control to work this way," he replies in Cantonese. "That comes only with experience."

Lee, who has worked in restaurants since he was fifteen years old, will be the first to tell you it is hard labor. He works a grueling twelve- to fourteen-hour shift, getting one day off every ten days. By the time his workday ends, his young children are fast asleep at home.

On busy nights he stir-fries 150 to 200 dishes nonstop in a cramped kitchen, using one wok. Standing by his side I time him, watching him cook a dish every minute to minute and a half. My favorite is his Sizzling Pepper and Salt Shrimp (page 104), local shrimp seared and juicy with the pungent flavor of fresh chilies and slightly caramelized garlic. I feel my body wilt under the sweltering heat of a relatively "cool" October night. Lee tells me this is nothing compared to the stifling conditions in the summer, when the temperature hovers above one hundred with high humidity and the kitchen reaches 130 degrees or more. "It's not exhausting until you sit down at the end of a shift. In a way it's exhilarating. To do this work you must have a passion for cooking," says Lee.

"The main difference between restaurant and home cooking is the intensity of the heat," says Chef Martin Yan. A Chinese restaurant stove has at least five times the heat of an American restaurant stove (at 15,000 to 30,000 BTUs) and far out-distances a home stove (at 8,000 to 14,000 BTUs). "It is the fierce heat necessary for oil-blanching that instantaneously sears the meat, poultry, or fish, concentrating the flavor," continues Yan. A restaurant wok stove makes it much easier for a chef compared to a home cook to create *wok hay*." Yan, who was born in Guangzhou, acknowledges that Cantonese chefs are the undisputed stir-fry experts. "They know how to use a powerful wok stove to its full advantage to achieve *wok hay*, the essence of aroma and breath."

Having always marveled at the superior quality of food in Hong Kong, I visit some of the best restaurant kitchens in hopes of discovering the stir-fry secrets of Cantonese chefs. After seeing several kitchens I comment to Chef Paray Li at the Peninsula hotel that their stoves sound like a 747 jet revving for take-off. "In Hong Kong, restaurant wok stoves produce a much stronger heat than American stoves. The gas is compressed, creating a more powerful roaring flame that enables the chef to achieve incredible *wok hay*," says Chef Li.

In fact, a Hong Kong restaurant stove's heat is so intense that a sturdy new carbon-steel wok will

Chef Lee Wan Ching stir-fries with the intense concentration of an experienced wok warrior.

Chef Ip Chi Cheung points out the muscles necessary for a chef to use the **pao** *action with a large restaurant wok; in order to gain arm strength and control he spent hours as an apprentice flipping a small metal bowl in a heavy Cantonese-style wok.*

大師
父將
軍

begin to warp within a few days, forcing the chef to rehammer the wok in order to prolong its life. Even with routine hammering, a wok can be reshaped only a limited number of times before holes form. A wok might last as little as one week or as long as one month before being discarded. In American restaurants, on the other hand, a new wok can be used for four to five months. Home woks sometimes withstand forty or fifty years of use.

"In the 1960s, both in Hong Kong and in San Fransisco's Chinatown, and, I assume, still in China, the true wok expert would turn the fire up so that flames were shooting two feet up all around the wok. The oil was so hot it often caught fire. Everything was seared instantly so it lost no flavor and retained all its moisture without a trace of grease," anthropology professor Eugene Anderson recalls. "Very few people can tolerate the heat," says Chef Martin Yan. "Chefs lose hair on their arms and repeatedly burn and scar their arms and hands," says Chef Yan as he shows me his eyebrow trimmed by the heat. "If not careful, a chef can burn his face," he warns.

Ability to withstand grueling heat and virtuosity with the wok are just two of the skills necessary for success as a wok warrior. Chef Kevin Chuk of CCTI teaches the fine knife skills essential for a young chef.

When working with such intense heat it is imperative that a chef be skillful and quick. "Without impeccable timing the food becomes like cinders. The great chefs are called 'masters of the wok,'" says Chinese food authority Ken Hom. "They are fantastic to watch."

Regardless of the punishing heat and physicality, restaurant cooking is a calling many Chinese chefs cannot deny. Chef Ming Tsai vividly remembers watching chefs stir-fry on his first trip to China in 1979. "I remember thinking these are the gods. Despite smoke and flames everywhere, the cooks maintained composure within their constant rhythm of stir-frying, then quickly washing the wok. Boom, wash, boom, wash—that's the pace," recalls Chef Tsai.

In Hong Kong and China a chef traditionally serves a long restaurant apprenticeship. An aspiring chef must work for three to five years before even being allowed to cook at the beginner wok position. Chef Martin Yan says that at the age of thirteen he began an apprenticeship at a well-established restaurant in Hong Kong. The best restaurant kitchens have four levels of wok chefs. Ideally an apprentice will build a relationship with the head chef, who will make him work for a long period of time before allowing him to observe the action of cooking at the wok. Nonetheless, some apprentices sneak over to the wok station in hopes of getting a glimpse of the action.

The head chef is a sort of "godfather." His responsibility is to keep a watchful eye on everything in the kitchen, tasting each chef's cooking and scrutinizing its quality. Many head chefs are known for their harsh discipline. "The Chinese system of culinary training instructs a chef not only in cooking skills but in character," says Nevin Lim, Hong Kong heritage researcher. Ideally, someone mentors a young chef, helping him build physical stamina and agility in addition to mental sharpness and unwavering focus for his work. A chef's knife skills must be fine; shreds must all match in uniformity. Every dish he cooks must satisfy the three criteria of color, aroma, and taste. What's more, the cooking must be consistent in quality, building flavors with precisely measured seasonings. The chef will later develop his own style and artistry. According to Chef Paray Li, he will cultivate a feeling for achieving the elusive *wok hay*.

In addition the chef must learn the subtle differences in heat—recognizing that each ingredient requires a different *fo hao*, or intensity of heat. Not everything stir-fries on high heat. This standard of excellence was illustrated a few weeks later when I dined in a fine restaurant in Guangzhou, China. Every dish arrived with a slip of paper identifying the chef who cooked the dish. I am impressed that if the cooking is unsatisfactory the chef is held accountable.

Late in the night after kitchen activity has been suspended, aspiring chefs often cook a snack for themselves. This is their opportunity to begin honing their wok skills. The weight of the classic 19-inch Cantonese-style two-ear wok is initially too heavy for most new chefs in a Cantonese kitchen to hold with one hand. Lifting a wok filled with ingredients requires substantial forearm strength. But a chef must also have a strong wrist for swirling the wok for pan-frying and to *pao* or toss the wok for stir-frying. The *pao* technique requires throwing the wok in a small circular motion in order to lift and catch the ingredients. This ensures that all of the ingredients receive an equal distribution of heat. Without the *pao* action food can easily burn.

As an eighteen-year-old apprentice, Chef Paray Li used to place a dampened kitchen towel, folded into a small square, in the wok and would then practice the *pao* motion for hours. Chef Ip Chi Cheung of Shang Palace restaurant in Kowloon practiced with a small stainless-steel bowl. If his action wasn't correct, the bowl would clatter onto the stove or floor.

The *pao* action is the most difficult to master. A stir-fry chef needs total body coordination; his knees control the gas lever, freeing his arms to *pao* and stir-fry with a ladle. The shoulder aches. The forearm aches the most. It is a wear and tear on the wrist that nothing can prepare you for. Even the hands will cramp. Practicing the *pao* motion is slightly easier

with a lightweight northern-style one-handle wok. "The most difficult is the heavier and larger Cantonese-style two-ear-handle wok, which requires not only wrist power but finger strength to grip the ears," says Chef Ip as he shows me the calluses on the inside crease of his thumb and on the palm at the base of his fourth finger, developed from years of work. The style of the two woks is so different that chefs cannot easily switch from one to the other.

After a three- to five-year training, an apprentice is designated worthy of working as the fourth wok chef. He will be allowed to stir-fry only a few dishes. The most elementary is fried rice, chosen because of its relative "safety." Its low-moisture ingredients are unlikely to cause oil spattering, yet the cooking demands mastery of the *pao* action. A fourth wok chef is also permitted to stir-fry rice noodles and simple vegetable dishes. If he does well, he can be promoted to third wok chef in one to two years, where he will learn more complex dishes. It will take him four to five years more to reach the rank of second wok chef. An additional five years are needed to become head chef, working the number one wok position.

Every chef I met with spoke of the years dedicated to methodically learning their craft, often enduring many hardships. For the restaurant chef, reaching each of the four levels of wok mastery is a proud life achievement. When I reflect on what I have learned, I have two clear images in my head. The first is of Chef Kevin Chuk, instructor at the Chinese Cuisine Training Institute in Hong Kong. A proud general standing in his Xian military-like chef's uniform complete with padded breast armor, he is ready to do battle at the stove with two trusted lieutenants by his side, each a student of CCTI. Then I think of Chef Lee Wan Ching of Yee Hen restaurant, a small, gentle man as stalwart and brave as he is resilient. As I regard their training, skill, creativity, and, not least, the enormous physical stamina demanded of these men hour after hour in a profession that requires ceaseless diligence, I recognize that they are not simply cooks but, indeed, wok warriors.

Stir-Frying **Fish** *and* **Shellfish**

Lee Wan Ching's Sizzling Pepper and Salt Shrimp

This is inspired by the incredible shrimp I had at the Yee Hen restaurant in Mui Wo, Lantau Island, Hong Kong. Chef Lee has a big jar of "chili pepper–salt mix" made up in his kitchen. I was pleased that my homemade concoction duplicates the wonderful salty hot flavor that coats the sweet shrimp. For the chilies, Chef Lee likes a moderately hot pepper such as an Anaheim. (photo page 102)

1 pound large shrimp
1 teaspoon salt
½ teaspoon sugar
¼ teaspoon chili powder
3 tablespoons vegetable oil
1 tablespoon minced garlic
1 tablespoon thinly sliced mild fresh chilies
2 scallions, chopped

1. Remove the shrimp legs, leaving the shells and tails on. Rinse the shrimp under cold water and set on several sheets of paper towels. With more paper towels, pat the shrimp dry. In a small bowl combine the salt, sugar, and chili powder.

2. Heat a 14-inch flat-bottomed wok over high heat until a bead of water vaporizes within 1 to 2 seconds of contact. Swirl in 1 tablespoon of the oil, add the garlic and sliced chilies, and stir-fry 30 seconds. Add the shrimp and 1 tablespoon of the oil and stir-fry 1 minute or until the shrimp just begin to turn pink. Swirl in the remaining 1 tablespoon oil, add the salt mixture, and stir-fry 1 to 2 minutes until the shrimp are just cooked. Stir in the scallions. *Serves 4 as part of a multicourse meal.*

Preceding pages:
Two of Chef Lee Wan Ching's specialties.
Left: Sizzling Pepper and Salt Shrimp
Right: Stir-Fried Clams in Bean Sauce with Chilies

Lee Wan Ching's Stir-Fried Clams in Bean Sauce with Chilies

Chef Lee Wan Ching stir-fries clams with bean sauce, a little wet bean curd (see page 228), and garlic. The sauce imparts a salty rich flavor with a touch of spicy heat from the fresh chilies. Use a mild chili such as an Anaheim. Many Chinese families insist on serving clams for the New Year's Eve dinner because clams signify good fortune. The shape of the shells is said to resemble ancient coins. (photo page 103)

1½ dozen littleneck clams
2 tablespoons bean sauce
1 small cube white wet bean curd
    (about 1 teaspoon)
¼ cup Homemade Chicken Broth (page 195)
2 tablespoons Shao Hsing rice wine or dry sherry
½ teaspoon sugar
2 tablespoons vegetable oil
1 tablespoon minced garlic
2 tablespoons thinly sliced mild fresh chilies
1 small green bell pepper, cut into 1-inch squares

1. Thoroughly wash the clams in several changes of cold water, discarding any open clams. Scrub the shells with a vegetable brush to remove grit and rinse well. Drain the clams in a colander. Lightly pat dry the shells with a paper towel. In a small bowl coarsely mash the bean sauce and wet bean curd with a fork. Stir in the broth, rice wine, and sugar.

2. Heat a 14-inch flat-bottomed wok over high heat until a bead of water vaporizes within 1 to 2 seconds of contact. Swirl in the oil, garlic, and chilies, and stir-fry 15 seconds or until fragrant. Add the clams and stir-fry 2 to 3 minutes. Add the bell pepper. Stir the broth mixture and swirl it into the wok. Cover the wok and cook 2 to 3 minutes or until the shells just begin to open. Transfer any opened clams to a platter and continue stir-frying, uncovered, over high heat until all the clams have opened and the broth is reduced slightly, 3 to 4 minutes. Discard any unopened clams. *Serves 4 as part of a multicourse meal.*

Ken Hom's Stir-Fried Peppers with Scallops

A scallop stir-fry, according to Chinese cooking authority Ken Hom, is perfect for a family meal or as the centerpiece for a dinner party. Scallops are fragile, sweet, delicate morsels that need very little preparation or cooking time. In this recipe, Hom combines them with nutritious and colorful red and green peppers, stir-frying them with peanut and olive oil. The result is a festive-looking dish that belies its ease of preparation.

1 pound fresh sea scallops
2 tablespoons Shao Hsing rice wine or dry sherry
1 tablespoon soy sauce
2 teaspoons bean sauce
1 teaspoon sugar
1 teaspoon sesame oil
1 tablespoon peanut oil
1 tablespoon olive oil
2 tablespoons chopped scallions
2 tablespoons chopped garlic
2 teaspoons minced ginger
1 large red bell pepper, cut into 1-inch squares
1 small green bell pepper, cut into 1-inch squares

1. Rinse the scallops under cold water, removing the muscle and any visible bits of shell or grit, and set on several sheets of paper towels. With more paper towels, pat the scallops dry. Halve any large scallops horizontally to match the size of the other scallops. In a small bowl combine the rice wine, soy sauce, bean sauce, sugar, and sesame oil.

2. Heat a 14-inch flat-bottomed wok over high heat until a bead of water vaporizes within 1 to 2 seconds of contact. Swirl in the peanut oil, add the scallops, and pan-fry 1 minute on each side. Transfer to a plate. Swirl in the olive oil. Add the scallions, garlic, and ginger, and stir-fry 30 seconds. Add the peppers and stir-fry 2 minutes. Return the scallops to the wok. Stir the rice wine mixture, swirl it into the wok, bring to a boil, and stir-fry until the scallops are just cooked, 30 seconds to 1 minute. *Serves 4 as part of a multicourse meal.*

Millie Chan's Chili Shrimp

Millie Chan uses chili bean sauce, a condiment made of capsicum, salt, and soybeans. If it is not available, chili sauce can be substituted, but the flavor is not as full. This shrimp has a wonderful balance of salty, sweet, peppery, and hot flavors and is an excellent appetizer served at room temperature.

1 tablespoon salt
1 pound large shrimp, peeled and deveined
2 tablespoons soy sauce
1 teaspoon chili bean sauce
½ teaspoon sugar
3 tablespoons vegetable oil
2 tablespoons Shao Hsing rice wine or dry sherry
2 tablespoons minced ginger
2 tablespoons chopped scallions
1 tablespoon minced mild fresh chilies, seeded
Cilantro sprigs

1. In a large bowl combine the salt with 3 cups cold water. Add the shrimp and let soak 1 hour. Drain the shrimp and set on several sheets of paper towels. With more paper towels, pat the shrimp dry. In a small bowl combine the soy sauce, chili bean sauce, and sugar.

2. Heat a 14-inch flat-bottomed wok over high heat until a bead of water vaporizes within 1 to 2 seconds of contact. Swirl in 2 tablespoons of the oil, add the shrimp, and stir-fry 1 minute or until the shrimp begin to turn pink. Swirl in the rice wine and immediately remove the wok from the heat. Transfer to a plate. Swirl the remaining 1 tablespoon oil into the wok over high heat, add the ginger, scallions, and chilies, and stir-fry 5 seconds. Stir the soy sauce mixture and swirl it into the wok. Return the shrimp to the wok and stir-fry 30 seconds to 1 minute or until the shrimp are just cooked. Garnish with the cilantro sprigs. *Serves 4 as part of a multicourse meal.*

Jean Yueh's Shanghai-Style Shrimp

Cookbook author and teacher Jean Yueh advises that the shrimp can be made ahead, transferred to a platter, and served at room temperature. Yueh tells me the shrimp are even better the next day after they absorb the sweet and savory Shanghai-style sauce.

1 pound large shrimp
3½ tablespoons soy sauce
1 teaspoon red wine vinegar
2 tablespoons vegetable oil
3 slices ginger
2 scallions, cut into 2-inch pieces
1 tablespoon dry sherry
3 tablespoons sugar, or to taste
1 tablespoon sesame oil, optional

1. Using kitchen shears, cut through the shrimp shells two-thirds of the length down the back of the shrimp. Remove the legs and devein the shrimp, leaving the shells and tails on. Rinse the unpeeled shrimp, drain, and set on several sheets of paper towels. With more paper towels, pat the shrimp dry. In a small bowl combine the soy sauce and vinegar.

2. Heat a 14-inch flat-bottomed wok over high heat until a bead of water vaporizes within 1 to 2 seconds of contact. Swirl in the vegetable oil, add the ginger and scallions, and stir-fry 30 seconds or until aromatic. Add the shrimp and stir-fry 30 seconds. Add the sherry and stir-fry a few seconds. Swirl in the soy sauce mixture and sprinkle in the sugar. Stir-fry the shrimp 1 to 2 minutes or until

Jean Yueh's custom-built home wok stove is large enough to accommodate an 18-inch wok. Like a hearth stove, it stabilizes the wok, allowing Jean to stir-fry without holding the wok. Opposite: Jean Yueh's Shanghai-Style Shrimp

the sauce is distributed and the shrimp are just cooked. Remove from the heat. Stir in the sesame oil if desired. Serve immediately or at room temperature. ***Serves 4 as part of a multicourse meal.***

Stir-Fried Shrimp with Garlic Sauce

Many Chinese cooks soak shrimp in saltwater. The brine soaking is said to give the shrimp a crisper texture, which the Chinese love. Make sure the shrimp are rinsed in fresh water and then patted dry before stir-frying. If there's moisture on them, the oil will spatter when they are added to the wok.

1 tablespoon salt
1 pound large shrimp, peeled and deveined
⅓ cup Homemade Chicken Broth (page 195)
2 teaspoons Shao Hsing rice wine or dry sherry
1½ teaspoons soy sauce
1½ teaspoons cornstarch
¾ teaspoon sugar
⅛ teaspoon ground white pepper
1 tablespoon vegetable oil
2 tablespoons minced garlic
1 teaspoon minced ginger
1 scallion, chopped

1. In a large bowl combine 2 cups cold water and the salt, stirring until the salt is dissolved. Add the shrimp and let stand 5 minutes. Rinse the shrimp under cold water and set on several sheets of paper towels. With more paper towels, pat the shrimp dry. In a small bowl combine the broth, rice wine, soy sauce, cornstarch, sugar, and pepper.

2. Heat a 14-inch flat-bottomed wok over high heat until a bead of water vaporizes within 1 to 2 seconds of contact. Swirl in the oil, add the shrimp, and stir-fry 1 minute or until the shrimp just begin to turn pink. Add the garlic and ginger and stir-fry 1 minute. Stir the cornstarch mixture, swirl it into the wok, and bring to a boil. Stir-fry until the shrimp are just cooked through and the sauce has thickened, 30 seconds to 1 minute. Stir in the scallion. ***Serves 4 as part of a multicourse meal.***

At home Chef Danny Chan stir-fries his Crabs with Black Bean Sauce (page 110) with a metal spatula. In restaurants, chefs use a ladle, making it easier for them to combine seasonings. Opposite: Julie Tay's Singapore-Style Squid (page 111).

Danny Chan's Crabs with Black Bean Sauce

Chef Danny Chan remembers eating crabs in China during the full moon. According to Chan the crabs are the fattest at that time. Stir-frying is excellent for keeping crabmeat moist and succulent. Adjust cooking times by the size of the crabs. (photo page 109)

4 live blue crabs (about 2 pounds)
1 tablespoon fermented black beans, rinsed
1 teaspoon cornstarch
2 tablespoons vegetable oil
4 slices ginger
2 scallions, cut into 2-inch pieces
2 tablespoons ground pork
⅓ cup Homemade Chicken Broth (page 195)
1 tablespoon soy sauce
½ teaspoon salt
¼ teaspoon ground white pepper
1 large egg, beaten

1. Put the crabs in a paper bag and put the bag in the freezer for about 1 hour or until the crabs are no longer moving. Put each crab shell side down on a cutting board and twist off the apron. Pull off the hard shell and remove the spongy gills on both sides. Cut the small legs off with a cleaver and discard. Cut each crab in half. Put the crabs in a colander and rinse under cold water. Shake off excess water. Roughly chop the black beans. In a small bowl combine the cornstarch with 2 tablespoons cold water. Set aside.

2. Heat a 14-inch flat-bottomed wok over high heat until a bead of water vaporizes within 1 to 2 seconds of contact. Swirl in the oil, add the ginger and just the white part of the scallions, and stir-fry 10 seconds or until fragrant. Add the black beans and stir-fry 10 seconds. Add the pork and stir-fry until it is no longer pink, about 20 seconds.

3. Add the halved crabs and stir-fry 20 seconds. Add the broth, cover, and cook 3 to 4 minutes or until the crabs begin to turn orange, stirring mid-

way. Add the soy sauce, salt, pepper, and the remaining scallion greens, stirring to combine. Cover and cook 1 minute. Stir the cornstarch mixture and swirl it into the wok with the egg. Stir-fry 30 seconds or until the crabs are just cooked through. *Serves 4 as part of a multicourse meal.*

Mandarin Fish Slices with Chrysanthemum CCTI

At the Chinese Cuisine Training Institute in Hong Kong an advanced cooking technique is taught: delicate matchsticks, or shreds, of fish and luffa (see page 222) are stir-fried using indirect heat. Only small quantities can be cooked in this manner, a total of about 2 cups of the mixture. This is a true culinary work of art when garnished with chrysanthemum petals, but rather than search for flowers that have not been sprayed or dipped in pesticide, I often make this without the garnish. (photo page 113)

12 ounces skinless sea bass fillet
1 tablespoon plus 1 teaspoon egg white
1½ teaspoons cornstarch
1½ teaspoons Shao Hsing rice wine or dry sherry
¾ teaspoon salt
¼ teaspoon ground white pepper
4 tablespoons vegetable oil
¼ cup Homemade Chicken Broth (page 195)
4 ounces luffa or zucchini
2 teaspoons minced ginger
½ teaspoon sesame oil
1 tablespoon edible chrysanthemum petals

1. Remove any visible bones from the fish. Halve the fish lengthwise, along the deep natural crease of the fillet, into 2 strips roughly 2 inches wide. One strip at a time, cut ¼-inch-thick slices across the strip on a slight diagonal. Stack the slices and cut into 2-inch-long matchsticks. Put the fish in a shallow bowl and add the egg white, 1 teaspoon of the cornstarch, 1 teaspoon of the rice wine, ¼ teaspoon of the salt, and the pepper. Gently stir to combine. Add 2 tablespoons of the vegetable oil with 1 teaspoon cold water, and gently combine.

2. In a small bowl combine the broth, the remaining ½ teaspoon cornstarch and ½ teaspoon rice wine, and ¼ teaspoon of the salt. Set aside. With a vegetable peeler, peel the luffa. If using zucchini the vegetable does not need to be peeled. Cut in half lengthwise. Cut each half on the diagonal into scant ¼-inch-thick slices. Stack the slices and cut into 2-inch-long matchsticks. You should have about ¾ cup.

3. Heat a 14-inch flat-bottomed wok over high heat until a bead of water vaporizes within 1 to 2 seconds of contact. Swirl in 1 tablespoon of the vegetable oil, add the ginger, and stir-fry 5 seconds. Add the fish slices, spreading them evenly in the wok. Cook undisturbed 10 seconds. Immediately turn off the heat. Gently stir-fry the fish slices in the wok with a metal spatula until they just turn white but are not cooked through, 1 to 2 minutes. Transfer to a plate.

4. Swirl the remaining 1 tablespoon vegetable oil into the wok over high heat, add the luffa and the remaining ¼ teaspoon salt, and stir-fry 30 seconds. Stir the broth mixture, swirl it into the wok, and bring to a boil, stirring gently until the sauce has thickened slightly, 20 to 30 seconds. Add the fish and turn off the heat. Gently stir-fry the ingredients until the fish is just cooked through, about 1 minute. Drizzle with the sesame oil. Garnish with the chrysanthemum petals. *Serves 4 as part of a multicourse meal.*

Julie Tay's Singapore-Style Squid

Julie Tay stir-fries squid, seasoning it with hot chilies and a little shrimp paste, duplicating the fiery, pungent flavors of Singapore cuisine. She uses belacan, also known as shrimp paste, which is sold in small bricks. Use a cleaver to shave off the amount you want, and warm it to bring out its flavor before cooking. I preheat the paste, wrapped in a small sheet of aluminum foil, in a dry wok over low heat 5 minutes or until fragrant. The heat brings out a fishy smell that may not appeal to everyone, but the flavor it adds is rich and mellow. (photo page 108)

12 ounces fresh squid
1 tablespoon black soy sauce
2 teaspoons soy sauce
1 teaspoon red wine vinegar
½ teaspoon salt
½ teaspoon sugar
2 tablespoons peanut oil
2 tablespoons thinly sliced garlic
3 tablespoons finely shredded ginger
1 teaspoon belacan shrimp paste
½ teaspoon minced fresh Thai chilies
¼ cup thinly sliced red onion
1 medium red bell pepper, cut into
    ¼-inch-wide strips

1. Cut off and reserve the tentacles attached to the squid heads. Remove the internal cartilage and heads from the bodies and discard. Peel off the purple membrane. Wash the squid in several changes of cold water and drain in a colander. Lightly pat dry the squid with paper towels to remove any excess moisture. Cut each body in half lengthwise. Using a very sharp knife, lightly score the inside of the bodies in a crisscross pattern. Cut the squid into 1½-inch squares and the tentacles into 2-inch pieces. Put the squid in a bowl and set aside. In a small bowl combine both types of soy sauce, the vinegar, salt, and sugar with 3 tablespoons cold water.

2. Heat a 14-inch flat-bottomed wok over high heat until a bead of water vaporizes within 1 to 2 seconds of contact. Swirl in the oil, add the garlic, and stir-fry 20 seconds. Add the ginger and stir-fry 10 seconds. Add the shrimp paste and stir-fry 10 seconds, breaking up the paste with a metal spatula. Add the chilies, red onion, and bell pepper and stir-fry 20 seconds. Add the squid and stir-fry 1 to 2 minutes or until it just begins to curl. Stir the soy sauce mixture, swirl it into the wok, and bring to a boil. Cover, reduce the heat to low, and cook 2 to 4 minutes or until the squid is just tender. *Serves 4 as part of a multicourse meal.*

Mrs. Miu's Stir-Fried Fish and Eggplant (page 114)
Opposite: Mandarin Fish Slices with Chrysanthemum CCTI (page 110)

Shrimp and Pine Nuts Shang Palace

This is inspired by an extraordinary dish I watched Chef Ip Chi Cheung prepare at the Shang Palace restaurant at the Shangri-La hotel in Kowloon. Chef Ip presents this dish in cups made from deep-fried spring roll wrappers. At home, this stir-fry is equally delicious served with steamed rice. (photo page 116)

2 tablespoons plus 1 teaspoon salt
1 pound large shrimp, peeled and deveined
1 tablespoon egg white
2 teaspoons cornstarch
1 teaspoon sesame oil
1/8 teaspoon ground white pepper
1/3 cup Homemade Chicken Broth (page 195)
1 tablespoon Shao Hsing rice wine or dry sherry
1/2 teaspoon sugar
2 tablespoons pine nuts
2 tablespoons vegetable oil
4 slices ginger
1 cup snow peas, strings removed (about
    3 ounces)
1 cup thinly sliced celery
1/2 cup red bell pepper, cut into 1-inch cubes

1. Dissolve 1 tablespoon of the salt in 1 quart cold water. Swish the shrimp in the saltwater and drain. Repeat the process with another tablespoon of the salt. Rinse the shrimp, drain, and set on several sheets of paper towels. With more paper towels, pat the shrimp dry. In a shallow bowl combine the shrimp, egg white, 1 1/2 teaspoons of the cornstarch, 1/2 teaspoon of the sesame oil, the pepper, and 1/2 teaspoon of the salt. In a small bowl combine the broth, rice wine, sugar, and the remaining 1/2 teaspoon sesame oil and 1/2 teaspoon cornstarch.

2. Heat a 14-inch flat-bottomed wok over medium heat 30 seconds. Add the pine nuts and toast, shaking the pan 1 to 2 minutes or until the nuts are light golden. Transfer to a small plate and set aside. Heat the wok over high heat until a bead of water vaporizes within 1 to 2 seconds of contact. Swirl in 1 tablespoon of the vegetable oil, add the ginger, and stir-fry 5 seconds. Carefully add the shrimp, spread-

ing them evenly in the wok. Cook undisturbed for 20 seconds, letting the shrimp begin to brown. Then, using a metal spatula, stir-fry 30 seconds to 1 minute or until the shrimp begin to turn pink but are not totally cooked through. Transfer to a plate.

3. Swirl the remaining 1 tablespoon vegetable oil into the wok over high heat. Add the snow peas, celery, and red pepper and stir-fry 1 minute. Add the shrimp. Stir the cornstarch mixture, and swirl it into the wok. Bring to a boil, and stir-fry constantly until the shrimp are just cooked and the sauce has thickened, about 1 minute. Sprinkle with the remaining 1/2 teaspoon salt and the pine nuts. ***Serves 4 as part of a multicourse meal.***

Mrs. Miu's Stir-Fried Fish and Eggplant

Mrs. Kam Toa Miu makes her own fish paste for this stir-fry by thinly slicing the fish with a sharp cleaver and then finely chopping it so that no bone is bigger than 1/8 inch. She then hand-chops the shrimp, adds it to the seasonings, and stirs by hand until the paste is stiff. With a food processor the results are almost as delicate. Just remember to check the paste with your fingers to be sure that all the bones have been finely minced. (photo page 112)

2 medium Asian eggplants (about 12 ounces)
8 ounces scrod fillet
4 ounces medium shrimp, peeled and deveined
1 tablespoon plus 1 teaspoon cornstarch
1 teaspoon sugar
1/2 teaspoon salt
1/8 teaspoon ground white pepper
2 teaspoons plus 2 tablespoons vegetable oil
1/4 cup minced scallions
2 teaspoons soy sauce
1 teaspoon Shao Hsing rice wine or dry sherry
1/2 teaspoon sesame oil
1 tablespoon minced garlic

1. Cut the eggplants in half lengthwise. Cut each half crosswise into 1/2-inch-thick slices. In a large pot bring 1 1/2 quarts water to a boil over high heat and add the eggplant. Blanch 1 to 2 minutes or until the eggplant slices are tender when pierced with a knife. Drain well in a colander.

2. Remove any visible bones from the fish. Finely chop the fish. Put the fish in a food processor and pulse 1 to 2 seconds. Add the shrimp and pulse 1 to 2 seconds or until finely chopped. Add the 1 tablespoon cornstarch, ¼ teaspoon of the sugar, the salt, pepper, the 2 teaspoons vegetable oil, and the scallions, and pulse 1 to 2 seconds until just combined. Add 2 tablespoons cold water and pulse 1 to 2 seconds or until the mixture is thick. In a small bowl combine the soy sauce, rice wine, sesame oil, the remaining ¾ teaspoon sugar, and the 1 teaspoon cornstarch with 1 tablespoon cold water.

3. Heat a 14-inch flat-bottomed wok over high heat until a bead of water vaporizes within 1 to 2 seconds of contact. Swirl in 1 tablespoon of the vegetable oil, add the garlic, and stir-fry 5 seconds. Add the eggplant and stir-fry 30 seconds to 1 minute. Transfer to a plate.

4. Swirl the remaining 1 tablespoon vegetable oil into the wok over high heat and add the fish paste by rounded teaspoonfuls, spreading it evenly. Reduce the heat to medium, and cook undisturbed 1 minute, letting the fish begin to brown. Increase the heat to high, add the eggplant, and stir-fry 30 seconds. The fish will break up a little once it's stir-fried with the eggplant. Stir the soy sauce mixture, swirl it into the wok, and bring to a boil. Stir-fry constantly until the fish is just cooked through, about 30 seconds. *Serves 4 as part of a multicourse meal.*

Che Chung Ng's Scallops with Asparagus

My Auntie Ivy's mother, Che Chung Ng, taught me this delicious and easy stir-fry. The key here is to rinse the scallops and dry them well. Excess moisture prevents them from absorbing the marinade and also causes the oil to spatter when stir-frying. The scallops take only a few minutes to cook. Make sure they are uniform in size and thickness for even cooking; cut any larger scallops in half horizontally so that all of the scallops have a similar thickness.

1 pound fresh sea scallops
1¼ teaspoons salt
1 pound asparagus, trimmed and cut into
    2-inch pieces
4 teaspoons Shao Hsing rice wine or dry sherry
2¼ teaspoons cornstarch
1½ teaspoons oyster sauce
1 teaspoon sesame oil
½ teaspoon ground white pepper
1 tablespoon vegetable oil
1 tablespoon minced garlic

1. Rinse the scallops under cold water, removing the muscle and any visible bits of shell or grit, and set on several sheets of paper towels. With more paper towels, pat the scallops dry. Halve any large scallops horizontally. In a 1½-quart saucepan bring 2 cups water and 1 teaspoon of the salt to a boil over high heat. Add the asparagus and return to a boil. Drain in a colander, and set aside.

2. In a small bowl combine 1 tablespoon of the rice wine, 1 teaspoon of the cornstarch, and the oyster sauce with ¼ cup cold water. In a shallow bowl combine the scallops, sesame oil, pepper, and the remaining 1¼ teaspoons cornstarch, 1 teaspoon rice wine, and ¼ teaspoon salt.

3. Heat a 14-inch flat-bottomed wok over high heat until a bead of water vaporizes within 1 to 2 seconds of contact. Swirl in the vegetable oil, add the garlic, and stir-fry 15 seconds or until golden. Add the scallops, carefully spreading them in the wok. Cook undisturbed 30 seconds, letting them begin to brown. Then, using a metal spatula, stir-fry 30 seconds to 1 minute or until the scallops are light golden but not cooked through. Add the asparagus. Stir the cornstarch mixture, swirl it into the wok, bring to a boil, and stir-fry until the scallops are just cooked through and the sauce has thickened, about 30 seconds. *Serves 4 as part of a multicourse meal.*

Stir-Frying
Rice *and*
Noodles

Yin Yang Rice Shang Palace

Inspired by the concept of yin yang harmony, Chef Ip Chi Cheung's signature dish at Shang Palace restaurant in the Shangri-La hotel in Kowloon combines two different rice grains, creating a contrast in color, taste, and texture. Rich black rice paired with shiitake mushrooms and wolfberries (see page 228) is the perfect contrast to the delicate taste of long-grain rice, crab, and egg whites. For simplicity I sometimes serve just the crab rice, but then I double the recipe. (photo page 117)

1 tablespoon pitted wolfberries
3 tablespoons vegetable oil
8 fresh shiitake mushrooms, stemmed and
    thinly sliced
¼ cup Homemade Chicken Broth (page 195)
1¼ teaspoons salt
¼ teaspoon ground white pepper
2 cups cold cooked Black Rice (below)
¼ cup minced scallions, green parts only, plus
    ¼ cup minced white parts
2 cups cold cooked long-grain rice (½ recipe
    Classic Rice, page 120)
⅓ cup minced celery
1 large egg white, beaten
4 ounces lump crabmeat, picked over to
    remove cartilage

1. Put the wolfberries in a small bowl, cover with cold water, and let sit 5 minutes. Drain.

2. Heat a 14-inch flat-bottomed wok over high heat until a bead of water vaporizes within 1 to 2 seconds of contact. Swirl in 1 tablespoon of the oil, add the mushrooms, and stir-fry 30 seconds. Swirl in the broth and stir-fry 30 seconds. Stir in ¼ teaspoon of the salt and ⅛ teaspoon of the pepper. Transfer to a plate. Rinse the wok and dry it thoroughly.

3. Heat the wok over high heat until a bead of water vaporizes within 1 to 2 seconds of contact. Swirl in 1 tablespoon of the oil. Add the black rice and stir-fry 1 minute, breaking up the rice with a metal spatula. Add the scallion greens, half the mushrooms, the wolfberries, and ½ teaspoon of the salt. Reduce the heat to medium and stir-fry 1 minute or until heated through. Transfer to a plate. Rinse the wok and dry it thoroughly.

4. Heat the wok over high heat until a bead of water vaporizes within 1 to 2 seconds of contact. Swirl in the remaining 1 tablespoon oil. Add the long-grain rice and celery and stir-fry, breaking up the rice with a spatula, 1 to 2 minutes, or until the rice is heated through. Add the egg white, crabmeat, white part of the scallions, the remaining mushrooms, ½ teaspoon salt, and ⅛ teaspoon pepper, and stir-fry 15 seconds. Remove from the heat and stir-fry 30 seconds or until the egg white is just cooked. Arrange on a serving platter so that the black rice is on one side and the white rice on the other, similar to a yin yang symbol. Place a spoonful of the black rice on the white rice and vice versa. *Serves 4 as part of a multicourse meal.*

Black Rice

Black rice is a glutinous rice with black and brown kernels. When it cooks it becomes almost burgundy-colored with a nutty flavor reminiscent of wild rice. The Chinese believe it promotes blood circulation and enhances health. Traditionally in Asia black rice is used only in desserts.

1 cup black rice

In a 1-quart saucepan combine the rice with 1 cup cold water. Bring to a boil over high heat. Cover, reduce the heat to low, and simmer 30 minutes or until the grains are tender. *Makes about 2 cups.*

Preceding pages:
Shang Palace restaurant in Kowloon is famous for traditional Chinese decor, innovative presentation, and fine cuisine.
Left: Shrimp and Pine Nuts Shang Palace (page 114)
Right: Yin Yang Rice Shang Palace

Ken Lo's Chow Fun with Beef and Broccoli

New York City cooking teacher Ken Lo created this recipe to duplicate the tastes of a favorite dish at a local Chiu Chow–style restaurant. It is essential to use fresh broad rice noodles, ho fan, available in 1-pound slabs in Chinese markets. Once the noodles are refrigerated, they become hard, and although this recipe will still work, unrefrigerated noodles are preferable.

6 ounces lean flank steak
1 tablespoon minced garlic
8 teaspoons canola oil
2 teaspoons plus 1 tablespoon Shao Hsing rice wine or dry sherry
3 teaspoons plus 1 tablespoon soy sauce
1 tablespoon plus 1 teaspoon cornstarch
¼ cup finely shredded ginger
12 ounces Chinese broccoli
1 slab fresh broad rice noodles (about 1 pound)
1 tablespoon oyster sauce
2 large eggs, beaten
2 scallions, chopped

1. Cut the beef with the grain into 2-inch-wide strips. Cut each strip across the grain into ¼-inch-thick slices. Put the beef in a shallow bowl and add the garlic, 2 teaspoons of the oil, the 2 teaspoons rice wine, 2 teaspoons of the soy sauce, the cornstarch, and ginger. Stir to combine and set aside. Cut the broccoli stalks in half lengthwise if more than ½ inch in diameter. Cut the stalks and leaves into 2-inch-long pieces, keeping the stalks separate from the leaves. Leaving the noodles as a slab, cut them crosswise into ½-inch-wide strips. Using your hands separate and loosen the noodles. In a small bowl combine the oyster sauce and 1 teaspoon of the soy sauce with ½ cup cold water. Set aside.

2. Heat a 14-inch flat-bottomed wok over high heat until a bead of water vaporizes within 1 to 2 seconds of contact. Swirl in 2 teaspoons of the oil and carefully add the beef, spreading it evenly in the wok. Cook undisturbed 30 seconds, letting the beef begin to brown. Then, using a metal spatula, stir-fry

1 minute until the beef is lightly browned but not cooked through. Transfer to a plate and set aside. Swirl 2 teaspoons of the oil into the wok, add the broccoli stalks, and stir-fry 30 seconds. Add the leaves and the remaining 1 tablespoon soy sauce and 1 tablespoon rice wine and stir-fry 1 to 2 minutes or until the stalks are bright green and the leaves just limp. Transfer to a plate. Rinse the wok and dry it thoroughly.

3. Heat the wok over high heat until a bead of water vaporizes within 1 to 2 seconds of contact. Swirl the remaining 2 teaspoons oil into the wok and add the noodles, spreading them evenly in the wok. Pan-fry undisturbed 30 seconds. Swirl in the eggs, tilting the pan so that the eggs cover the surface. Pan-fry 1 to 1½ minutes until the bottom is browned, using a spatula to loosen the noodle cake. Slide the noodles onto a 10-inch plate. Place another plate over the noodles and flip both plates over. Slide the noodles back into the wok browned side up and pan-fry 30 seconds until the bottom is golden. Transfer to a platter.

4. Return the broccoli and beef to the wok. Swirl in the oyster sauce mixture, add the scallions, and stir-fry 1 to 1½ minutes or until the sauce comes to a boil and has thickened slightly. Pour the beef and broccoli mixture over the noodles. *Serves 4 as part of a multicourse meal.*

Classic Rice

Traditionally, in China many families had a wok just for cooking rice. Rice cooked in a wok is said to be fragrant (see sidebar). However, if you have only one wok, reserve it for cooking and prepare the rice in a saucepan. When washing rice, remember to save the water for washing the wok after cooking. The starchy water is the best cleanser you'll ever use for a cast-iron or carbon-steel wok (see page 55).

1⅓ cups long-grain rice

Put the rice in a 1½-quart heavy saucepan. Wash the rice in several changes of cold water until the water runs clear. Drain. Level the rice and add enough cold water to cover by ¾ inch. (or add 2 cups water). Bring the water to a boil over high heat, reduce the heat to medium-high, and boil the rice until most of the water has evaporated and little craters appear on the surface, 4 to 5 minutes. Reduce the heat to low, cover, and simmer 10 minutes or until all of the water is absorbed. Turn off the heat and let stand 5 minutes before serving. *Makes about 4 cups; serves 4 as part of a multicourse meal.*

Fried Rice with Ham, Egg, and Scallions

The egg in this fried rice is cooked by a super easy method. Rather than being made like the classic egg "crêpe," the egg is cooked right in the well of the rice, which creates a much more delicate texture.

2 tablespoons vegetable oil
1 tablespoon minced garlic
½ cup chopped scallions
4 cups cold cooked Classic Rice (above)
¾ cup frozen peas
1 large egg, beaten
1 cup diced smoked ham
½ teaspoon salt
¼ teaspoon ground white pepper

Cooking Rice in a Wok

"In Guangzhou, China, in 1955 one of my jobs as a student was to cook rice in a wok for 140 people twice a day," recalls Dr. Kam Toa Miu. "I always needed the help of another young man. The wok was so enormous that between the two of us it was impossible to put our arms around it. First we would fill the wok with water—it looked like a swimming pool. Then we would burn wood in the stove's fire chamber." Meanwhile, as the water slowly heated, the two men poured 150 pounds of rice into a giant bamboo basket, hosing it down with water to rinse the rice. "In those days we ate about a pound of rice at each meal, with very little else to eat. In later years, with constant food shortages, we were lucky to have four ounces of rice each day," says Dr. Miu. "Once the water boiled we used shovels to scoop the wet rice grains into the wok. Then we placed a huge wooden lid on the wok along with wet rags around the edges to seal the wok and prevent any steam from escaping. We quickly removed the burning wood from the fire chamber. By then the wok was so hot that if we left the wood in the stove the rice would've easily burned. In twenty minutes the rice was ready."

1. Heat a 14-inch flat-bottomed wok over high heat until a bead of water vaporizes within 1 to 2 seconds of contact. Swirl in 1 tablespoon of the oil, add the garlic and scallions, and stir-fry 10 seconds. Add the rice and the peas and stir-fry 2 to 3 minutes, breaking up the rice with a metal spatula.

Cooking rice in a wok is slightly different from cooking it in a saucepan. My friend Peipei Chang says it is essential that the wok lid not be removed during cooking to ensure that no steam heat is lost. As the rice simmers she also likes to give the wok a quarter turn every 3 to 4 minutes, which Peipei explains helps the rice grains cook evenly.

1¼ cups long-grain rice

1. In a 14-inch flat-bottomed wok wash the rice in several changes of cold water until the water runs clear. Drain. Add 2 cups cold water to the wok and level the rice. Soak the rice 5 minutes.

2. Place the wok lid on the wok and set the pan over high heat. In about 4 to 5 minutes when the water comes to a boil, you'll see big boiling bubbles around the edges of the lid. Do not remove the wok's lid until the rice has finished cooking. Boil, covered, until the bubbles disappear around the lid, about 5 minutes. Reduce the heat to medium-low and simmer, covered, 15 minutes, giving the wok a quarter turn every 3 to 4 minutes. Turn off the heat and let sit 5 minutes before serving. *Makes a scant 4 cups.*

2. Make a well in the rice, exposing the bottom of the wok. Add the remaining 1 tablespoon oil and the egg. Immediately stir-fry to incorporate the egg throughout the rice, 1 to 2 minutes or until the egg is almost cooked through. Add the ham, salt, and pepper and stir-fry 1 to 2 minutes until heated through. *Serves 4 as part of a multicourse meal.*

Ming Tsai's Mandarin Fried Rice

Chef Ming Tsai recalls that the first dish he learned to stir-fry as a ten-year-old child was Mandarin fried rice, perhaps inspired by his mother's restaurant, the Mandarin Kitchen, in Dayton, Ohio. Chinese sausage, lop chong, has a sweet flavor well suited to fried rice. The hard pork sausage looks like skinny salami and is sold in Chinese butcher shops and in some Asian markets. Chef Tsai suggests substituting 4 strips of crumbled cooked bacon if the sausage is unavailable.

2 tablespoons canola oil
1 teaspoon sesame oil
2 large eggs, beaten
2 tablespoons minced garlic
2 tablespoons minced ginger
1 Chinese sausage, cut into ⅛-inch dice
½ cup sliced scallions
4 cups cold cooked Classic Rice (opposite)
2 tablespoons soy sauce
½ teaspoon salt
¼ teaspoon ground white pepper

1. Heat a 14-inch flat-bottomed wok over high heat until a bead of water vaporizes within 1 to 2 seconds of contact. Swirl in 1 tablespoon of the canola oil, the sesame oil, and eggs, and cook 30 seconds to 1 minute, tilting the pan so that the eggs cover the surface as thinly as possible to make a pancake. When the bottom is just beginning to brown and the pancake is just set, with a metal spatula, flip the pancake and allow it to set, 5 seconds. Transfer it to a cutting board and cut into shreds.

2. Swirl the remaining 1 tablespoon canola oil into the wok over high heat, add the garlic and ginger, and stir-fry 30 seconds. Add the Chinese sausage and stir-fry 1 minute. Add the scallions and rice and stir-fry 2 to 3 minutes or until heated through. Add the soy sauce, salt, pepper, and egg shreds and toss to combine. *Serves 4 as part of a multicourse meal.*

Mama's Noodles with Mushrooms and Ham

Mama often makes this noodle dish for lunch. The Cantonese like using spare amounts of Smithfield ham; its flavor resembles that of a famous ham from Yunnan province in China. If you want to prepare this with Smithfield ham, follow the boiling and steaming directions for the ham in Mama's Fuzzy Melon with Dried Scallops (page 178). But for such a small amount I use prosciutto to save time.

6 dried shiitake mushrooms
8 ounces flat dried rice noodles
1 tablespoon vegetable oil
1 tablespoon finely shredded ginger
8 ounces mung bean sprouts (about 4 cups)
1 teaspoon salt
¼ teaspoon sugar
2 teaspoons sesame oil
3 teaspoons soy sauce
2 ounces prosciutto, julienned
1 scallion, thinly sliced
Cilantro sprigs

1. In a medium shallow bowl soak the mushrooms in ¾ cup cold water 30 minutes or until softened. Drain and squeeze dry, reserving the soaking liquid. Cut off and discard the stems and thinly slice the caps. Set aside. Soak the noodles in a bowl with enough warm water to cover 20 minutes or until they are soft and pliable. Drain and set aside.

2. Heat a 14-inch flat-bottomed wok over high heat until a bead of water vaporizes within 1 to 2 seconds of contact. Swirl in the vegetable oil, add the ginger, and stir-fry 10 seconds. Add the bean sprouts and stir-fry 1 minute. Add the mushrooms, ½ teaspoon of the salt, and the sugar and stir-fry 1 minute or until the sprouts are cooked but still crisp. Transfer to a shallow bowl and toss with 1 teaspoon of the sesame oil and 2 teaspoons of the soy sauce.

3. Add ½ cup of the reserved mushroom soaking liquid, the remaining 1 teaspoon soy sauce, and 1 teaspoon sesame oil to the unwashed wok.

Add the rice noodles and warm over medium heat, stirring constantly, 2 to 3 minutes until all the liquid is absorbed and the noodles are just tender. Add the bean sprout mixture and the remaining ½ teaspoon salt, and stir-fry 1 minute until combined. Transfer to a platter. Sprinkle on the shredded ham, scallion, and cilantro sprigs. *Serves 4 as part of a multicourse meal.*

Aromatic Vegetarian Fried Rice

If you want to add a little protein to this dish, make an egg pancake with 1 or 2 beaten eggs (see page 121). Finely shred the pancake and add it to the rice during the last minute of cooking. Vary the vegetables according to what is seasonally available. I like to add asparagus, green beans, and cherry tomatoes.

2 tablespoons vegetable oil
⅓ cup chopped shallots
2 tablespoons minced mild fresh chilies
1 tablespoon minced garlic
1 cup diced carrots
4 cups cold cooked Classic Rice (page 120)
½ cup diced red bell pepper
½ cup diced celery
1 tablespoon soy sauce
1 teaspoon salt
¼ teaspoon ground white pepper
2 tablespoons chopped cilantro
2 teaspoons sesame oil

Heat a 14-inch flat-bottomed wok over high heat until a bead of water vaporizes within 1 to 2 seconds of contact. Swirl in the vegetable oil, add the shallots, chilies, and garlic, and stir-fry 10 seconds. Add the carrots, reduce the heat to medium, and stir-fry 2 to 3 minutes until the shallots begin to brown. Add the rice, bell pepper, celery, soy sauce, salt, and pepper. Increase the heat to medium-high and stir-fry 2 to 3 minutes, breaking up the rice with a metal spatula until it is heated through. Remove from the heat. Stir in the cilantro and drizzle on the sesame oil. *Serves 4 as part of a multicourse meal.*

Dickson Hee's Oyster Lo Mein

When I visited Dickson Hee at the Hong Hop Noodle Company in New York's Chinatown, the employees prepared this during a work break. Hee fondly remembers his father cooking this classic Cantonese comfort food when he was a child. It is important to rinse the cooked noodles in cold water to remove excess starch. (photo page 127)

1 teaspoon salt
One 1-pound package fresh lo mein noodles
3 tablespoons oyster sauce
2 teaspoons soy sauce
2 teaspoons sesame oil
¼ teaspoon sugar
2 tablespoons vegetable oil
1 tablespoon minced garlic
1 scallion, finely shredded
½ cup julienned carrots, optional

1. In a large pot bring 3 quarts water to a boil over high heat. When the water comes to a rolling boil, add the salt and noodles. Return to a rolling boil and boil about 1 minute or according to package directions

A stir-fry requires the freshest noodles. Dickson Hee presides over the Hong Hop Noodle Company, started by his granduncle, which has been providing fresh noodles to New York City's Chinatown since 1910.

until al dente. Carefully pour the hot water from the pot and add several changes of cold water, swishing the noodles to remove surface starch. Drain thoroughly in a colander. In the unwashed pot combine the oyster sauce, soy sauce, sesame oil, and sugar. Add the drained noodles and toss to combine.

2. Heat a 14-inch flat-bottomed wok over high heat until a bead of water vaporizes within 1 to 2 seconds of contact. Swirl in the vegetable oil, add the garlic, and stir-fry 20 seconds or until the garlic begins to brown. Add the lo mein, reduce the heat to medium, and stir-fry 2 to 3 minutes until heated through and well combined. Remove from the heat, add the scallion and carrots, if desired, and toss to combine. *Serves 4 as part of a multicourse meal.*

Scallion and Ginger Lo Mein

Although called lo mein, this classic Hong Kong–style dish typically uses won ton noodles as thin as vermicelli. If fresh won ton noodles are unavailable, Italian dried angel hair pasta can be substituted. Boiling water is poured over the cooked noodles to reheat them before they are combined with the sauce ingredients.

1 teaspoon oyster sauce
1 teaspoon sesame oil
1 teaspoon soy sauce
1½ teaspoons salt
¼ teaspoon ground white pepper
12 ounces fresh won ton noodles
1½ quarts boiling water
2 tablespoons vegetable oil
6 scallions, finely shredded
3 tablespoons finely shredded ginger

1. In a shallow serving bowl combine the oyster sauce, sesame oil, soy sauce, ½ teaspoon of the salt, and the pepper.

2. In a large pot bring 3 quarts water to a boil over high heat. When the water comes to a rolling boil, add the remaining 1 teaspoon salt and the noodles.

Return to a rolling boil and boil 15 seconds or according to package directions until al dente. Carefully pour out the hot water and add several changes of cold water, swishing the noodles to remove surface starch. Drain thoroughly in a colander. Pour the 1½ quarts boiling water over the noodles and again drain thoroughly. Transfer to the serving bowl containing the oyster sauce mixture and toss to combine.

3. Heat a 14-inch flat-bottomed wok over high heat until a bead of water vaporizes within 1 to 2 seconds of contact. Swirl in the vegetable oil, add the scallions and ginger, and stir-fry 30 to 40 seconds or until the scallions are just wilted but still bright green. Spoon over the noodles and pour in any remaining oil from the wok. Toss to combine. *Serves 4 as part of a multicourse meal.*

Chicken Lo Mein

Any kind of fresh Chinese-style egg noodle can be used for lo mein. Be careful not to overcook thin chow mein noodles. When tossing the noodles with the chicken and vegetables, I use a pair of chopsticks in one hand and a metal spatula in the other.

1¼ teaspoons salt
One 1-pound package fresh lo mein noodles
1 teaspoon sesame oil
8 ounces skinless, boneless chicken thigh, cut into
    ¼-inch-thick bite-sized slices
½ teaspoon plus 1 tablespoon Shao Hsing rice
    wine or dry sherry
¾ teaspoon cornstarch
½ teaspoon plus 2 tablespoons soy sauce
¼ teaspoon sugar
¼ teaspoon ground white pepper
1 tablespoon oyster sauce
2 tablespoons vegetable oil
2 tablespoons minced garlic
1 stalk celery, thinly sliced
1 cup thinly sliced carrots
1 green bell pepper, cut into ¼-inch-wide strips

1. In a large pot bring 3 quarts water to a boil over high heat. When the water comes to a rolling boil, add 1 teaspoon of the salt and the noodles. Return to a rolling boil and boil about 1 minute or according to package directions until al dente. Carefully pour out the hot water and add several changes of cold water, swishing the noodles to remove surface starch. Drain in a colander. In the unwashed pot combine the sesame oil and drained noodles and toss to combine. Set aside.

2. Put the chicken in a shallow bowl and add the ½ teaspoon rice wine, the cornstarch, the ½ teaspoon soy sauce, the sugar, white pepper, and remaining ¼ teaspoon salt. In a small bowl combine the oyster sauce and the remaining 1 tablespoon rice wine and 2 tablespoons soy sauce.

3. Heat a 14-inch flat-bottomed wok over high heat until a bead of water vaporizes within 1 to 2 seconds of contact. Swirl in 1 tablespoon of the vegetable oil, add the garlic, and stir-fry 10 seconds. Carefully add the chicken mixture, spreading it evenly in the wok. Cook undisturbed 30 seconds, letting the chicken begin to brown. Then, using a metal spatula, stir-fry 1 minute or until the chicken is lightly browned. Transfer to a plate. Swirl the remaining 1 tablespoon vegetable oil into the wok, add the celery, carrots, and bell pepper, and stir-fry 1 minute. Add the chicken. Stir the oyster sauce mixture, swirl it into the wok, add the drained noodles, and stir-fry 1 to 2 minutes or until the chicken is cooked through and the noodles are heated. *Serves 4 as part of a multicourse meal.*

Chinese workers like this nineteenth-century street vendor with a portable wok brought their cooking traditions to America. Today that heritage survives in Western kitchens. Opposite: a traditional stir-fry of oyster lo mein (page 124) at the Hong Hop Noodle Company, New York City.

The Wok in America: the 1800s

Finding information on the wok in America in the nineteenth century is challenging, for there is little documentation on the everyday habits of the Chinese. Many researchers speculate that the wok was brought by Chinese immigrants who came to work in the gold mines or on the railroad. As early as the 1850s, records from the U.S. Customs House in San Francisco show that food items and culinary implements such as iron and copper pots, bamboo ware, and chopsticks were imported from Hong Kong.

Unable to speak English, immigrants preferred to eat their own food and to cook in the manner they were accustomed to. Lisa See, curator of the Smithsonian exhibit "On Gold Mountain," wrote me, "There are many photographs of Chinese immigrants on boat decks. They brought all of their own food with them and their cooking utensils as well. (After all, they wouldn't have wanted to eat the standard fare on the ship even if they had been allowed in the dining room, which, as steerage passengers, they wouldn't have been. However, if a Chinese traveled first or second class, then he would have had access to the dining room. Still, Chinese food was not prepared for those passengers.)"

"Woks were used on the Hawaiian plantations," says Maxine Chan, a food historian with a specialty in Chinese American foodways. "The Chinese arrived in Hawaii in the late 1880s. Typically, the Chinese housing provided by the plantation owner would have a separate house/structure for the kitchen. Many times the wok was placed outside due to smoke. The wok was positioned on top of brick or some material that would not burn. It was not uncommon to have two or more."

Professor Priscilla Wegars, who has conducted archaeological digs in Chinese mining camps in Granite, Oregon, writes, "The Chinese usually used cast-iron woks for cooking, and fragments of four different ones were found at the site. These could be differentiated because of their different diameters . . . ." According to Professor Wegars, most of the artifacts found in the "Ah Hing" camp could be dated from the 1860s to the early 1900s. It is possible these woks were made by Chinese blacksmiths in America.

Maxine Chan recalls seeing European-style cookware next to Chinese cookware at the mining sites she visited. According to Chan, it reflects the resourceful nature of the Chinese to adapt to "whatever was at hand to do their cooking." It is compelling to know that the shift to Western-style cookware began so early in the Chinese American story.

The Wok as a **Musical Instrument**

鑊
鏟
交
響
樂

Since the art of cooking appeals to all the senses, it's perhaps not so surprising that I am seduced by the musicality of stir-frying in a wok—a sound uniquely its own. Years ago when I got my first answering machine I often changed my message, in search of something clever or funny. I decided one day that an intriguing recording to tease the senses would be the sound of stir-frying in a wok. I had the illusion that the message could convey the vitality I associate with stir-frying.

Looking back, it was a comical scene. There I was busily prepping the ingredients, firing up the wok, timing the pressing of the record button, stir-frying, reciting my message, a little more stir-frying, hitting the stop button, and then quickly replaying the machine to evaluate the recording. Once I missed the cue to begin stir-frying. Another time I was so anxious I jumbled my voice message. Sadly each recording was too distant and flat. The answering machine couldn't pick up the musical rhythms I hear when stir-frying in a wok.

A stir-fry has a distinct musical progression. I've heard it walking down streets in Chinatown and in Asia, especially in alleyways where restaurant doors are flung open to cool the kitchen. If I listen carefully, I can often hear not one but several cooks stir-frying, creating an orchestra of woks that roar. Jean Yueh remembers that when she lived in Hong Kong, she relished hearing "the cacophony of clamoring spatulas and sizzling oil coming from cooks stir-frying in high-rise apartment buildings at dinnertime."

I find this sound so distinct that you could blindfold me and put me in a room with someone stir-frying with a wok and I would know immediately what they were doing. I often hear before I even sample a dish whether it will taste right or not.

Of course, my ears cannot discern the quantity of seasonings or the freshness of the food, but if there is barely a crackle when the ingredients are added and the spatula has an off-key sluggish sound, I can predict the stir-fry won't taste right.

The wok evokes a variety of instrumental sounds. If the cook has formidable virtuosity, the culinary rhythms have elements of jazz improvisation with a fierce percussion—highly textured and a little wild. The first steady, sizzling beats occur when the garlic or ginger strikes the hot oil. Then the loud, thunderous bang as a big handful of vegetables is added resembles cymbals crashing. The metal spatula strokes the carbon-steel sides like a snare drum, its sharp, fast rhythms marking time against the beat of the vegetables crackling in oil. A more muted splashing bang mimics the cymbals as the sauce ingredients are swirled in. Sometimes there's the clang of the lid being popped on for a beat or two. The three- to four-minute musical riff ends with a hushed silence once the wok is pulled off the heat.

"In the old days, some chefs would finish a stir-fry with a *pao* motion, tossing the ingredients in the air, then catching the food with a large ladle," says renowned Chinese food authority Cecilia Chiang. "After quickly transferring the food to a serving plate, the chef would knock several times on the wok's metal handle with the ladle. This signaled the waiter that the dish was ready to be served. It was quite a performance," says Chiang

When done properly, a stir-fry does feel like a performance, and I find that the little routines exact simple pleasures. Practicing these "wok riffs" not only produces the music but indulges the senses. I savor with long, deep breaths the moment the ginger is added. My appetite grows with the aroma of the other ingredients searing. Watching the plain raw ingredients turn golden and glisten,

Attentive to the sound, sight, and smell of his stir-fry, my parents' dear friend Ray Lee orchestrates the heat and timing for a perfect stir-fry of choy sum.

it's hard not to sneak a taste. And all the while as I experience this transformation I'm conducting it with my spatula, drawing the ingredients up with each stroke into the wok's well, feeling with all my senses everything change before my eyes.

I truly believe that those who stir-fry in a non-stick wok miss out on half the experience. I think it's like baking cookies in a toy oven. There is a difference in taste when food isn't cooked in an authentic manner. But further, what kind of sound can a plastic spatula stroking a nonstick surface make? What can stir-frying be without all the lively clamor?

My parents proved to me years ago that stir-frying in a skillet also works, especially on an electric range. Yet, while a skillet can certainly do the job, I think the spirit of cooking in a wok is a culinary pleasure that transports the cook beyond the confines of the modern kitchen to another way of life. Stir-frying in a wok honors a centuries-old culinary ritual. For that reason, I can never be persuaded to eat Chinese food with fork and knife.

Mastering the art and craft of cooking in a wok holds a special reward. The wok is an instrument. It's impossible to simply take it up and play it like a true artist on the first try. With effort and practice the sound grows richer and more beautiful—a pleasure one can savor with every bite.

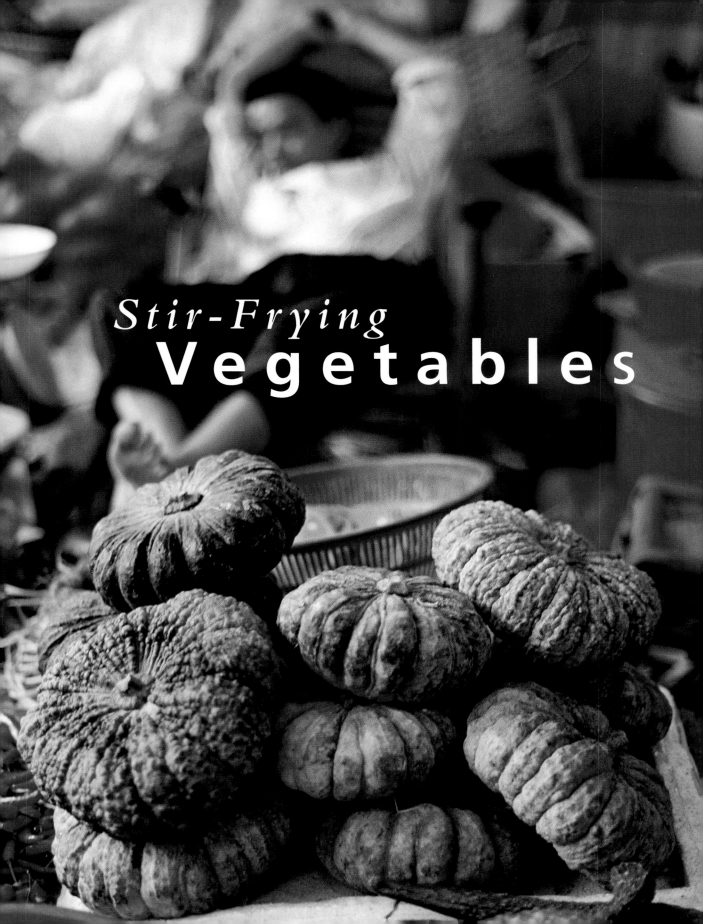

Stir-Frying
Vegetables

Stir-Frying Vegetables

Preceding pages:
Chinese markets are filled with both the familiar and the not-so-familiar. A motorcycle is used as a stand for selling watermelons, and a vendor slumbers behind a stack of kabocha squash.

Left: Liang Nian Xiu chops pork belly. Opposite: She stir-fries her Snow Peas, Tomatoes, and Chilies.

Liang Nian Xiu's Snow Peas, Tomatoes, and Chilies

My friend Liang Nian Xiu likes to stir-fry snow peas with minced ginger, garlic, chilies, and a little chopped pork belly. It's a flavorful fiery mix that's also visually appealing. She calls for about an ounce of pork belly, which adds remarkable richness. If I don't have it on hand, I use a little salt pork or a slice of bacon and reduce the salt.

1 tablespoon vegetable oil
2 tablespoons chopped boneless pork belly
    (about 1 ounce)
2 tablespoons minced ginger
1 tablespoon minced garlic
1 fresh Thai chili, minced
¾ teaspoon salt
1 pound snow peas, strings removed
1 ripe medium tomato, roughly chopped
¼ teaspoon sugar

Heat a 14-inch flat-bottomed wok over high heat until a bead of water vaporizes within 1 to 2 seconds of contact. Swirl in the oil, add the pork, ginger, garlic, chili, and ½ teaspoon of the salt, and stir-fry 1 minute. Add the snow peas and stir-fry 1 minute. Add the chopped tomato, sugar, and the remaining ¼ teaspoon salt, and stir-fry 1 to 2 minutes or until the vegetables are just tender. *Serves 4 as part of a multicourse meal.*

Liang Nian Xiu's Moon Hill Corn and Beans

Liang Nian Xiu and I shopped for these vegetables in her local market in Moon Hill village in Guangxi province. Liang showed me a variation, adding a tablespoon or two of chopped pork with cilantro and Chinese chives, but I prefer the stir-fry without meat. In the summertime, with corn, beans, and tomatoes at their peak of sweetness, this delicious combination needs no additional ingredients.

1 tablespoon vegetable oil
1 tablespoon minced garlic
1 tablespoon minced ginger
1 tablespoon minced mild fresh chilies
3 medium ears corn, kernels scraped off
    (about 2½ cups)
⅓ cup roughly chopped green beans
¾ teaspoon salt
1 ripe medium tomato, cut into thin wedges
¼ teaspoon sugar

Heat a 14-inch flat-bottomed wok over high heat until a bead of water vaporizes within 1 to 2 seconds of contact. Swirl in the oil and add the garlic, ginger, and chilies and stir-fry 30 seconds. Add the corn, green beans, and salt and stir-fry 1 minute. Add the tomato wedges and stir-fry 1 minute. Add 2 tablespoons cold water and the sugar and stir-fry 1 to 2 minutes more or until the tomatoes are just wilted and the vegetables are tender. *Serves 4 as part of a multicourse meal.*

Above: Mary Chau's Shanghai-Style Snow Cabbage and Edamame. Right: Mary uses fresh edamame when they are available.

Mary Chau's Shanghai-Style Snow Cabbage and Edamame

I had never cooked with edamame (soybeans) until Mary Chau taught me this recipe, a favorite of her family's in Shanghai. Fresh edamame are preferred, but frozen are more readily available (see page 221). Mary sometimes omits the pork and five-spice tofu. She uses very little salt because preserved snow cabbage (see page 226) contains salt.

4 ounces lean pork butt
3 teaspoons Shao Hsing rice wine or dry sherry
1 teaspoon cornstarch
2½ teaspoons soy sauce
¼ teaspoon salt
3 tablespoons vegetable oil
One 1-pound package frozen shelled
    edamame, defrosted
¼ cup thinly sliced shallots
½ cup diced green bell pepper
2 pieces five-spice tofu (about 8 ounces), cut into
    ¼-inch dice
One 6.5-ounce can preserved snow cabbage,
    well drained

1. Cut the pork into 2-inch-wide strips, then cut into ¼-inch-thick slices. Stack the slices and cut into 2-inch-long matchsticks. Put the pork in a shallow bowl and add 1 teaspoon of the rice wine, the cornstarch, ½ teaspoon of the soy sauce, and the salt.

2. Heat a 14-inch flat-bottomed wok over high heat until a bead of water vaporizes within 1 to 2 seconds of contact. Swirl in 2 tablespoons of the oil, add the edamame, and stir-fry 3 minutes or until the beans are just beginning to brown. Transfer to a plate. Rinse the wok and dry it thoroughly.

3. Swirl the remaining 1 tablespoon oil into the wok over high heat, add the shallots, and stir-fry 10 seconds. Add the pork. Cook undisturbed 15 seconds. Then, using a metal spatula, stir-fry 1 minute or until the pork is no longer pink. Add the remaining 2 teaspoons rice wine, cover, and cook over medium heat 30 seconds. Add the

pepper, tofu, and edamame to the wok, increase the heat to high, and stir-fry 1 minute. Add the cabbage and stir-fry 1 minute. Add the remaining 2 teaspoons soy sauce. Cover, reduce the heat to medium, and cook 2 minutes or until the vegetables are just tender, stirring occasionally. *Serves 4 as part of a multicourse meal.*

Stir-Fried Sugar Snap Peas with Water Chestnuts

In classic Chinese cooking, soy sauce is seldom added to a dish with water chestnuts as it mars their beautiful ivory color. The seasonings here are deliberately light to accentuate the sugar snap peas and fresh water chestnuts. If the sugar snaps are very young, there is no need to remove the strings.

4 fresh water chestnuts
1 tablespoon Shao Hsing rice wine or dry sherry
1 teaspoon salt
¾ teaspoon sugar
¼ teaspoon ground white pepper
1 tablespoon vegetable oil
3 slices ginger
3 cups sugar snap peas, strings removed (about
    8 ounces)
1 teaspoon sesame oil

1. Peel the water chestnuts with a paring knife and then thinly slice to make about ½ cup. In a small bowl combine the rice wine, salt, sugar, and pepper with 1 tablespoon cold water.

2. Heat a 14-inch flat-bottomed wok over high heat until a bead of water vaporizes within 1 to 2 seconds of contact. Swirl in the vegetable oil, add the ginger, and stir-fry 5 seconds or until fragrant. Add the sugar snaps and water chestnuts and stir-fry 1 minute. Stir the rice wine mixture, swirl it into the wok, and stir-fry 30 seconds to 1 minute or until the vegetables are just tender. Remove from the heat and stir in the sesame oil. *Serves 4 as part of a multicourse meal.*

Chinese markets offer a seemingly endless variety of greens for stir-frying. Freshly picked amaranth with the root still attached is brought to market each morning. Opposite: Southern China has an ideal climate for growing tropical fruits and vegetables.

Auntie Yi's Stir-Fried Garlic Spinach

On a home stove it's impossible to stir-fry more than 10 ounces of spinach at one time. More than that won't fit in the wok and, most important, the temperature of the wok will drop too drastically. Since 10 ounces makes only about 2 cups, if more is needed, my Auntie Yi of Foshan recommends making two separate batches of the recipe.

2 tablespoons vegetable oil
1 tablespoon minced garlic
1 bunch spinach (about 10 ounces)
½ teaspoon salt
½ teaspoon sugar
1 tablespoon Shao Hsing rice wine or dry sherry

Heat a 14-inch flat-bottomed wok over high heat until a bead of water vaporizes within 1 to 2 seconds of contact. Swirl in the oil, add the garlic, and stir-fry 10 seconds. Add all the spinach and stir-fry 10 seconds. Add the salt, sugar, and rice wine and stir-fry 1 to 2 minutes or until the spinach is just tender but still bright green. ***Serves 4 as part of a multicourse meal.***

Stir-Fried Bok Choy

I prefer bok choy that is no more than 8 inches in length. The larger bunches tend to be tough and old. Select bok choy that has unblemished leaves and closed buds. Yellow flowers are an indication that the bok choy is past its prime.

1 pound bok choy
¼ cup Homemade Chicken Broth (page 195)
1 tablespoon Shao Hsing rice wine or dry sherry
¾ teaspoon salt
½ teaspoon sugar
1 tablespoon vegetable oil
3 slices ginger
1 teaspoon sesame oil

1. Separate the bok choy into stalks. Trim ¼ inch from the bottom of each stalk. Cut the stalks and leaves into 2-inch-long pieces. In a small bowl combine the broth, rice wine, salt, and sugar.

2. Heat a 14-inch flat-bottomed wok over high heat until a bead of water vaporizes within 1 to 2 seconds of contact. Swirl in the vegetable oil, add the ginger, and stir-fry 10 seconds. Add the bok choy and stir-fry 1 to 2 minutes or until the leaves are just limp and the bok choy is bright green. Stir the broth mixture and swirl it into the wok. Stir-fry 1 to 2 minutes or until the bok choy is just cooked. Drizzle with the sesame oil. ***Serves 4 as part of a multicourse meal.***

Stir-Fried Watercress

In New York's Chinatown stir-fried watercress is often served at dim sum restaurants. It is a welcome treat to balance the rich array of fried dumplings. Rather than aromatics like garlic and ginger, watercress is more likely to be stir-fried with shallots. If the watercress is not dry to the touch, the excess water will turn the stir-fry into a braise.

1 tablespoon Shao Hsing rice wine or dry wine
1 tablespoon soy sauce
½ teaspoon salt
½ teaspoon sugar
2 tablespoons vegetable oil
2 medium shallots, thinly sliced (about ⅓ cup)
2 bunches watercress (about 7 ounces)

1. In a small bowl combine the rice wine, soy sauce, salt, and sugar.

2. Heat a 14-inch flat-bottomed wok over high heat until a bead of water vaporizes within 1 to 2 seconds of contact. Swirl in the oil, add the shallots, and stir-fry 30 seconds. Add the watercress and stir-fry 1 minute or until it just begins to wilt. Stir the rice wine mixture, swirl it into the wok, and stir-fry 1 to 2 minutes or until the watercress is just tender but still bright green. ***Serves 4 as part of a multicourse meal.***

Henry Hugh's Lotus Root with Sugar Snaps

Chef Henry Hugh's stir-fry has a variety of crisp textures ranging from the lotus root (see page 222) to the cloud ears, carrots, celery, and sugar snaps. The seasonings accentuate the natural sweetness of each vegetable. Slicing the lotus root in half lengthwise can be difficult. Chef Hugh rocks the cleaver or chef's knife gently back and forth to cut the root.

¼ cup cloud ears
1 large section lotus root (about 6 ounces)
2 tablespoons Homemade Chicken Broth
    (page 195)
2 teaspoons Shao Hsing rice wine or dry sherry
2 teaspoons oyster sauce
1 teaspoon salt
⅛ teaspoon ground white pepper
1 cup sugar snap peas, strings removed (about
    3 ounces)
½ cup thinly sliced carrots
1 cup thinly sliced celery
1 tablespoon canola oil
1 tablespoon minced garlic
4 scallions, halved lengthwise and cut into
    2-inch pieces

1. Put the cloud ears in a medium bowl with enough cold water to cover. Let stand 30 minutes or until softened. Drain thoroughly. Remove the hard spots from the cloud ears and cut into bite-sized pieces. Using a vegetable peeler, peel the lotus root, removing the rootlike strands, and rinse under cold water. Slice the lotus root lengthwise in half. Cut each half into ¼-inch-thick half moons. Rinse again in case there is any mud, and set aside to drain well. In a small bowl combine the broth, rice wine, oyster sauce, ½ teaspoon of the salt, and the pepper. Set aside.

2. In a large saucepan bring 1 quart water to a boil over high heat. Add the remaining ½ teaspoon salt and the lotus root. Cook 30 seconds, then add the sugar snaps. Cook 30 seconds, then add the carrots. Cook 30 seconds, then add the celery. Immediately drain all the vegetables in a colander. Run under cold water. Drain thoroughly.

3. Heat a 14-inch flat-bottomed wok over high heat until a bead of water vaporizes within 1 to 2 seconds of contact. Swirl in the oil, add the garlic and scallions, and stir-fry 5 seconds. Add the drained vegetables and cloud ears and stir-fry 1 minute. Stir the rice wine mixture, swirl it into the wok, and stir-fry 1 minute. *Serves 4 as part of a multicourse meal.*

Stir-Fried Garlic Lettuce

Lettuce is an auspicious vegetable to stir-fry for the Lunar New Year. The word for lettuce in Cantonese, saang choy, sounds like "growing fortune." Iceberg is most commonly used for stir-fries, but I prefer heart of Romaine. It has crunch and sweetness, while still being tender. The garlic cloves are edible and delicious, too.

1 tablespoon Shao Hsing rice wine or dry sherry
1 tablespoon soy sauce
¾ teaspoon sugar
½ teaspoon salt
2 tablespoons vegetable oil
5 medium garlic cloves, smashed
1 pound hearts of Romaine, cut crosswise into
    1-inch-wide pieces
1 teaspoon sesame oil

1. In a small bowl, combine the rice wine, soy sauce, sugar, and salt.

2. Heat a 14-inch flat-bottomed wok over high heat until a bead of water vaporizes within 1 to 2 seconds of contact. Swirl in the vegetable oil, add the garlic, and stir-fry 5 seconds. Add the lettuce and stir-fry 1 to 2 minutes or until the lettuce is just limp. Stir the sauce, swirl it into the wok, and stir-fry 30 seconds to 1 minute or until the lettuce is just tender and still bright green. Remove from the heat and drizzle on the sesame oil. *Serves 4 as part of a multicourse meal.*

Susan Lin's Summer Long Beans with Eggs

Susan Lin, a respected herbalist at Lin Sister Herb Shop in New York's Chinatown, taught me this recipe. The Chinese regard long beans as a neutral vegetable, neither too yin nor too yang. Lin says this is an excellent dish to cook in the summer when long beans are in season; it is considered ching, *or purifying for the body. Long beans are sold in Chinese produce stores and can be either dark green or pale green.*

5 large eggs
½ teaspoon salt
2 tablespoons olive oil
8 ounces Chinese long beans, cut into
    ½-inch pieces

1. In a medium bowl beat the eggs with ¼ teaspoon of the salt.

2. Heat a 14-inch flat-bottomed wok over high heat until a bead of water vaporizes within 1 to 2 seconds of contact. Swirl in the oil, add the long beans and the remaining ¼ teaspoon salt, and stir-fry 1 minute. Swirl in the eggs and stir-fry, constantly turning the mixture with a metal spatula, allowing the uncooked egg to run to the bottom of the wok, until the eggs are just set but not dry, 1 to 2 minutes. *Serves 4 as part of a multicourse meal.*

After years of cooking with a traditional wok, Susan Lin switched to a five-layer wok, but it took a lot of adjustment. The five-layer wok takes much longer to heat than a carbon-steel or cast-iron wok.

Lee Wan Ching's Chinese Broccoli with Ginger Sauce

Chef Lee Wan Ching of Yee Hen restaurant on Lantau Island, Hong Kong, taught me this recipe. Traditionally ginger is always cooked with broccoli— its warmth balances the coolness of yin vegetables such as broccoli. Just a small amount of ginger juice intensifies the flavor of the vegetables. To make ginger juice, grate a small amount of ginger and then squeeze it with your fingers to extract the juice.

6 medium stalks Chinese broccoli (about
    12 ounces)
¼ cup Homemade Chicken Broth (page 195)
1½ teaspoons Shao Hsing rice wine or dry sherry
1 teaspoon ginger juice
½ teaspoon cornstarch
¼ teaspoon salt
⅛ teaspoon sugar
1 tablespoon vegetable oil
3 slices ginger

1. Cut the broccoli stalks in half lengthwise if more than ½ inch in diameter. Cut the stalks and leaves into 2-inch-long pieces, keeping the stalk ends separate from the leaves. In a small bowl combine the broth, rice wine, ginger juice, cornstarch, salt, and sugar.

2. Heat a 14-inch flat-bottomed wok over high heat until a bead of water vaporizes within 1 to 2 seconds of contact. Swirl in the oil, add the ginger, and stir-fry 10 seconds or until the ginger is fragrant. Add only the broccoli stalks and stir-fry 1 to 1½ minutes until the stalks are bright green. Add the leaves and stir-fry 1 minute until the leaves are just limp. Stir the broth mixture and swirl it into the wok. Stir-fry 1 minute or until the sauce has thickened slightly and lightly coats the vegetables. *Serves 4 as part of a multicourse meal.*

Lee Wan Ching's Chinese Broccoli with Ginger Sauce

Susanna Foo's Tofu, Eggplant, Mushrooms, and Sun-Dried Tomatoes

This is one of my favorite dishes at Susanna Foo restaurant in Philadelphia. Chef Foo says the key to making this dish is to cook the eggplant until soft. The tofu and mushrooms must sear in the hot flavored garlic oil. It is critical not to add the sauce until these three ingredients are cooked. Foo likes eggplant and mushrooms cooked with olive or corn oil. The sun-dried tomatoes are dried, not the oil-soaked variety.

2 squares firm tofu (about 7 ounces), rinsed
4 sun-dried tomato halves
2 tablespoons soy sauce
1 tablespoon sake or vodka
1 teaspoon Chinkiang or balsamic vinegar
1 teaspoon sugar
3 tablespoons olive oil or corn oil
3 medium garlic cloves, thinly sliced
2 small jalapeño peppers, thinly sliced
1 small Chinese eggplant, halved lengthwise and
    cut into ¼-inch-thick slices
½ cup small button mushrooms, halved
¼ cup julienned red bell pepper
1 small zucchini, halved lengthwise and cut into
    ¼-inch-thick slices
½ cup sugar snap peas, strings removed and cut
    diagonally in half
Purple basil and baby basil sprigs, optional

1. Put the tofu squares on several sheets of paper towels and set aside. In a small bowl soak the sun-dried tomatoes in ¼ cup warm water to cover until softened, about 10 minutes. Pour out the soaking water, and cut each tomato half into 3 pieces. In a small bowl combine the soy sauce, sake, vinegar, and sugar. Set aside. Cut each tofu square in half. Cut each half into 4 pieces, to make a total of 16 pieces.

2. Heat a 14-inch flat-bottomed wok over medium-high heat until a bead of water vaporizes within 1 to 2 seconds of contact. Swirl in the oil, add the garlic and jalapeño peppers, and stir-fry about 1 minute until the garlic starts to brown. Add the eggplant and sun-dried tomatoes, reduce the heat to

medium, and cook until the eggplant is soft, about 3 minutes. Add the tofu, mushrooms, and bell pepper, and stir-fry until the tofu begins to brown, about 3 minutes. (The wok will be dry when the tofu and vegetables are added, and there may be a little sticking.) Stir the sauce, swirl it into the wok, and stir-fry until the tofu, mushrooms, and eggplant are coated with sauce. Increase the heat to high, add the zucchini and sugar snaps, and stir-fry until the vegetables are tender but still bright green, 1 to 2 minutes. Garnish with the basil sprigs if desired. *Serves 4 as part of a multicourse meal.*

Florence Lin's Slow Stir-Fried Red Peppers

When Florence Lin slowly stir-fries red bell peppers, she starts them over high heat for 2 minutes and then adjusts the temperature down to medium and medium-high. On my stove that heat setting was too high, and the peppers started to char. Experiment with the heat levels until you find the highest heat that won't char the peppers. It's also critical to continually turn the peppers with a spatula. Lin says this technique is also excellent with fresh shiitake mushrooms, and with green bell peppers. The peppers should be as thick and meaty as possible. She advises against using too much oil in the beginning, because it prevents the peppers from browning.

2 to 3 tablespoons canola oil or corn oil
2 large red bell peppers, cut into 1-inch squares
¼ teaspoon sugar
¼ teaspoon salt

Heat a 14-inch flat-bottomed wok over high heat until a bead of water vaporizes within 1 to 2 seconds of contact. Swirl in 1 tablespoon of the oil, add the peppers, and stir-fry 1 minute, continually moving them with a spatula. Continue to stir-fry 8 to 10 minutes, adjusting the heat between medium and low as the peppers begin to brown. Add a little more oil if necessary. The peppers are almost ready when their skins begin to wrinkle. Increase the heat to medium-high and stir-fry 1 minute more. Sprinkle on the sugar and salt. *Serves 4 as part of a multicourse meal.*

Florence Lin's Slow Stir-Fried Red Peppers

Spicy Garlic Eggplant

Typically when eggplant is stir-fried it requires a cup or more of oil. Steaming the eggplant reduces the amount of oil and yet the eggplant retains a rich flavor. Serve hot, at room temperature, or even chilled.

4 medium Asian eggplants (about 1¼ pounds)
¼ cup soy sauce
2 tablespoons Chinkiang or balsamic vinegar
2 tablespoons Shao Hsing rice wine or dry sherry
1 tablespoon sugar
1 teaspoon salt
1 teaspoon red pepper flakes
3 tablespoons vegetable oil
¼ cup minced garlic
¼ cup minced ginger
1 teaspoon sesame oil
¼ cup finely minced scallions

1. Cut the eggplants into 2-inch sections, then halve each section lengthwise. Cut each half lengthwise into thirds to make sticks. In a small bowl combine the soy sauce, vinegar, rice wine, sugar, salt, and pepper flakes. Set aside.

2. Put the eggplant in a shallow, heatproof bowl. Place a 1-inch-high steamer rack in a 14-inch flat-bottomed wok. Add water to a depth of ¾ inch and bring to a boil over high heat. Carefully put the bowl on the rack, cover, and steam on high heat 5 to 8 minutes or until the eggplant is tender when pierced with a knife. Be sure to check the water level from time to time and replenish, if necessary, with boiling water. Carefully remove the bowl from the wok. Pour out the water from the wok and dry the pan.

3. Heat the wok over high heat until a bead of water vaporizes within 1 to 2 seconds of contact. Swirl in the vegetable oil, add the garlic and ginger, and stir-fry 10 seconds. Add the eggplant and stir-fry 20 seconds. Stir the sauce, swirl it into the wok, and stir-fry until the eggplant is heated through, about 1 minute. Drizzle on the sesame oil and scallions. ***Serves 4 as part of a multicourse meal.***

David Camacho's Stir-Fried Shiitake Mushrooms

This easy recipe is from my friend David Camacho of Hong Kong. After the broth mixture is added and the wok is covered, David describes the technique of shaking the wok as similar to shaking a pot of popcorn over high heat. This recipe is so delicious I often make two separate batches, since a pound of mushrooms cooks down to about 2 cups.

1 pound fresh shiitake or button mushrooms
¼ cup Homemade Chicken Broth (page 195)
¼ cup Shao Hsing rice wine or dry sherry
1 teaspoon soy sauce
3 tablespoons vegetable oil
2 tablespoons minced ginger
1 tablespoon sesame oil
½ teaspoon salt

1. Trim the mushroom stems. Cut the mushrooms in half. Quarter any large mushrooms. In a small bowl combine the broth, rice wine, and soy sauce.

2. Heat a 14-inch flat-bottomed wok over high heat until a bead of water vaporizes within 1 to 2 seconds of contact. Swirl in the vegetable oil, add the ginger, and stir-fry 10 seconds. Add the mushrooms and stir-fry 30 seconds to 1 minute. Swirl in the broth mixture, cover, and shake the wok over high heat 4 to 5 minutes or until the liquid is absorbed and the mushrooms are firm but tender. Remove from the heat and stir in the sesame oil and salt. ***Serves 4 as part of a multicourse meal.***

In Chinese markets shiitake mushrooms are weighed using a traditional scale with weights.

Cecilia Chiang's Asparagus with Gingko Nuts and Wolfberries

When Cecilia Chiang stir-fries asparagus, she likes adding classic Chinese ingredients revered not only for their taste but for their health attributes. Gingko nuts (see page 222) are said to strengthen the lungs and wolfberries (see page 228) are good for the eyes. Shelled, fresh gingko nuts are now available in some Asian markets in Cryovac packages. Chiang likes to soak them in boiling water to freshen them before stir-frying. (photo page 149)

1 tablespoon pitted wolfberries
One 3.5-ounce package shelled fresh gingko nuts
2 tablespoons peanut oil
¾ teaspoon salt
1 pound asparagus, peeled and cut into
    2-inch pieces
⅛ teaspoon sugar
¼ teaspoon sesame oil

1. Put the wolfberries in a small bowl and cover with cold water for 5 minutes. Drain and set aside. In a 1-quart saucepan bring 2 cups water to a boil over high heat. Add the gingko nuts and remove from the heat. Let stand 3 minutes. Drain the gingko nuts in a colander, shaking well to remove excess water. Set aside.

2. Heat a 14-inch flat-bottomed wok over high heat until a bead of water vaporizes within 1 to 2 seconds of contact. Swirl in the peanut oil, add ¼ teaspoon of the salt and the asparagus, and stir-fry 30 seconds. Add the remaining ½ teaspoon salt and stir-fry 1 to 2 minutes or until the asparagus is bright green. Add the gingko nuts and stir-fry 15 seconds. Add the drained wolfberries and stir-fry 1 minute. Add the sugar and stir-fry 10 seconds or until the asparagus is just tender. Remove from the heat. Drizzle on the sesame oil. *Serves 4 as part of a multicourse meal.*

Stir-Fried Bean Sprouts and Scallions

Remember to remove excess moisture from the mung bean sprouts to prevent the stir-fry from becoming watery. Either wash the sprouts early in the day and allow them to air-dry in a colander or use a salad spinner. This is also excellent with soybean sprouts, but increase the cooking time by a minute or two.

2 tablespoons vegetable oil
2 tablespoons minced ginger
12 ounces mung bean sprouts (about 6 cups)
1 teaspoon salt
¼ teaspoon sugar
1 teaspoon sesame oil
2 scallions, chopped

Heat a 14-inch flat-bottomed wok over high heat until a bead of water vaporizes within 1 to 2 seconds of contact. Swirl in the vegetable oil, add the ginger, and stir-fry 10 seconds. Add the bean sprouts and stir-fry 1 minute. Add the salt and sugar and stir-fry 30 seconds to 1 minute or until the sprouts are cooked but still crisp. Do not overcook. Stir in the sesame oil and scallions. *Serves 4 as part of a multicourse meal.*

Sweet and Sour Cabbage

Easy to make, this sweet and sour cabbage has a lovely accent of ginger heat. If you desire a more subtle ginger flavor, rather than mince the ginger, add 2 or 3 slices. This is excellent served warm or chilled.

1 tablespoon Shao Hsing rice wine or dry sherry
1 tablespoon soy sauce
2 teaspoons Chinkiang or balsamic vinegar
2 teaspoons sugar
1 teaspoon salt
½ teaspoon cornstarch
2 tablespoons vegetable oil
2 tablespoons minced ginger
1 pound Napa cabbage, cut crosswise into
    ¼-inch-wide shreds
1 cup thinly sliced carrots
2 tablespoons minced scallions

1. In a small bowl combine the rice wine, soy sauce, vinegar, sugar, salt, and cornstarch.

2. Heat a 14-inch flat-bottomed wok over high heat until a bead of water vaporizes within 1 to 2 seconds of contact. Swirl in the oil, add the ginger, and stir-fry 10 seconds. Add the cabbage and carrots and stir-fry 1 to 2 minutes or until the vegetables are just limp. Stir the rice wine mixture, swirl it into the wok, and bring to a boil, stirring constantly, about 30 seconds. Sprinkle with the scallions. *Serves 4 as part of a multicourse meal.*

Auntie Lil's Stir-Fried Lotus Root with Chinese Bacon

Auntie Lil's daughter Cindy recalls that as a child she called this "wagon wheel" stir-fry because the lacy pattern of the lotus root slices (see page 222) reminded her of wagon wheels. There are many varieties of salted turnip (see page 225). For this dish you must ask for teem choy pou. *These words do not appear on the package. The only English you will likely see is "salted turnip." Chinese bacon (see page 220) is available in Chinese butcher shops. (photo page 167)*

3 ounces Chinese bacon
1/3 cup cloud ears
6 pieces salted turnip (about 2 ounces)
1 large section lotus root (about 6 ounces)
2 tablespoons Shao Hsing rice wine or dry sherry
2 teaspoons soy sauce
3/4 teaspoon sugar
1/2 teaspoon salt
1/2 teaspoon cornstarch
2 tablespoons vegetable oil
10 sugar snap peas, strings removed
1 teaspoon minced garlic
1 teaspoon minced ginger
1/2 small onion, thinly sliced
Chopped scallions, optional

1. Put the bacon in a small heatproof dish. Put a 1-inch-high steamer rack in a 14-inch flat-bottomed wok. Add water to a depth of 3/4 inch and bring to a boil over high heat. Carefully put the dish on the rack, cover, and steam over high heat 20 minutes. Be sure to check the water level from time to time and replenish, if necessary, with boiling water. Carefully remove the dish from the steamer, pouring out any juices. When the bacon is cool enough to handle, remove the hard rind. Thinly slice the bacon into scant 1/4-inch-thick slices. Pour out the water from the wok and dry the pan.

2. Put the cloud ears and salted turnip in separate bowls. Add enough cold water to each bowl to cover. Let stand 30 minutes. When softened, pour out the water. Remove the hard spots from the cloud ears and cut into bite-sized pieces. Cut each piece of salted turnip in half crosswise, then thinly cut lengthwise. Set aside.

3. Using a vegetable peeler, peel the lotus root, removing the rootlike strands, and rinse under cold water. Slice the lotus root into 1/4-inch-thick rounds. Rinse again in case there is any mud. Set aside to drain well. In a small bowl combine the rice wine, soy sauce, sugar, and salt. Set aside. In a separate small bowl combine the cornstarch with 3 tablespoons cold water. Set aside.

4. Heat the wok over high heat until a bead of water vaporizes within 1 to 2 seconds of contact. Swirl in 1 tablespoon of the oil, add the cloud ears and lotus root, and stir-fry 1 minute. Add the salted turnip and sugar snaps with 1 tablespoon cold water and stir-fry 1 minute. Transfer to a plate. Swirl the remaining 1 tablespoon oil into the wok over high heat, add the garlic and ginger, and stir-fry 15 seconds. Add the onion slices and bacon and stir-fry 1 minute. Add the vegetables. Stir the rice wine mixture, swirl it into the wok, and stir-fry 1 minute. Stir the cornstarch mixture, swirl it into the wok, and stir-fry 1 minute. Garnish with the scallions, if desired. *Serves 4 as part of a multicourse meal.*

Cecilia Chiang brings her natural elegance even to a simple stir-fry such as her Asparagus with Gingko Nuts and Wolfberries (page 146) by choosing intriguing ingredients and presenting them on an antique Qing dynasty plate.

Cecilia Chiang and The Mandarin

In 1961 legendary restaurateur Cecilia Chiang opened The Mandarin in San Francisco and revolutionized the Chinese restaurant scene. Chiang recalls that when she first came to San Francisco, Westerners knew only simple Americanized Cantonese food. Chiang's high-style gourmet restaurant elevated the perception of Chinese food and at the same time introduced America to the tastes of Beijing-Shandong and Sichuan-Hunan—the foods that she had grown up eating in China.

In her desire to present authentic northern Chinese food, Chiang went to great lengths to equip her kitchens with northern-style woks. "Chinatown in those days had only Cantonese-style woks, a reflection of the fact that 90 percent of the Chinese population was Cantonese," recalls Chiang. "A Cantonese-style wok is shallow and wide, which spreads the heat. I wanted the northern style, concentrating the heat on the bottom. The pan is deeper, perfect for braises and for tossing food when stir-frying. Some chefs don't even use a ladle. When they toss the wok, the food tumbles back like the tide from the ocean," says Chiang. It was difficult to find the smaller northern-style woks but, eventually, Chiang found some in Taiwan and had them sent to San Francisco. But then she faced the problem that all the restaurant stoves were constructed for the big Cantonese-style woks. Bob Yick, whose company specializes in restaurant stove fabrication, adapted the design for Chiang, creating smaller rings of fire and lifting the base.

Chiang's other challenge was that she had never cooked. Like many privileged women in China, she barely knew where the kitchen was in her home. In old China, wealthy homes had their kitchens at the far end of the house. Chiang recalls that in her home in Beijing, she and her eleven brothers and sisters were not permitted into the kitchen. Only her mother went each morning to discuss the day's menus with the family cook. Chiang remembers the spacious room was dark and stuffy, equipped with several old-fashioned stoves made of mud and brick and fueled by coal. There were northern-style woks and steam woks; all were made of cast iron. One wok was used just for cooking rice. In order to serve piping-hot food, the fourteen servants formed a line to pass the dishes quickly from the kitchen to the dining room.

When Chiang emigrated to America, she missed the foods she had grown up eating. "You always long for your own food," says Chiang. "My parents knew how to eat. I have a very good palate and I always remember the flavor of foods I enjoy." With determination she learned her way around the kitchen, eventually training a staff that could duplicate her refined tastes, producing high-quality authentic dishes and, in turn, pioneering a new perception of Chinese cuisine in America.

Tina Yao Lu's Shanghai-Style Crabs and Rice Cakes (page 182)
Opposite: Chef In Chi Cheung holding his Pan-Fried Noodles with Pork Shang Palace (page 164)

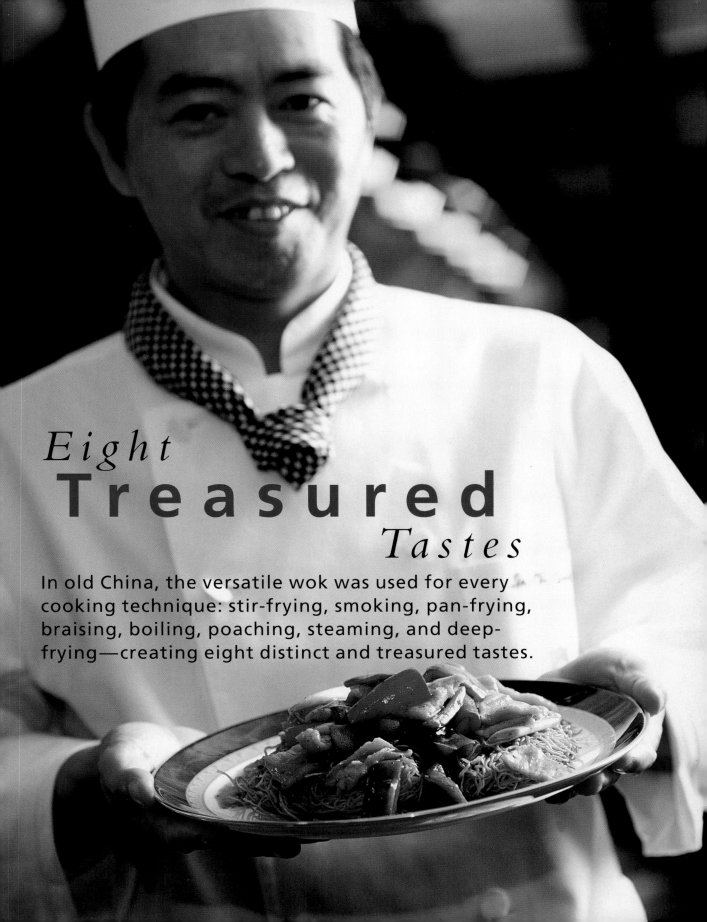

Eight
Treasured
Tastes

In old China, the versatile wok was used for every cooking technique: stir-frying, smoking, pan-frying, braising, boiling, poaching, steaming, and deep-frying—creating eight distinct and treasured tastes.

The *Master Lesson*

循
循
善
誘

For years I regretted the missed opportunity to study with the legendary Chinese culinary expert Florence Lin. When I first moved to Manhattan I had no idea my apartment was a five-minute walk from China Institute, where Lin taught Chinese cooking for over thirty years. Fresh from university, I was creating a life deliberately separate and distinct from that of my Chinese upbringing. Studying Chinese cooking was the farthest thing from my mind. By the time my interest in Chinese cuisine evolved, Florence Lin had retired. From time to time I would hear about the extraordinary cooking classes that even Craig Claiborne attended. All that was left to me was to collect her remarkable cookbooks.

Years later, Lin's close friend and former student Millie Chan learns of my desire to meet the revered teacher and offers to contact her on my behalf. "After all the years Florence spent in the public eye she is now shy of interviews," Chan explains. "Still, she loves to teach. Undoubtedly she would enjoy hearing about your wok project." Miraculously Chan arranges not only an interview but a cooking lesson. When I speak with Lin she suggests cooking three unique dishes for our session: Smoked Chicken and Eggs, Tofu with Cilantro Relish, and Slow Stir-Fried Red Peppers.

Lin meets me at her door and immediately puts me at ease with the request that I call her Florence. She is a petite woman, and her youthful appearance defies any reference to age. Casually dressed in slacks and a simple cotton Chinese top, she has a natural elegance. In fact, Lin has none of the reserve I am accustomed to finding in the Chinese of her generation. She is candid, happy to answer my cooking questions, and clearly proud to be a native of Ningbo, a port city near Shanghai.

"My family had a big kitchen with an enor-

mous wok set on a traditional hearth stove," Lin tells me. "In that part of China it was customary to cook an entire meal in the wok. We put a layer of raw rice and water on the bottom of the wok. Above the rice was a bamboo steaming rack that held four dishes—perhaps a fish, two different vegetables, and a soup. The wok was covered with a domed lid. We fed the stove with rice stalks; this was my favorite chore in the wintertime," Lin recalls. "In China fuel is very expensive and nothing is wasted. To cook the four dishes separately would have required five times the amount of fuel. Instead, the wok cooked everything efficiently in twenty minutes. In this manner we could feed six or seven people twice a day. Fresh food was not always plentiful in Ningbo, so we were forced to eat more salt-preserved foods, preferring to braise or steam. We stir-fried only every other day."

As she talks, Lin brings me into her small, modestly equipped kitchen, without a professional range or custom-made wok stove. I am surprised to see an electric range, the very same model my parents used for thirty years. I realize that I'm about to see the claim that Chinese food is impossible to cook in a wok set on an electric range clearly refuted. The kitchen is simple in all respects except for a forty-year-old wok with a beautiful patina sitting on the front burner. Lin observes me admiring the wok. As if she can read my mind, she says, "With one wok we can do everything."

I examine the heavy carbon-steel wok and am surprised Lin has a Cantonese-style wok. "No, no!" she says emphatically. "This is *not* Cantonese—

Florence Lin understands the subtleties of wok cooking. Here she uses a slow stir-fry to bring out the sweetness of red peppers, preserve their natural crunch, and add a robust roasted flavor (page 143).

循
循
善
誘

this is a home-style wok!" Though the pan resembles the Cantonese-style wok with two ear handles, she points out that it is slightly deeper and rounder and has the small flat bottom necessary for use on an electric range. In China, there are regional differences in the cuisine and cookware. Clearly, it matters greatly to Lin to distinguish the differences regardless of the degree of subtlety.

The day is warm and in accordance with the Chinese principles of harmony, Lin has thoughtfully made chrysanthemum tea, the perfect drink to cool the body. Once my tea is poured I cannot resist posing one of my favorite culinary questions. Does she use the traditional method of seasoning a new wok with Chinese chives? Lin barely suppresses a laugh. "I cook chives for eating. Why waste good ingredients to clean a wok?" She explains that for her the care of a cast-iron skillet is essentially the same as that for a carbon-steel pan. "The wok is indestructible. In China I've

even seen cooks use a brick to clean away sticky residue," says Lin.

Poised and unhurried, Lin assembles the ingredients for the smoked chicken. She explains to me that cooking two whole legs is more practical than cooking an entire chicken for just the two of us. I love her practicality (besides, I much prefer dark meat). The chicken legs must be steamed before smoking. To save time Lin has steamed the chicken, but she has set up her wok to demonstrate the steaming technique with raw chicken. She has also soft-boiled a few eggs ahead of time. An exceptional teacher, she is attentive to every detail.

As she peels the soft-boiled eggs, Lin recounts her experiences as the principal consultant on the famous *Cooking of China* volume in the Time-Life Foods of the World series. I know the book well, having studied its text and photographs countless times. As it turns out, Lin was also the hand model for all of the complicated step-by-step how-to

Above left: Florence Lin lines a carbon-steel wok with foil, pressing it down with her hands so that it lies flat against the bottom of the wok. Above right: She tends the covered wok, using temperature, sound, and smell to know when the smoking is complete. Right: Florence lifts the foil-lined lid to reveal the richly colored chicken and eggs supported above the smoking chips by bamboo chopsticks (page 156).

photographs. No wonder these graceful hands are so familiar.

"See how the yolk is creamy and soft, just barely beginning to firm up," Lin says, showing me a soft-boiled egg she has just cut. "After this is marinated in a soy sauce mixture and smoked it is so delicious." I can nearly taste the sublime perfection.

Next, Lin lines the wok with foil and adds a handful of hickory chips. Other traditional smoking materials that can be used are camphor chips or a combination of tea, rice, and sugar. Then she sets two pairs of "take-out" chopsticks in a tic-tac-toe formation in the center of the wok. She places the steamed chicken and marinated eggs directly on the chopstick rack and says playfully, "Mother and child." How can anyone be so efficient and adorable at the same time?

Once the wok is heated and covered with the lid, smoking requires only a few minutes. Lin watches the kitchen clock, listens for the cooking sounds coming from the wok, and smells the aroma with deep breaths. The smoky fragrance is at first faint but soon builds. Knowing exactly when the smoking is complete, Lin lifts the lid to reveal the magnificent golden-brown chicken and eggs, blanketed by a light cloud of smoke. She smiles, pleased at the results as she slices a little chicken for each of us to taste. The chicken is juicy, perfumed with an irresistible smoky rich flavor. "If it's oversmoked the taste is bitter," she says.

I ask Lin how the smoke from her family's kitchen stove was exhausted in China. The American sensibility of my question clearly amuses her. "In China a kitchen with delicious cooking smells is a good thing. It shows that the household is well-to-do. As a child I loved to be in the kitchen with our cook, observing all the activities. My father also allowed me to accompany him on business trips where I learned to eat the very best foods. In order to become a good cook it's essential to develop a discerning palate," Lin tells me. "My cooking was influenced by my desire to duplicate the foods I'd grown up eating in China."

Florence Lin Recipes

Florence Lin's Slow Stir-Fried Red Peppers (page 143)

Florence Lin's Smoked Chicken and Eggs (page 156)

Florence Lin's Tofu with Cilantro Relish (page 161)

Returning to the tasks at hand, Lin lifts the aluminum foil and its charred contents out of the wok. Then she cuts two large peppers into bite-sized pieces, showing me that they are meaty and not thin. Lin stir-fries the peppers with a little oil in a wok that "isn't too hot," constantly moving them with a metal spatula until they are a brilliant red hue. "The technique of slow stir-frying is a specialty of Ningbo," Lin explains, as we sample the peppers. They have a delicious roasted flavor—their texture slightly crunchy with a center so tender it nearly melts in my mouth.

I realize that in this remarkably short amount of time, Lin has demonstrated the wok's astounding versatility, using it to steam, smoke, pan-fry, and stir-fry. No fancy equipment or cooking gadgets. I cannot help marveling that her lesson plan is so perfectly conceived for me, the "wok student." While her recipe instructions are straightforward, it is her storytelling that helps me most understand Chinese culinary culture. The long-awaited cooking lesson far exceeds my stellar expectations.

Toward the end of our visit I admire an exquisite Chinese watercolor of lichees hung in Lin's living room. Simple and spare, it is both delicate and powerful. "I painted this many years ago," she tells me. I am not surprised to discover she is a gifted artist, too. Recognizing my appreciation, she proudly shows me a book of extraordinary traditional Chinese paintings. Admiring the beauty in the paintings, she points out the economy of strokes. "This is achieved only by an accomplished painter. In old China the best way for a student to learn was to copy a master's work," Lin explains. I understand.

Eight Treasured Tastes   155

煙 Smoking

Florence Lin's Smoked Chicken and Eggs

Florence Lin uses either a handful of hickory chips or this tea mixture to smoke chicken. I prefer the tea mixture because I always have the ingredients on hand. This recipe can be used on a whole 4-pound chicken: marinate the chicken in 3 tablespoons salt for 2 days in the refrigerator, turning once. Increase the chicken steaming time to 45 minutes and the smoking time to 8 to 10 minutes. Lin taught me that after the chicken steams it cannot be smoked immediately because it is too juicy. Let it rest for at least 15 minutes.

2 whole chicken legs (about 1½ pounds)
2½ teaspoons salt
3 large eggs
2 tablespoons soy sauce
½ teaspoon plus 1 tablespoon sugar
2 teaspoons sesame oil
¼ cup loose black tea leaves
¼ cup raw long-grain rice

1. Rinse the chicken under cold water and pat dry with paper towels. Gently rub the chicken with 2 teaspoons of the salt. Cover with plastic wrap and refrigerate for 8 to 24 hours. Rinse and dry with paper towels.

2. About 1 hour before you are ready to cook the chicken, puncture a tiny hole in the wide end of each egg with a pin. In a medium saucepan bring enough water to a boil to cover the eggs by 1 inch. With a slotted spoon, gently lower the eggs one at a time into the boiling water. Return to a boil and then reduce the heat to a simmer. Simmer the eggs 6 minutes uncovered. Pour off the hot water and cover the eggs with cold water. Gently crack the cooked eggs and leave them in the cold water 1 minute, then peel.

3. In a medium bowl combine the soy sauce, the ½ teaspoon sugar, 1 teaspoon of the sesame oil, and the remaining ½ teaspoon salt. Coat the eggs in the mixture and let stand 1 hour or more, turning the eggs from time to time to coat evenly.

4. Put the whole chicken legs in a 9-inch shallow heatproof bowl. Put a 1-inch-high steamer rack in a 14-inch flat-bottomed wok. Add water to a depth of ¾ inch and bring to a boil over high heat. Carefully put the bowl on the rack, cover, and steam on high heat 20 to 25 minutes or until a meat thermometer registers 170°F when inserted at the meatiest point of the thigh but not touching the bone. Be sure to check the water level from time to time and replenish, if necessary, with boiling water.

5. Carefully remove the bowl from the steamer. Pour out the chicken broth and save for other uses, such as soup. Cool the chicken in the refrigerator 10 to 15 minutes. Pour out the water from the wok and dry the pan.

6. Line the inside of the wok and its lid with heavy-duty aluminum foil, allowing a 1-inch overhang for the wok. Be sure the foil is flat against the bottom of the wok—if it is not, the mixture will not smoke. Sprinkle the tea, rice, and remaining 1 tablespoon sugar evenly across the bottom of the wok. Put two pairs of 10-inch-long bamboo chopsticks in a tic-tac-toe formation about 1 inch apart in the center of the wok, or use an oiled rack. Gently pat dry the chicken and eggs with paper towels to remove any excess liquid. Put the chicken and eggs on the rack.

7. Open the window and turn the exhaust fan on high. Heat the wok over high heat and wait until the mixture just begins to show a faint wisp of smoke, 1 to 2 minutes. Put the lid on tightly, folding up the overhang of foil to seal in the smoke, and cook over high heat 2 to 4 minutes or until the chicken and eggs are golden brown. The longer the smoking time, the darker the color, but remember that too much smoking imparts a bitter taste. Turn off the heat.

8. Remove the chicken and eggs to a plate and brush the chicken lightly with the remaining 1 teaspoon sesame oil. Bone the chicken and cut into bite-sized pieces. Wrap up the foil packet and discard. Serve warm or at room temperature, or refrigerate and serve cold. When ready to serve, halve the eggs. Smoked chicken can be made several days in advance; keep well covered in the refrigerator. *Serves 4 as part of a multicourse meal.*

Smoked Striped Bass

This fish is infused with aromatic ginger and scallions when it is steamed; then it is smoked in a blend of black tea, rice, and roasted Sichuan peppercorns.

One 1½-pound striped bass, cleaned and gutted, with head and tail intact
1½ teaspoons salt
4 scallions
5 slices ginger
¼ cup loose black tea leaves
¼ cup raw long-grain rice
1 tablespoon sugar
1 teaspoon roasted and ground Sichuan peppercorns (optional; see page 9)
2 teaspoons soy sauce
2 teaspoons sesame oil

1. Thoroughly rinse the fish in cold water and drain. Gently rub the cavity and outside of the fish with 1 teaspoon of the salt and rinse again. Rub the remaining ½ teaspoon salt in the cavity and on the outside of the fish. Put 1 whole scallion and the ginger slices in the cavity. Put the remaining 3 scallions lengthwise down the center of a heatproof oval platter. Put the fish directly on the scallions.

2. Put a 1-inch-high steamer rack in a 14-inch flat-bottomed wok. Add water to a depth of ¾ inch and bring to a boil over high heat. Carefully put the platter on the rack, cover, and steam 8 to

10 minutes on high heat or until the fish flakes when tested. Check the water level and replenish, if necessary, with boiling water. Test the fish for doneness by poking the thickest part with a fork or chopstick; the fish should flake. If not, steam 1 to 2 minutes more, or just until the fish flakes. Carefully remove the platter.

3. Carefully transfer the fish to a lightly oiled 1-inch-high round cake rack and allow the fish to cool, 15 to 30 minutes. Discard the scallions. Using paper towels, lightly pat the bottom of the fish, through the rack, to remove any excess moisture. If the fish is dripping it will be impossible to smoke. Pour out the water from the wok and dry the pan.

4. Line the inside of the wok and its lid with heavy-duty aluminum foil, allowing a 1-inch overhang for the wok. Be sure the foil is flat against the bottom of the wok—if it is not, the mixture will not smoke. Sprinkle the tea, rice, sugar, and peppercorns over the bottom of the foil. Center the rack in the bottom of the wok.

5. Open the window and turn the exhaust fan on high. Heat the wok over high heat and wait until the mixture just begins to show a faint wisp of smoke, 1 to 2 minutes. Put the lid on tightly, folding up the overhang of foil to seal in the smoke, and cook over high heat 2 to 4 minutes or until the fish is golden. Turn off the heat and allow the fish to sit in the covered wok an additional 2 to 4 minutes. The longer the smoking time, the darker the color; too much smoking imparts a bitter taste.

6. Remove the fish to a plate and drizzle the soy sauce and sesame oil over the fish. Wrap up the foil and discard. Serve warm or at room temperature, or refrigerate and serve cold. The smoked fish can be made several days in advance; keep well covered in the refrigerator. *Serves 4 as part of a multicourse meal.*

Chef Siu Chah Lung opens large meaty oysters for his Ginger and Scallion Oysters Lichee Garden (page 160).
Opposite: Virginia Yee's Dry-Fried Sichuan String Beans (page 160)

Pan-Frying

Ginger and Scallion Oysters Lichee Garden

Chef Siu Chah Lung of Lichee Garden restaurant in San Francisco shucks plump oysters just seconds before he cooks them (see page 159). He pan-fries the oysters in his giant wok before adding the sauce and gives the wok a quick pao *motion. Within a few minutes the oysters are cooked to perfection. Chef Siu prefers dusting the oysters lightly with potato starch, which is difficult to find. Cornstarch is an adequate substitute.*

6 large shucked fresh oysters
1 tablespoon oyster sauce
2 teaspoons soy sauce
¾ teaspoon sugar
¼ teaspoon sesame oil
1¼ teaspoons potato starch or cornstarch
⅛ teaspoon ground white pepper
1 bunch scallions
1 tablespoon vegetable oil
¼ cup thinly sliced ginger, smashed
1 tablespoon Shao Hsing rice wine or dry sherry
1 tablespoon Homemade Chicken Broth
    (page 195)

1. In a medium saucepan bring 2 cups water to a boil over high heat. Add the oysters and cook 30 seconds. Drain and rinse under cold water. Allow the oysters to air-dry on a rack.

2. In a small bowl combine the oyster sauce, soy sauce, sugar, sesame oil, ¼ teaspoon of the potato starch, and the pepper with 3 tablespoons cold water.

3. Lightly pound the white ends of the scallions. Cut the scallions into 2-inch pieces, separating the white from the green part. Lightly dust the remaining 1 teaspoon potato starch over both sides of the oysters.

4. Heat a 14-inch flat-bottomed wok over high heat until a bead of water vaporizes within 1 to 2 seconds of contact. Swirl in the vegetable oil, add the ginger, and stir-fry 1 minute until light golden. Add the white part of the scallions and cook 5 seconds. Carefully add the oysters, spreading them evenly in the wok. Cook undisturbed 1 minute, letting the oysters begin to brown. Then, using a metal spatula, press lightly on the oysters. Turn over and pan-fry 1 minute on the other side.

5. Swirl the rice wine and broth into the wok and cook 15 seconds. Add the green part of the scallions. Stir the oyster sauce mixture, swirl it into the wok, and bring to a boil, stirring constantly, until the oysters are just cooked and the sauce has thickened, 15 seconds. *Serves 4 as part of a multicourse meal.*

Virginia Yee's Dry-Fried Sichuan String Beans

Virginia Yee either pan-fries or deep-fries these beans, but no matter which technique, the beans must be fried until they begin to wrinkle. She stresses the importance of buying young string beans. For the best flavor, let the beans stand several hours before serving. (photo page 158)

¼ cup Homemade Chicken Broth (page 195)
1 tablespoon sugar
1 teaspoon salt
4 tablespoons vegetable oil
1 pound string beans or Chinese long beans
2 tablespoons minced ginger
2 ounces ground pork (about ¼ cup)
1 tablespoon Chinkiang or balsamic vinegar
1 teaspoon sesame oil
1 tablespoon chopped scallion

1. In a bowl combine the broth, sugar, and salt.

2. Heat a 14-inch flat-bottomed wok over high heat until a bead of water vaporizes within 1 to 2 seconds of contact. Swirl in 2 tablespoons of the vegetable oil and add half the beans. Reduce the heat to medium and pan-fry, turning the beans with a metal spatula, until they have brown spots and begin to wrinkle, 3 to 4 minutes. Transfer to a plate with a slotted spoon. Pan-fry the remaining beans with 1 tablespoon of the vegetable oil in the same manner.

3. If the unwashed wok is dry, swirl in the remaining 1 tablespoon vegetable oil over medium heat. Add the ginger and ground pork and stir-fry until the pork is no longer pink, breaking up the pork with a spatula, about 1 minute. Stir the broth mixture and swirl it into the wok. Bring to a boil over high heat and add the beans, tossing to combine, and cook until most of the liquid has evaporated, 1 to 2 minutes. Add the vinegar, sesame oil, and scallion and remove from the heat. Serve at room temperature. *Serves 4 as part of a multicourse meal.*

Florence Lin's Tofu with Cilantro Relish

Florence Lin recommends salting tofu before cooking it to remove excess water and to bring out the flavor and texture. The cilantro relish can be made ahead and stored in the refrigerator for up to a week. This fragrant relish is also delicious served as a condiment.

4 squares firm tofu (about 14 ounces), rinsed
1¼ teaspoons salt
⅓ cup finely chopped cilantro
Pinch plus ½ teaspoon sugar
1½ teaspoons plus 2 tablespoons canola oil
1 tablespoon minced ginger
1 tablespoon soy sauce
2 tablespoons Homemade Chicken Broth
    (page 195)

1. Cut each square of tofu into 3 equal strips. Put the strips on a rack set over a plate. Sprinkle with 1 teaspoon of the salt and let stand 30 minutes. Put the tofu on a cutting board lined with paper towels and pat dry.

2. In a small bowl combine the cilantro, pinch of sugar, the 1½ teaspoons oil, and the remaining ¼ teaspoon salt. Set aside.

3. Heat a 14-inch flat-bottomed wok over high heat until a bead of water vaporizes within 1 to 2 seconds of contact. Swirl in 1 tablespoon of the oil and half the tofu, and reduce the heat to medium. Pan-fry the tofu

about 1 minute per side until light golden. Transfer to a plate. Repeat with the remaining 1 tablespoon oil and tofu. Add the ginger to the wok and stir-fry 30 seconds or until fragrant. Return the tofu to the wok, add the soy sauce, broth, and the remaining ½ teaspoon sugar and shake the pan to coat the tofu evenly. Cook 2 minutes, basting the tofu with the sauce. Add the cilantro relish. *Serves 4 as part of a multicourse meal.*

Cousin Sylvia's Drumsticks with Caramelized Onions

This is my cousin Sylvia's version of a recipe her father used to cook. The combination of sweet caramelized onions and rich oyster sauce is reminiscent of my Uncle Tommy's extraordinary home cooking.

1 tablespoon vegetable oil
2 tablespoons thinly sliced garlic
1 tablespoon finely shredded ginger
1 small onion, halved and thinly sliced
¾ teaspoon salt
¼ teaspoon ground white pepper
8 chicken drumsticks (about 2 pounds)
⅓ cup finely shredded scallions
2 tablespoons oyster sauce
½ teaspoon sesame oil

Heat a 14-inch flat-bottomed wok over high heat until a bead of water vaporizes within 1 to 2 seconds of contact. Swirl in the vegetable oil, add the garlic and ginger, and stir-fry 10 seconds. Add the onion, ½ teaspoon of the salt, and the pepper, and stir-fry on medium heat 3 to 4 minutes or until light golden. Transfer to a plate. Add the drumsticks, spreading them evenly in the wok, and pan-fry 20 to 25 minutes over medium heat, continually turning the drumsticks until browned on all sides and the chicken is cooked through. Add the cooked onions and the remaining ¼ teaspoon salt and stir until well combined. Add the scallions, oyster sauce, and sesame oil, stirring over low heat until well combined. *Serves 4 as part of a multicourse meal.*

Uncle Lang's Pan-Fried Sea Bass

My uncle's method for pan-frying fish is fast and simple and keeps the fish moist and flavorful. The Cantonese call this technique of cooking on high heat in a wok with the lid on "roasting" because it produces a seared, roasted taste.

1 pound sea bass fillets
3 scallions, cut into 2-inch pieces
Three ½-inch-thick slices ginger, smashed
3 tablespoons minced garlic
2 teaspoons Shao Hsing rice wine or dry sherry
¾ teaspoon salt
½ teaspoon sugar
¼ teaspoon ground white pepper
2 tablespoons vegetable oil
¼ cup Homemade Chicken Broth (page 195)
1 teaspoon soy sauce
½ teaspoon cornstarch
⅓ cup sliced mild fresh chilies

1. Cut the fish fillets crosswise into 1-inch pieces. In a shallow bowl combine the fish, scallions, ginger, garlic, rice wine, salt, sugar, pepper, and 1 tablespoon of the oil. In a small bowl combine the broth, soy sauce, and cornstarch.

2. Heat a 14-inch flat-bottomed wok over high heat until a bead of water vaporizes within 1 to 2 seconds of contact. Swirl in the remaining 1 tablespoon oil and add the fish skin side down, spreading the pieces evenly in the wok. Cover and cook 30 seconds over high heat. Uncover and loosen the pieces with a metal spatula.

3. Add the chilies, cover, reduce the heat to medium, and cook 1 minute. Increase the heat to high, stir the broth mixture, and swirl it into the wok. Turn the fish pieces over. Cover, remove from the heat, and let stand 1 to 2 minutes. Test the fish for doneness by poking the thickest part with a fork or chopstick; the fish should flake. If not, cover and cook over low heat 1 to 2 minutes or until the fish flakes. *Serves 4 as part of a multicourse meal.*

Auntie Bertha's Ginger Drumettes with Oyster Sauce

For this recipe my Auntie Bertha likes chicken wing drumettes, perfect as an appetizer. Select drumettes similar in size so that the cooking time will be the same. Remember that the drumettes can't be pan-fried on high heat or they will burn. (photo page 171)

14 chicken drumettes (about 1½ pounds)
2 tablespoons thinly sliced ginger
1 tablespoon cornstarch
1 tablespoon black soy sauce
2 tablespoons oyster sauce
1 large egg
½ cup unseasoned dry breadcrumbs
3 tablespoons vegetable oil
1 scallion, thinly sliced
2 cups shredded iceberg lettuce

1. In a bowl combine the drumettes, ginger, cornstarch, black soy sauce, and 1 tablespoon of the oyster sauce with 1 tablespoon cold water. Cover and refrigerate 4 hours. Allow the drumettes to come to room temperature 30 minutes before cooking. In a shallow bowl beat the egg. Put the breadcrumbs in a plate. Dip the drumettes in the egg and then lightly dredge in the breadcrumbs.

2. Heat a 14-inch flat-bottomed wok over high heat until a bead of water vaporizes within 1 to 2 seconds of contact. Swirl in 1 tablespoon of the oil and add the drumettes, spreading them evenly in the wok. Pan-fry 15 to 20 minutes, adjusting the heat between medium and medium-low, continually turning the drumettes until browned on all sides and cooked through. When the wok becomes dry swirl in the remaining oil—1 to 2 tablespoons, as needed. Add the scallion and the remaining tablespoon of oyster sauce and stir-fry 1 minute. Transfer to a platter lined with the shredded lettuce. *Serves 4 as part of a multicourse meal.*

My Uncle Yang Lang Ping working at his powerful two-burner gas stove in Foshan, China. The lower counter level puts the wok at the perfect height for cooking.

Pan-Fried Noodles with Pork Shang Palace

Chef Ip of the Shang Palace restaurant in Kowloon swirls the wok masterfully when he fries a noodle pancake. This is my version of Chef Ip's recipe, using Hong Kong–style pan-fried noodles (see page 225). The fresh noodles are pre-cooked, no boiling required. If you have difficulty turning the pancake over in the wok, slide the pancake onto a dinner plate. Place another plate over the noodles and flip both plates over before sliding the noodles back into the wok. (photo page 151)

12 ounces lean pork butt, cut into ¼-inch-thick
   bite-sized slices
1½ teaspoons Shao Hsing rice wine or dry sherry
2¼ teaspoons cornstarch
½ teaspoon soy sauce
¾ teaspoon sesame oil
1 teaspoon salt
⅓ cup Homemade Chicken Broth (page 195)
¼ teaspoon sugar
4 tablespoons vegetable oil
8 ounces fresh Hong Kong–style pan-fried noodles
2 tablespoons thinly sliced garlic
1 small red bell pepper, cut into 1-inch pieces
1 small green bell pepper, cut into 1-inch pieces

1. In a shallow bowl combine the pork, rice wine, cornstarch, soy sauce, sesame oil, and ½ teaspoon of the salt. In a small bowl combine the broth, sugar, and remaining ½ teaspoon salt.

2. Heat a 14-inch flat-bottomed wok over high heat until a bead of water vaporizes within 1 to 2 seconds of contact. Swirl in 1 tablespoon of the vegetable oil and add the noodles, spreading them to form a 9-inch pancake. Reduce the heat to medium and pan-fry 30 seconds, shaking the pan. Swirl in ¼ cup cold water and pan-fry, pressing the pancake with a metal spatula, 2 minutes. Swirl in an additional ¼ cup water and pan-fry 2 minutes or until golden. Using the spatula, loosen the pancake and turn it over. Swirl in 1 tablespoon of the vegetable oil with ⅓ cup water and pan-fry, shaking the pan and pressing the pancake with the spatula, until golden brown,

3 to 4 minutes. Transfer to a heatproof platter and place in a warm oven. Rinse the wok and dry it thoroughly.

3. Heat the wok over high heat until a bead of water vaporizes within 1 to 2 seconds of contact. Swirl in 1 tablespoon of the vegetable oil and add the garlic and pork, spreading it evenly in the wok. Cook undisturbed 20 seconds, letting the pork begin to brown. Then, using a metal spatula, stir-fry, separating the pork until it is browned but still slightly rare, 1 to 2 minutes. Transfer to a plate. Swirl in the remaining 1 tablespoon vegetable oil, add the peppers, and stir-fry 1 to 2 minutes or until the vegetables are just limp. Stir the broth mixture and swirl it into the wok. Add the pork and stir-fry 1 minute or until the pork is cooked through. Spoon over the warm noodles. *Serves 4 as part of a multicourse meal.*

Che Chung Ng's Water Chestnut and Pork Omelets

My Auntie Ivy's mother, Che Chung Ng, is well known for her delicate half-moon-shaped omelets. Auntie Ivy arranged a special cooking session with her mom so that we could both learn this extraordinary but simple recipe. If fresh water chestnuts are unavailable, I use Asian pear or jicama.

6 ounces ground pork (about ¾ cup)
1 tablespoon plus 2 teaspoons cornstarch
2 teaspoons Shao Hsing rice wine or dry sherry
1 teaspoon soy sauce
1 teaspoon sesame oil
½ teaspoon sugar
½ teaspoon ground white pepper
¾ teaspoon salt
1 tablespoon plus 3 teaspoons vegetable oil
3 fresh water chestnuts
4 large eggs

1. In an 8-inch shallow heatproof bowl combine the pork, cornstarch, rice wine, soy sauce, sesame oil, sugar, pepper, and ¼ teaspoon of the salt. The mixture will be very dry. Stir in the 1 tablespoon vegetable oil until well mixed. Spread the mixture evenly to within 1 inch of the edge of the bowl.

2. Put a 1-inch-high steamer rack in a 14-inch flat-bottomed wok. Add water to a depth of ¾ inch and bring to a boil over high heat. Carefully put the bowl on the rack, cover, reduce the heat to medium-low, and steam 10 to 12 minutes, until all of the meat is just cooked through, breaking up the mixture with a spoon midway through cooking. Be sure to check the water level from time to time and replenish, if necessary, with boiling water. Carefully remove the bowl from the wok and set aside to cool slightly. Pour out the water from the wok and dry the pan.

3. Rinse the water chestnuts under cold water. Peel and then finely chop. In a medium bowl beat the eggs and the remaining ½ teaspoon salt. Stir in the water chestnuts and hot pork mixture.

4. Heat the wok over high heat until a bead of water vaporizes within 1 to 2 seconds of contact. Swirl in 1 teaspoon of the vegetable oil. Using a measuring cup, pour three scant ¼-cup portions of the eggs into the wok like pancake batter. Cook on medium to medium-low heat 1 to 2 minutes until just set. Using a metal spatula, fold each pancake in half to form a half moon. Turn over and cook 1 to 2 minutes until just set and light golden. Turn over and cook 30 seconds or until just set. Transfer to a platter. Repeat with the remaining vegetable oil and egg mixture. *Makes 9 mini-omelets; serves 4 as part of a multicourse meal.*

Henry Hugh's Chinkiang Pork Chops

This recipe is adapted from one Chef Henry Hugh of The New School Culinary Arts in New York City taught me. The sauce is sweet and sour but with a rich flavor that comes from Chinkiang vinegar—a black vinegar similar to balsamic. Chef Hugh chops through the bone, cutting each pork chop into three pieces. I prefer to cut the chop into three pieces but leave the whole bone attached to one of the pieces.

Three ½-inch-thick lean blade rib pork chops
   (about 1 pound)
2 tablespoons Shao Hsing rice wine or dry sherry
1 teaspoon soy sauce
¾ teaspoon salt
1 large egg, beaten
½ teaspoon plus ¼ cup cornstarch
3 tablespoons Chinkiang or balsamic vinegar
3 tablespoons sugar
1 tablespoon ketchup
¼ teaspoon A.1. sauce
¼ teaspoon Tabasco
2 tablespoons plus 2 teaspoons canola oil
2 teaspoons minced garlic

1. Put the pork chops on a cutting board and, using the blunt side of a cleaver blade or a meat pounder, pound the meat portion of the chops in a crisscross pattern. Turn the chops over and continue pounding until they are about ¼ inch thick. Cut each pork chop into three pieces, leaving the bone attached to one piece. In a shallow medium bowl combine the rice wine, soy sauce, ½ teaspoon of the salt, the egg, and the ½ teaspoon cornstarch. Add the pork and marinate 30 minutes.

2. In a small bowl combine the vinegar, sugar, ketchup, A.1. sauce, Tabasco, and remaining ¼ teaspoon salt. Set aside. Put the remaining ¼ cup cornstarch in a dish and lightly dredge the pork.

3. Heat a 14-inch flat-bottomed wok over high heat until a bead of water vaporizes within 1 to 2 seconds of contact. Swirl in 1 tablespoon of the oil and carefully add the pork. Pan-fry 1 minute over medium heat. Swirl in 1 tablespoon of the oil and continue pan-frying 1 to 2 minutes or until golden. Turn the pork over and fry 1 to 2 minutes or until golden. Transfer to a plate. Swirl in the remaining 2 teaspoons oil, add the garlic, and stir-fry 10 seconds until fragrant. Stir the vinegar mixture, swirl it into the wok, and bring to a boil. Add the pork, reduce the heat to medium-low, and cook until the pork is just cooked through, 2 to 4 minutes. *Serves 4 as part of a multicourse meal.*

The Family **Wok-a-thon**

大
獻
身
手

It was my cousin Fred's idea, casually mentioned at a family function. Immediately I knew it was brilliant. "Gracie, you ought to gather the older and younger generations together to cook using a wok, and then record the recipes." The idea of sampling two generations' home cooking was tempting enough, but to compare the Chinese culinary customs of my aunts and uncles—all born and raised in San Francisco's Chinatown in the 1920s and 1930s—was even more alluring. In our family, these relatives are the first generation of Cantonese Chinese Americans, and they are famous for being great cooks. My cousins, like me, are postwar baby boomers and are entirely assimilated to Western culture. What would the culinary differences and similarities possibly be?

I began contacting family for the "wok-a-thon" months before my trip home to San Francisco. The only criterion I gave them was that any chosen recipe be cooked in a wok or skillet. After many weeks a few cousins responded positively, but there was a great wall of silence from the aunties and uncles. Finally, Auntie Betty and Uncle Roy offered to host the event at their home, but they were reluctant to cook. "We have nothing special to show you," they claimed. As I pursued the other aunties and uncles, they were equally self-effacing. I came to realize that I had to overcome their natural humility and their deference to me as a culinary professional. I also had to reassure them that what I wanted was exactly the thing only they could teach me. They believed that their everyday cooking could not compare to a complicated dish like Peking duck, beggar's chicken, or dim sum. I assured all of them that I was not in search of something "exotic." I wanted family home cooking. My family's home cooking.

Once Auntie Betty and Uncle Roy were

enlisted, the event began to take shape. Still dubious about what they could teach me, my cousins, aunties, and uncles were nonetheless eager for a family get-together.

Finally, on a gorgeous San Francisco Sunday, eighteen members of my large family gather for the "wok-a-thon." Each cook arrives with loud and happy fanfare, carrying a large tote filled with ingredients and condiments. I am surprised and saddened to see that many of them have brought skillets: except for Auntie Betty's, there is not a wok among them.

The kitchen activities begin at eleven A.M. as Auntie Betty fires up her custom-built wok stove and pulls out a wok with a richly colored surface. "Food tastes better when cooked in a wok," she explains. "Experienced cooks say it's the secret to achieving *wok hay*, and it's true." I am gratified to see the day is beginning with the traditional Chinese cooking tool, and I edge into the kitchen to watch the cooks prepare for an all-day tasting feast.

Auntie Betty cooks the first dish, a savory braise of cellophane noodles, shiitake mushrooms, cloud ears, barbecued pork, egg pancake, and scallions seasoned with oyster sauce that she prepares in less than 15 minutes. The dish is magnificent with a sublime blend of tastes and textures. Everyone is stunned at the ease with which such an impressive dish is made. They break into spontaneous applause. Auntie Betty smiles shyly while Doreen proudly tells me this is just one of many favorites her mother makes. I am relieved I didn't allow Auntie Betty to escape cooking. The dish is passed around on small plates and quickly disappears amid sounds of happy eating.

To my delight Auntie Betty begins describing how she learned to cook from her father, George Jew, when she was nine years old. She explains how every day she would shop for groceries after

Auntie Lil, surrounded by Doreen, Cindy, and Mel, shows off her Stir-Fried Lotus Root with Chinese Bacon (page 147).

大
獻
身
手

school in Chinatown. Then her father would stand beside her in the kitchen teaching her all the "basics." "By the time I was twelve I was the sole cook for our family of eight," says Auntie Betty. "In those days it was common for Chinese children to assume household responsibilities."

"If you could stand straight, you could cook," says Auntie Frances. Uncle Sherman adds that he and his brother started cooking as young boys. They were taught by their mother so she could help out at the family fur business. Auntie Lil tells me that her father, Lum Bo Fay, was twelve years old when he began cooking in a fancy twenty-four-hour restaurant on Grant Avenue. "He slept in the kitchen. When a stir-fry order came in, he stood on a specially made stool in order to reach the wok." By the time her father was nineteen, he opened one of Chinatown's most successful restaurants, Sun Hung Heung on Washington Street.

The familiar storytelling of my elders briefly transports me to life in "old Chinatown." I soon realize Uncle Sherman is preparing to cook, lining up his ingredients on the counter. He cuts a fine figure at the stove—tall, lean, and ruggedly handsome, he makes me think of Gary Cooper with a wok in hand. It takes a few moments for Uncle Sherman to adjust Auntie Betty's high-powered wok stove to his liking. Holding his open palm over the empty wok he checks the heat level, explaining to the hushed crowd that every stove heats differently. It must be hot to make the flavors right. Satisfied that he has reached an optimum temperature, Uncle Sherman quickly adds marinated chicken slices to the wok. Then the crack and sizzle of fresh ginger and garlic release an explosion of aromas and flavors into the room, reigniting the conversation as anticipation for the second dish builds.

At the completion of each dish, every cook receives thunderous applause. Pride and joy is evident in the cook's face. A chorus of "ooohhs" and "ahhhs" follows as the scrumptious concoction reaches the audience of discerning tasters. I note

how the presentation of every dish has the casual beauty and artistry natural to home cooks.

When it is Auntie Bertha's turn to present her fried ginger chicken drumettes, she confesses that she rehearsed her dish the day before. Shy like all the others, she modestly says, "I hope this is good enough." Our response is to empty the platter within minutes. We all have an insatiable appetite for the robust, hearty taste of Chinese comfort food, and we are treated to a tour de force of braises, stir-fries, and pan-fried dishes. By the third or fourth course, my cousins David and Judy observe that because there are so many delectable sauces, we must cook rice so not a drop is lost.

A few hours into the "wok-a-thon" the mood of the party has grown boisterous. The cooking continues as the waiting cooks and family reminisce. The cooks are bombarded with questions, and there is serious discussion about different marinades and ingredients, the elder generation assuming a mentoring role. When Auntie Betty sees Kathy opening a can of water chestnuts she asks, "Do you ever use fresh water chestnuts?" Kathy is surprised and shy to admit that she didn't even know they were available fresh. I notice that a couple of cousins and Auntie Betty's friend Gladys are even taking notes.

As the afternoon gives way to evening, the talk returns to remembrance. Auntie Betty and Auntie Frances recall how in the 1930s, their father's shrimp store on Sacramento Street in Chinatown had a traditional Chinese hearth stove fitted with two large woks. One was used only for cooking rice, the other for steaming or stir-frying dishes to feed the family and the store's employees. But to my surprise, they tell me they have no recollection of ever seeing a wok in any Chinese home in the 1930s. "A wok! We didn't even have a refrigerator. We put our food outside the window to stay cool. We made do with what we had," says Auntie Frances. "The kitchens in Chinatown were so small in those days that there was no way a wok could fit. Everyone was so poor. It was normal for four and five families to

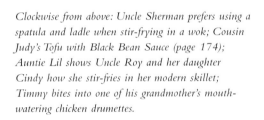

Clockwise from above: Uncle Sherman prefers using a spatula and ladle when stir-frying in a wok; Cousin Judy's Tofu with Black Bean Sauce (page 174); Auntie Lil shows Uncle Roy and her daughter Cindy how she stir-fries in her modern skillet; Timmy bites into one of his grandmother's mouth-watering chicken drumettes.

大
獻
身
手

live on one floor, using a common kitchen with only two or three burners. Woks weren't even available for us to buy when I was a young girl, so I learned to stir-fry using a skillet. Even if we'd been able to have a wok, the burners didn't have the high flame necessary for Chinese cooking," Auntie Betty explains.

Uncle William remembers that the block on Sacramento Street in front of the family shrimp store had only three parked cars, two of which were his father's Packard and the family's store truck. Uncle Roy speaks of Grant Avenue when it was a two-way street and there were cable cars not only on California Street but also on Sacramento and Clay streets. Auntie Lil tells the story of how her mother made moonshine and she and her nine-year-old sister were the "runners." Auntie Lil also remembers Greer Garson having a favorite table at her father's restaurant. I love being reminded of how dramatically different life was one generation ago and to remember how much of that family history has to do with food and cooking and family gatherings. "So many great moments in the family center around food. It brings us together. We share the experience and renew ourselves," says Sylvia. I note with gratitude that the family's culinary heritage is being passed along.

My aunties and uncles have prepared mainly Cantonese fare for the "wok-a thon," dishes they have cooked for more than fifty years, favorites of their children and grandchildren. But their cooking has changed over the years. Auntie Frances and Uncle Sherman have added non-Asian vegetables like cauliflower and broccoli to their stir-fries, but they still prefer cooking with the carbon-steel wok they bought when they married in 1953. Auntie Lil now steams Chinese bacon, *laab yuk*, before stir-frying in order to remove excess fat. Auntie Bertha's recipe is the most modern: she rolls soy sauce and ginger-marinated chicken drumettes in breadcrumbs before pan-frying them until crisp. When I ask Auntie Betty if her braised cellophane noodles with shiitake mushrooms and barbecued pork is similar to the dishes her father

taught her, she gently tells me this dish has many more "luxury" ingredients than what her family could afford when she was young.

The cousins have strayed even further from traditional Chinese cooking. Having come from the generation of Americans that embraced take-out and restaurant dining as alternatives to home cooking, these cousins were not taught to cook as children and are less inclined to cook every day. In fact, my cousins cook Chinese food only occasionally, and then mainly dishes they remember eating as children. Doreen's black bean sauce spareribs is a version of a dish her mother used to prepare. Sylvia's chicken and onions is based on a favorite dish her father used to cook. She has recently modified the recipe at the suggestion of her son Thomas by adding ginger. My cousin Cindy, who used to cook with a wok, switched to a high-end skillet. Seeing Auntie Betty's wok and hearing our reminiscing has reminded her of the importance of continuing the "old Chinese" customs. Cindy resolves not only to return to using her wok but to buy woks for her grown children.

At one point in the cooking I overhear Auntie Bertha tell her daughter Kathy how delicious the Lion's Head tasted. Auntie Bertha recalls that it was once a staple of her own cooking repertoire but she has forgotten how to make it. She remembers that my Uncle Tommy would effortlessly hand-chop the pork with two cleavers. Auntie Bertha marvels that Kathy improvised the recipe from a cookbook, pleased that Kathy cared enough to find the recipe and learn to cook it. She smiled and asked Kathy to teach her the recipe.

At its best, cooking is a vessel of memory. The aroma, the taste, the image are all transporting. "Food, no matter what style, evokes family," says Cindy wisely. Chinese banquets traditionally serve nine courses, an auspicious symbol of longevity. By chance our party has produced nine propitious dishes. We have spent the day laughing, eating wonderful food, and sharing a lifetime of culinary knowledge. And the stories, the extraordinary stories. Did everyone really believe they had nothing special to share?

Right: The elder generation—Uncle Roy, Auntie Betty, Auntie Bertha, Uncle Sherman, Auntie Lil, Uncle William, and Auntie Frances—pose with their skillets and wok. Bottom right: Auntie Bertha's Ginger Drumettes with Oyster Sauce (page 162). Bottom left: The younger generation—Judy, Sylvia, Thomas, Fred, Kathy, Doreen, David, and Timmy (in front)—pose with their skillets. Below: Timmy is curious to see if his grandmother's dish is ready yet.

Family Wok-a-thon Recipes

炆 Braising

Auntie Betty's Cellophane Noodles, Mushrooms, and Barbecued Pork

My Auntie Betty has enough room in her enormous Cantonese-style wok to double this recipe for parties. It is essential to thinly slice all the ingredients; the fine shreds make the dish much more pleasing to eat.

6 dried shiitake mushrooms
½ cup cloud ears
One 3.5-ounce package cellophane noodles
2 tablespoons vegetable oil
2 large eggs, beaten
¼ teaspoon salt
1 teaspoon black soy sauce
1¾ to 2¼ cups Homemade Chicken Broth
    (page 195)
2 teaspoons oyster sauce
4 ounces Chinese Barbecued Pork (opposite),
    or store-bought, julienned
½ cup shredded scallions

1. Put the mushrooms and cloud ears in separate bowls. Pour about ½ cup cold water over the mushrooms and about 2 cups cold water over the cloud ears, and soak about 30 minutes or until softened. Pour out the cloud ear soaking water, but reserve the mushroom liquid. Drain and squeeze the mushrooms dry. Cut off and discard the stems and thinly slice the caps. In another bowl, soak the cellophane noodles in cold water to cover, 15 minutes or until softened. Drain thoroughly.

2. Heat a 14-inch flat-bottomed wok over high heat until a bead of water vaporizes within 1 to 2 seconds of contact. Swirl in 1 tablespoon of the oil, add the eggs, and cook 30 seconds to 1 minute, tilting the pan so that the egg covers the surface as thinly as possible to make a pancake. When the bottom is just beginning to brown and the pancake is just set, use a metal spatula to flip the pancake and allow it to set, about 5 seconds. Transfer it to a cutting board and remove the wok from the heat. Cut the egg pancake into fine shreds. Set aside.

3. Swirl the remaining 1 tablespoon oil into the cooled wok. Add the drained noodles, salt, and soy sauce, and turn the heat to medium-low, tossing the noodles with two metal spatulas, as you would a salad. Continue tossing over medium-low heat until the soy sauce is evenly distributed, about 1 minute. Add the mushrooms, tossing to combine. Add 1½ cups broth and bring to a boil over high heat. Cover, reduce the heat to medium-low, and simmer, stirring occasionally, 8 to 10 minutes, or until the noodles are just tender. If the noodles absorb all the broth, add ¼ to ¾ cup more as needed. The mixture should be wet but not soupy.

4. Add the oyster sauce, ¼ cup reserved mushroom liquid, and the cloud ears, tossing together. Bring to a boil over high heat and cook 1 minute or until the cloud ears are just softened. Add half the barbecued pork, half the eggs, and half the scallions and toss to combine. Transfer to a platter. Decorate with the remaining barbecued pork, egg shreds, and scallions. *Serves 4 to 6 as part of a multicourse meal.*

Uncle Roy reaches for a taste of Auntie Betty's Cellophane Noodles, Mushrooms, and Barbecued Pork.

Chinese Barbecued Pork

Barbecued pork is sold in some restaurants in Chinatown. However, if you don't live near a restaurant source, here is an easy recipe for making your own at home that is actually far superior. This makes more than you need for Auntie Betty's Cellophane Noodles, Mushrooms, and Barbecued Pork, but you'll find homemade barbecued pork is an excellent appetizer simply served warmed.

1 pound lean pork butt
2 tablespoons sugar
1 tablespoon soy sauce
1 tablespoon hoisin sauce
1 tablespoon black soy sauce
1 tablespoon Shao Hsing rice wine or dry sherry
1 tablespoon bean sauce
1 teaspoon sesame oil
⅛ teaspoon ground white pepper
1 tablespoon honey

1. Quarter the pork lengthwise. Rub with 1 tablespoon of the sugar. Put it in a large bowl and set aside for 15 minutes. Pour off any excess liquid. In a bowl, combine the soy sauce, hoisin sauce, black soy sauce, rice wine, bean sauce, sesame oil, pepper, and remaining 1 tablespoon sugar. Pour the mixture over the pork, making sure the pork is well coated. Cover loosely with plastic wrap and refrigerate 6 to 8 hours, turning the pork from time to time.

2. When ready to roast, let the pork come to room temperature. Preheat the broiler. Put a rack in a roasting pan and add water to a depth of ¼ inch. Remove the pork from the marinade, reserving the marinade. Using your hands, evenly spread the honey on the pork. Put the pork on the rack, leaving about 1 inch of space between the pieces.

3. Carefully place the pan under the broiler (the pork should be about 4 inches from the broiler element), and broil until the meat is just beginning to char slightly, 7 to 10 minutes. Monitor the water level in the roasting pan to make sure it never falls below ¼ inch. Turn the pork, brush with the reserved marinade, and broil until the meat is just beginning to char, 7 to 10 minutes, or until the pork registers 155°F when tested with a meat thermometer. If the pork is getting too charred, cover loosely with a small piece of aluminum foil. Carefully remove the pork from the broiler and set on a cutting board to cool 10 minutes. Slice ¼ inch thick and serve warm or at room temperature. *Serves 4 as part of a multicourse meal.*

Right: Cousins Sylvia and Fred hard at work; their son Thomas watches from behind. Center right: Uncle William gives Cousin Kathy a hand with her recipe. Far right: Cousins David and Judy cook together as a team.

Cousin Doreen's Braised Spareribs and Asparagus

For this recipe my cousin Doreen uses boneless spareribs, available in Chinatown in San Francisco. In New York City boneless spareribs are not available, but Chinatown butchers typically sell spareribs cut across the bones into 1-inch pieces. Once home I cut them between the bones into individual squares.

1½ pounds lean spareribs, cut into bite-sized
    pieces
2 tablespoons fermented black beans, rinsed
2 teaspoons cornstarch
1 teaspoon vegetable oil
1 tablespoon minced garlic
1 tablespoon soy sauce
8 ounces asparagus, cut into 2-inch pieces
¼ teaspoon salt

1. Wash the spareribs in several changes of cold water and drain in a colander. Pat dry with paper towels. In a small bowl mash the black beans with a fork. In a separate small bowl combine the cornstarch with 1 tablespoon cold water.

2. Heat a 14-inch flat-bottomed wok over high heat until a bead of water vaporizes within 1 to 2 seconds of contact. Swirl in the oil and add the spareribs, spreading them in the wok. Cook undisturbed 30 seconds, letting the spareribs begin to brown. Then, using a metal spatula, stir-fry 1 to 2 minutes or until the spareribs are lightly browned.

3. Add the garlic and the black beans and stir-fry 1 minute. Add the soy sauce with ¾ cup cold water. Bring to a boil, cover, reduce the heat to low, and simmer, stirring occasionally, 10 minutes or until the spareribs are just tender. Stir in the asparagus and salt and return to a boil over high heat. Cover and cook 1 to 2 minutes or until the asparagus is just tender. Stir the cornstarch mixture, swirl it into the wok, and bring to a boil, stirring constantly, until the sauce has thickened, about 30 seconds. *Serves 4 as part of a multicourse meal.*

Cousin Judy's Tofu with Black Bean Sauce

My cousin David and his wife, Judy, cook this dish at least once a week; it is their son Timothy's favorite Chinese meal. Judy recalls her father cooking tofu this way with ground pork and fermented black beans (see page 221). She now prefers to eat less meat and has switched to ground turkey. (photo page 169)

4 squares firm tofu (about 14 ounces), rinsed
½ teaspoon salt
1 cup Homemade Chicken Broth (page 195)
1 tablespoon oyster sauce
1 teaspoon sugar
1½ teaspoons cornstarch
2 tablespoons fermented black beans, rinsed
1 tablespoon minced garlic
1 teaspoon Shao Hsing rice wine or dry sherry
1 tablespoon soy sauce
⅛ teaspoon ground white pepper
2 tablespoons vegetable oil
½ pound ground turkey
2 scallions, thinly sliced

1. Cut each tofu square in half. Put the halves on several sheets of paper towels. Sprinkle the salt evenly over the tofu and set aside. In a medium bowl combine the broth, oyster sauce, sugar, and cornstarch. Set aside. In a separate small bowl mash the black beans and garlic with a fork. Stir in the rice wine, soy sauce, and pepper.

2. Heat a 14-inch flat-bottomed wok over high heat until a bead of water vaporizes within 1 to 2 seconds of contact. Swirl in 1 tablespoon of the oil and add the turkey, spreading it in the wok. Cook undisturbed 30 seconds, letting the turkey begin to brown. Then, using a metal spatula, stir-fry 1 to 2 minutes or until the turkey is no longer pink but is not cooked through. Transfer to a plate. Rinse the wok and dry it thoroughly.

3. Heat the wok over high heat until a bead of water vaporizes within 1 to 2 seconds of contact.

Swirl in the remaining 1 tablespoon of oil, carefully add the tofu, and reduce the heat to medium. Pan-fry the tofu 1 minute per side. Add the black bean mixture and stir-fry 30 seconds or until fragrant. Stir the broth mixture, swirl it into the wok, and bring to a boil over high heat, stirring constantly, until the sauce has thickened. Cover, reduce the heat to low, and simmer 2 to 3 minutes. Increase the heat to high, stir in the turkey and scallions, and cook 1 minute or until the turkey is just cooked through. *Serves 4 as part of a multicourse meal.*

Cousin Kathy's Lion's Head

My cousin Kathy's children, Mark and Sarah, are fond of eating Lion's Head—the Chinese believe the meatball resembles a lion's head with a cabbage mane. Kathy discovered the trick to keeping the pork meatballs juicy: mix them lightly with your hands.

8 dried shiitake mushrooms
1 pound ground pork
¼ cup minced canned or peeled fresh water
  chestnuts
¼ cup minced bamboo shoots
½ cup minced scallions
6 teaspoons cornstarch
2 tablespoons Shao Hsing rice wine or dry sherry
3 tablespoons soy sauce
1 teaspoon sugar
½ teaspoon salt
⅛ teaspoon ground white pepper
½ cup Homemade Chicken Broth (page 195)
2 teaspoons plus 1 tablespoon vegetable oil
1 pound Napa cabbage, cut crosswise into
  2-inch-wide pieces

1. In a medium bowl soak the mushrooms in 1 cup cold water for 30 minutes or until softened. Drain and squeeze dry, reserving the soaking liquid. Cut off and discard the stems and mince the caps.

2. In a large bowl combine the ground pork, water chestnuts, bamboo shoots, scallions, 4 teaspoons of the cornstarch, 1 tablespoon of the rice wine, 2 tablespoons of the soy sauce, ½ teaspoon of the sugar, the salt, pepper, and minced mushrooms with your hands. Divide the mixture into 4 equal portions and shape into large meatballs. In a bowl, combine the broth, remaining 1 tablespoon rice wine, 1 tablespoon soy sauce, and ½ teaspoon sugar, and ½ cup of the reserved mushroom soaking liquid. Set aside the sauce. In a separate small bowl combine the remaining 2 teaspoons cornstarch with 1 tablespoon cold water. Set aside.

3. Heat a 14-inch flat-bottomed wok over high heat until a bead of water vaporizes within 1 to 2 seconds of contact. Swirl in the 2 teaspoons oil, add the meatballs, reduce the heat to medium, and brown the meatballs on all sides, 7 to 10 minutes. Remove from the heat and carefully transfer to a plate.

4. Swirl the remaining 1 tablespoon oil into the unwashed wok over high heat, add the cabbage, and stir-fry 1 to 2 minutes or until the cabbage is slightly softened. Stir the broth mixture, swirl it into the wok, and bring to a boil over high heat. Carefully return the meatballs to the wok. Cover, reduce the heat to medium-low, and simmer 20 minutes, turning the meatballs midway through cooking. Check one meatball for doneness by cutting into the meatball. The center should be cooked through and the meat no loger pink.

5. Transfer the cabbage to a serving bowl and spoon the meatballs on top. Bring the sauce to a boil over high heat. Stir the cornstarch mixture, swirl it into the wok, and bring to a boil, stirring, about 30 seconds or until the sauce is slightly thickened. Pour over the meatballs. *Serves 4 as part of a multicourse meal.*

Henry Hugh's Cantonese Stuffed Tofu (page 178)
Opposite: Mama holds a platter of her Fuzzy Melon with Dried Scallops (page 178)

Mama's Fuzzy Melon with Dried Scallops

Rich in flavor, Chinese dried scallops (see page 225) and Smithfield ham (see page 226) are the perfect counterpoint for mild fuzzy melon (see page 222). Smithfield ham steaks are sold in Chinese butcher stores. Even though the ham is rinsed, it can still be very salty, and little additional salt is needed. Mama cooks fuzzy melon in the summertime when it is in its prime. She likes melons that have fine, prickly hairs and are about 2 inches wide. (photo page 176)

6 dried scallops (about 1½ ounces)
1 ounce Smithfield ham
2 teaspoons light brown sugar
1½ pounds fuzzy melon
1 tablespoon vegetable oil
3 slices ginger
¼ teaspoon salt
Cilantro sprigs

1. In a small bowl soak the dried scallops in ½ cup cold water for 2 hours or until softened. Drain, reserving the soaking liquid. There should be about ⅓ cup. Remove the small hard muscle from the sides of the scallops. Finely shred the scallops.

2. Rinse the ham in cold water. In a small saucepan bring 1 cup cold water to a boil over high heat. Add the ham and return to a boil. Reduce the heat to medium-low, cover, and simmer 20 minutes. Drain the ham and rinse under cold water. Pat dry with paper towels. Put the ham in a small heatproof dish and add the brown sugar.

3. Put a 1-inch-high round steamer rack in a 14-inch flat-bottomed wok. Add water to a depth of ¾ inch and bring to a boil over high heat. Carefully put the dish on the rack, cover, reduce the heat to medium, and steam 20 minutes or until the ham is softened. Be sure to check the water level from time to time and replenish, if necessary, with boiling water. Carefully remove the dish from the steamer and set the ham aside to cool. Pour out any juices accumulated in the dish. Pour out the water from the wok and dry the pan. Slice the ham into paper-thin slices. Stack a few slices at a time and cut into fine shreds. Set aside. Peel the fuzzy melon and cut into 2-inch sections. Cut each section into quarters lengthwise.

4. Heat the wok over high heat until a bead of water vaporizes within 1 to 2 seconds of contact. Swirl in the oil, add the ginger, and stir-fry 10 seconds. Add the fuzzy melon and stir-fry 1 minute. Add the scallops and reserved soaking liquid to the wok and bring to a boil over high heat. Cover, reduce the heat to low, and simmer 20 to 25 minutes or until the fuzzy melon is just tender. Stir the vegetables occasionally and if the liquid evaporates, add up to ¼ cup water. Stir in the salt. Scatter the ham shreds and cilantro sprigs over the top. *Serves 4 as part of a multicourse meal.*

Henry Hugh's Cantonese Stuffed Tofu

Chef Henry Hugh's recipe for this classic Cantonese home-style dish includes a little dried shrimp (see page 226), which brings out the sweetness of the pork in the filling. Bean curd is often braised, as it readily absorbs the strong, rich flavors of a hearty sauce. (photo page 177)

1 tablespoon dried shrimp
4 squares firm tofu (about 14 ounces), rinsed
¾ teaspoon salt
4 ounces ground pork (about ½ cup)
2 teaspoons cornstarch
¼ teaspoon sugar
⅛ teaspoon ground white pepper
1 teaspoon sesame oil
¼ cup minced scallions
2 tablespoons canola oil
1 garlic clove, thinly sliced
¾ cup Homemade Chicken Broth (page 195)
2 teaspoons soy sauce
1 teaspoon black soy sauce
1 tablespoon oyster sauce
Cilantro sprigs, optional

1. In a small saucepan bring ½ cup water to a boil over high heat. Add the shrimp, reduce the heat to low, and simmer 1 minute. Drain, reserving the water. Finely mince the shrimp. Set aside.

2. Put the tofu squares on several sheets of paper towels. Sprinkle ½ teaspoon of the salt evenly over the tofu and set aside. In a medium bowl combine the pork, 1 teaspoon of the cornstarch, the sugar, pepper, remaining ¼ teaspoon salt, and minced shrimp. Stir in ½ teaspoon of the sesame oil, the scallions, and 1 tablespoon of the reserved shrimp liquid with 1 tablespoon cold water.

3. Cut each tofu square diagonally into 2 triangles. Using a paring knife, cut a shallow pocket laterally along the cut edge, removing some of the bean curd. The pocket should be about 2½ inches long and ½ inch deep. Discard the excess tofu. Stuff each triangle with about 1 tablespoon of the filling, packing it to extend beyond the pocket.

4. Heat a 14-inch flat-bottomed wok over high heat until a bead of water vaporizes within 1 to 2 seconds of contact. Swirl in the canola oil and add each tofu triangle pork side down. Reduce the heat to medium and pan-fry about 2 minutes. Scatter the garlic in the pan and cook 1 minute. Swirl in the broth with ¼ cup cold water and bring to a boil over high heat. Cover, reduce the heat to medium-low, and simmer about 3 minutes. Then, using a metal spatula, carefully loosen each triangle and turn onto its side. Swirl in the soy sauce, cover, and continue simmering about 4 minutes, turning midway. Stir in the black soy sauce, oyster sauce, and remaining ½ teaspoon sesame oil.

5. In a small bowl combine the remaining 1 teaspoon cornstarch with 1 tablespoon cold water. Increase the heat to high, swirl the cornstarch mixture into the wok, and cook, gently stirring, 30 seconds or until the sauce is slightly thickened and the pork is cooked through. Garnish with cilantro if desired. *Serves 4 as part of a multicourse meal.*

Curried Cauliflower, Napa Cabbage, and Carrots

Cauliflower, Napa cabbage, and carrots are ideal for absorbing the flavors of ginger and curry. I cut the cauliflower into small florets so that they will cook quickly. This is a great dish to make ahead, equally delicious served hot or at room temperature.

½ cup Homemade Chicken Broth (page 195)
¾ teaspoon salt
½ teaspoon sugar
¼ teaspoon cornstarch
1 tablespoon vegetable oil
3 slices ginger
1 small cauliflower (about 4 cups florets)
½ cup thinly sliced carrots
2 cups shredded Napa cabbage
1 teaspoon curry powder

1. In a small bowl combine the broth, salt, sugar, and cornstarch.

2. Heat a 14-inch flat-bottomed wok over high heat until a bead of water vaporizes within 1 to 2 seconds of contact. Swirl in the oil, add the ginger, and stir-fry 15 seconds. Add the cauliflower, carrots, and cabbage, and stir-fry 1 minute. Add the curry powder and stir-fry 1 minute or until fragrant. Stir the cornstarch mixture, swirl it into the wok, and bring to a boil, stirring until well combined. Cover and cook over high heat 1 to 2 minutes or until the vegetables are just tender. *Serves 4 as part of a multicourse meal.*

Liang Nian Xiu's Farm-Style Omelets

Liang Nian Xiu pan-fries and then braises her omelets briefly on medium heat on her hearth stove. If either the cooking time or heat is increased, these omelets become dry and tough. Be sure the pork is not icy cold, or the omelets will require more time to cook.

3 dried shiitake mushrooms
4 ounces ground pork (about ½ cup)
¼ cup finely minced scallions
¼ cup finely chopped cilantro
2 tablespoons minced garlic
1 tablespoon finely minced hot fresh chilies
½ teaspoon salt
2 teaspoons vegetable oil
4 large eggs, beaten

1. In a small bowl, soak the mushrooms in ⅓ cup cold water 30 minutes or until softened. Drain and squeeze dry, reserving the soaking liquid. Cut off and discard the stems and finely mince the caps. In a small bowl combine the pork, scallions, cilantro, garlic, chilies, salt, and minced mushrooms.

2. Heat a 14-inch flat-bottomed wok over high heat until a bead of water vaporizes within 1 to 2 seconds of contact. Swirl in 1 teaspoon of the oil, then using a measuring cup, pour two ¼-cup portions of the eggs into the wok like pancake batter. Cook on medium to medium-low heat 20 seconds until bubbles form around the edges. Put about a scant ¼ cup pork mixture on each pancake and, using a metal spatula, fold in half. Fold in half again to form a flat cigar shape and cook 1 to 2 minutes until golden. Transfer to a plate.

3. Continue forming omelets with the remaining oil, eggs, and pork mixture. When all the eggs are cooked, return the omelets to the wok, increase the heat to high, and add the reserved mushroom liquid. Cover, reduce the heat to medium, and cook 2 minutes. Turn the omelets, cover, and cook 2 minutes or until the pork is no longer pink and just cooked through. *Makes 4 mini-omelets; serves 4 as part of a multicourse meal.*

Omelets braise in the mushroom liquid. Liang Nian Xiu has stopped adding rice stalks to the fire at this point, and the fire has died down to allow a slow braise.

Tina Yao Lu's Shanghai-Style Crabs and Rice Cakes

Arriving in Shanghai in October, I was invited to dinner at my Auntie Linda's home, where her talented daughter Tina prepared this dish with hairy crabs, a Shanghainese specialty—but the recipe is delicious with any type of crab. Fresh rice cakes (see page 225) are also unique to Shanghai and are sold stateside in some Chinese markets in the refrigerator section. If they are unavailable omit them from the recipe. (photo page 150)

4 live blue crabs (about 2 pounds)
2 tablespoons all-purpose flour
2 cups Homemade Chicken Broth (page 195)
2 tablespoons Shao Hsing rice wine or dry sherry
1 tablespoon black soy sauce
½ teaspoon sugar
1 tablespoon cornstarch
2 tablespoons vegetable oil
Five ½-inch-thick slices ginger
2 cups fresh rice cakes (about 10 ounces)
½ teaspoon salt

1. Put the crabs in a paper bag and put the bag in the freezer for about 1 hour or until the crabs are no longer moving. Put each crab shell side down on a cutting board and twist off the apron. Pull off the hard shell, and remove the spongy gills on both sides. Cut the small legs off with a cleaver and discard. Cut each crab in half. Put in a colander and rinse under cold water. Shake off excess water. Put the flour in a shallow bowl. Lightly dust only the cut sides of the crab in flour. In a medium bowl combine the broth, rice wine, soy sauce, and sugar. In a small bowl combine the cornstarch with 2 tablespoons cold water. Set aside.

2. Heat a 14-inch flat-bottomed wok over high heat until a bead of water vaporizes within 1 to 2 seconds of contact. Swirl in the oil and carefully add the crabs floured side down. Reduce the heat to medium and cook 1 minute or until the crabs begin to brown. Add the ginger and stir-fry 30 seconds. Stir the broth mixture and swirl it into the

wok. Cover, bring to a boil over high heat, and cook until the crabs just turn orange, 1 minute. Add the rice cakes and salt. Cook uncovered 1 to 2 minutes, stirring constantly. Stir the cornstarch mixture, swirl it into the wok, and bring it to a boil, stirring constantly, until the sauce has thickened and the crabs and rice cakes are just cooked through, about 1 minute. *Serves 4 as part of a multicourse meal.*

Margaret Loo's Braised Tofu and Mushrooms

For years my Auntie Anna has raved about her friend Margaret Loo's home cooking. Raised in Hong Kong in a household with servants, Margaret Loo remembers that when she ventured near the kitchen the servants would chase her out. She learned to cook when she came to America in 1950. Today, she has six children, nine grandchildren, and two great-grandchildren, and cooking huge meals is routine.

4 squares firm tofu (about 14 ounces), rinsed
½ teaspoon salt
4 ounces ground pork (about ½ cup)
1½ teaspoons cornstarch
1½ teaspoons soy sauce
2 tablespoons vegetable oil
2 tablespoons minced garlic
4 button mushrooms, thinly sliced
⅔ cup Homemade Chicken Broth (page 195)
2 tablespoons oyster sauce
1 tablespoon chopped cilantro

1. Cut each tofu square in half. Cut each half into 4 equal pieces. Put the tofu on several sheets of paper towels. Sprinkle the salt evenly over the tofu and set aside. In a small bowl combine the ground pork, 1 teaspoon of the cornstarch, and the soy sauce. In a separate small bowl combine the remaining ½ teaspoon cornstarch with 1 tablespoon cold water.

2. Heat a 14-inch flat-bottomed wok over high heat until a bead of water vaporizes within 1 to 2 seconds of contact. Swirl in 1 tablespoon of the oil and add the tofu. Reduce the heat to medium and pan-fry the tofu 2 to 3 minutes on each side until light golden. Transfer to a plate.

3. Increase the heat to high and swirl the remaining 1 tablespoon of oil into the wok. Add the garlic and the pork mixture, breaking it up with a metal spatula. Stir-fry 1 minute or until the pork is no longer pink. Add the mushrooms and stir-fry 1 minute. Add the tofu and stir-fry 30 seconds. Swirl in the broth and oyster sauce, and bring to a boil over high heat. Cover and cook 2 minutes. Stir the cornstarch mixture, swirl it into the wok, and bring to a boil, stirring, 30 seconds or until the sauce is slightly thickened. Sprinkle on the cilantro. *Serves 4 as part of a multicourse meal.*

Uncle Lang's Three Teacup Chicken

I was charmed when my uncle brought a small Chinese teacup to measure the soy sauce, vinegar, and sugar for this recipe. He typically browns a whole chicken in the wok, which requires skill to do. I prefer to use split chicken breasts or whole legs. If using the Sichuan peppercorns, they must be dry-roasted in a wok for a few minutes to bring out their flavor and then finely crushed before being cooked.

3 whole star anise
¼ cup soy sauce
¼ cup rice vinegar
¼ cup sugar
2 tablespoons Shao Hsing rice wine or dry sherry
½ teaspoon vegetable oil
4 small chicken breast halves on the bone or
    4 whole legs (about 2 pounds)
3 medium garlic cloves, smashed
6 slices ginger
1 teaspoon roasted and ground Sichuan
    peppercorns (optional; see page 9)
½ cup Homemade Chicken Broth (page 195)

1. In a medium bowl combine the star anise, soy sauce, vinegar, sugar, and rice wine. Set aside.

2. Heat a 14-inch flat-bottomed wok over high heat until a bead of water vaporizes within 1 to 2 seconds of contact. Swirl in the oil and carefully add the chicken skin side down, spreading it evenly in the wok. Cook undisturbed 3 to 4 minutes, adjusting the heat between medium and medium-high to let the chicken brown.

3. Add the garlic and ginger. Then, using a metal spatula, turn the chicken over, and pan-fry 3 to 4 minutes or until the chicken is browned but not cooked through. Sprinkle on the ground peppercorns. Stir the soy sauce mixture, and swirl it into wok. Turn the chicken over. It should be golden brown. Swirl the broth into the wok, cover, reduce the heat to low, and cook 5 minutes for the breast and 8 minutes for the legs. Turn the chicken and cook 5 to 8 minutes or until the juices run clear when the chicken is pierced, the chicken is cooked through, and the sauce is reduced. *Serves 4 as part of a multicourse meal.*

Uncle Lang's Three Teacup Chicken

One-Wok Curry Chicken

A high-quality curry is key to this recipe's success. I prefer curry paste, which I think has greater depth of flavor than curry powder. Be sure to stir the coconut milk in the can; the cream always floats to the top.

½ teaspoon vegetable oil
One 3½-pound chicken, cut up
1 cup thinly sliced shallots
3 tablespoons yellow curry paste or
    1 tablespoon curry powder
½ cup canned unsweetened coconut milk
¾ cup Homemade Chicken Broth (page 195)
2 all-purpose potatoes, peeled, quartered, and
    cut into 1/4-inch-thick slices
1 green bell pepper, cut into ¼-inch-wide strips
1 teaspoon salt
¼ teaspoon ground white pepper

1. Heat a 14-inch flat-bottomed wok over high heat until a bead of water vaporizes within 1 to 2 seconds of contact. Swirl in the oil and add the chicken pieces skin side down, spreading them in the wok. Cook undisturbed 3 to 4 minutes, adjusting the heat between medium and medium-high as the chicken browns. Then, using a metal spatula, turn the chicken over and pan-fry 3 to 4 minutes or until the chicken is browned on the other side but not cooked through. Remove to a plate, leaving the pan drippings.

2. Add the shallots to the pan drippings, and cook over medium heat 2 to 3 minutes or until just softened. Add the curry paste or powder and cook, stirring, 30 seconds or until fragrant. (With curry paste, the drippings may spatter a little; with curry powder, the ingredients become dry and the pan may begin to smoke.)

3. Return the chicken to the wok and stir until well combined with the shallots. Add the coconut milk and broth and bring to a boil over high heat, uncovered. Add the potatoes, bell pepper, salt, and pepper and stir to combine. Cover, reduce the heat

to medium-low, and simmer 15 minutes. Turn the chicken and simmer 15 minutes or until the chicken is cooked through and the potatoes are tender. *Serves 4 as part of a multicourse meal.*

Danny Chan's Ginger and Scallion Crabs

Chef Danny Chan says that high heat and a short cooking time bring out the sweetness in crabs. He prefers blue crabs, but any kind of crab can be substituted— adjust cooking time by the size of the crabs.

4 live blue crabs (about 2 pounds)
1 tablespoon vegetable oil
1 large walnut-sized knob of ginger, smashed
2 scallions, cut into 2-inch pieces
1 cup Homemade Chicken Broth (page 195)
2 teaspoons soy sauce
1 teaspoon sesame oil
½ teaspoon salt
½ teaspoon ground white pepper
Cilantro sprigs, optional

1. Put the crabs in a paper bag and put the bag in the freezer for about 1 hour or until the crabs are no longer moving. Put each crab shell side down on a cutting board and twist off the apron. Pull off the hard shell and remove the spongy gills on both sides. Cut the small legs off with a cleaver and discard. Cut each crab in half. Put in a colander and rinse under cold water. Shake off excess water.

2. Heat a 14-inch flat-bottomed wok over high heat until a bead of water vaporizes within 1 to 2 seconds of contact. Swirl in the vegetable oil, add the ginger and the white part of the scallions only, and stir-fry 10 seconds or until fragrant. Add the crabs and stir-fry 20 seconds. Add the broth and immediately cover. Cook over high heat 5 minutes. Add the soy sauce, sesame oil, salt, pepper, and the scallion greens, stirring to combine. Cook, stirring, 30 seconds or until the crabs are just cooked through. Garnish with cilantro sprigs, if desired. *Serves 4 as part of a multicourse meal.*

Uncle Lang's Oyster Sauce Mushrooms

Uncle Lang uses dried shiitake mushrooms with thick caps about 3 inches in diameter for this braise. The thicker caps are more expensive but they are also meatier, absorbing the rich, concentrated flavors of the oyster sauce. The soaking time for thicker mushrooms is 3 to 4 hours. It helps to turn them occasionally, thus ensuring that the mushroom caps completely soften. For thinner caps soak no more than 30 minutes.

16 dried shiitake mushrooms with thick caps
½ teaspoon sugar
1 tablespoon vegetable oil
3 tablespoons chopped garlic
2 tablespoons oyster sauce
½ cup Homemade Chicken Broth (page 195)
½ teaspoon sesame oil

1. In a shallow medium bowl soak the mushrooms in 1½ cups cold water and ¼ teaspoon of the sugar 3 to 4 hours or until softened. Drain and squeeze dry, reserving the soaking liquid. Cut off the stems, leaving the caps whole.

2. Heat a 14-inch flat-bottomed wok over high heat until a bead of water vaporizes within 1 to 2 seconds of contact. Swirl in the vegetable oil, add the garlic, and stir-fry 15 seconds until it begins to brown. Add the mushroom caps and oyster sauce and stir-fry 1 minute. Add ¼ cup reserved mushroom liquid, the broth, and remaining ¼ teaspoon sugar, and bring to a boil over high heat. Cover, reduce the heat to medium-low, and simmer until the sauce is slightly thickened and clings to the mushrooms, about 30 minutes. (Check occasionally to make sure there is just enough liquid to simmer the mushrooms. Add up to ¼ cup water if necessary.) Transfer to a platter and drizzle on the sesame oil. *Serves 4 as part of a multicourse meal.*

Virginia Yee's Beef Short Ribs with Scallions

Virginia Yee's Beef Short Ribs with Scallions

This is a filling wintertime dish. Virginia Yee either pan-fries or deep-fries these beef short ribs and scallions before braising them. The short ribs are tender and the sauce is fragrant and rich. Choose short ribs that are well trimmed, or they will release too much fat during the pan-frying and cause spattering.

6 lean beef short ribs (about 3 pounds)
20 scallions, roots trimmed
1 tablespoon vegetable oil
¼ cup Shao Hsing rice wine or dry sherry
¼ cup soy sauce
2 tablespoons sugar

1. Rinse the short ribs in cold water, set on paper towels, and pat dry. The ribs must be bone-dry before pan-frying. Dry the scallions with paper towels until bone-dry.

2. Heat a 14-inch flat-bottomed wok over high heat until a bead of water vaporizes within 1 to 2 seconds of contact. Swirl in the oil, add the scallions, and pan-fry until wilted and brown, 3 to 5 minutes, continually turning with bamboo chopsticks or tongs. The scallions should be as dark as possible without being burned. Transfer to a plate and pour off the oil from the wok.

3. Add the short ribs to the wok (no additional oil is necessary, as the short ribs will release fat) and pan-fry over medium to medium-high heat until well browned on all sides, 7 to 10 minutes. Pour off any excess fat. Swirl in the rice wine, soy sauce, sugar, and cooked scallions with 2 cups cold water and bring to a boil over high heat. Cover, reduce the heat to medium, and cook at a medium simmer 2 hours, turning the ribs from time to time until tender. For the last 10 minutes, increase the heat to medium-high, remove the cover, and cook until the sauce is reduced to about ¾ cup. Transfer the ribs and the scallions to a platter. Skim the fat from the sauce and serve with the ribs. *Serves 4 as part of a multicourse meal.*

Walter Kei's Sweet and Sour Spareribs

Walter Kei of Hong Kong likes to flour these spareribs and then deep-fry them, but I prefer pan-frying and then braising them. Kei finishes the sauce with lime juice and butter; this twist reflects the innovative style of Hong Kong cooks.

1 teaspoon salt
½ teaspoon sugar
1 teaspoon cornstarch
1 teaspoon Shao Hsing rice wine or dry sherry
½ teaspoon soy sauce
½ teaspoon plus 1 tablespoon olive oil
1½ pounds lean baby back pork spareribs, cut
    into single ribs
⅓ cup packed dark brown sugar
⅓ cup Chinkiang or balsamic vinegar
1 teaspoon unsalted butter
½ teaspoon lime juice
1 teaspoon lime zest, optional

1. In a large bowl combine ½ teaspoon of the salt, the sugar, cornstarch, rice wine, soy sauce, and the ½ teaspoon oil. Add the spareribs and combine. Marinate 1 hour. Pat dry completely with paper towels.

2. Heat a 14-inch flat-bottomed wok over high heat until a bead of water vaporizes within 1 to 2 seconds of contact. Swirl in the remaining 1 tablespoon oil and add the spareribs meat side down, spreading them in the wok. Reduce the heat to medium and pan-fry undisturbed 5 minutes, letting the spareribs brown. Then, using a spatula, turn the spareribs over and pan-fry an additional 2 minutes.

3. Add the brown sugar, vinegar, and the remaining ½ teaspoon salt with ⅓ cup water to the wok and bring to a boil over medium-high heat. Turn the ribs meat side down. Cover, reduce the heat to low, and simmer 1 to 1½ hours, until the meat is tender. Add the butter and lime juice and stir to combine. Garnish with lime zest if desired. *Serves 4 as part of a multicourse meal.*

Martin Yan's Mandarin Five-Flavored Boneless Pork Chops

Chef Martin Yan uses the blunt side of his cleaver to lightly pound the pork to tenderize the meat. With effortless precision he then finely minces and chops the aromatics and vegetables.

2 tablespoons soy sauce
2 tablespoons dry sherry
2 teaspoons cornstarch
¼ teaspoon Chinese five-spice powder
Four ½-inch-thick boneless pork chops
    (about 1 pound)
1 tablespoon vegetable oil
1 teaspoon minced ginger
1 teaspoon minced garlic
¼ cup chopped celery
¼ cup chopped onions
1 fresh red Thai chili, minced (about ½ teaspoon)

1. In a shallow bowl combine the soy sauce, sherry, cornstarch, and five-spice powder. Put the pork on a cutting board. Using the blunt side of a cleaver blade or a meat pounder, lightly pound the pork in a crisscross pattern. Turn the pork over and repeat. Add the pork to the marinade, coating both sides well. Marinate 30 minutes. Shake the marinade off the pork and put on a plate. Gently pat the pork with paper towels. Add ½ cup cold water to the marinade and set aside.

2. Heat a 14-inch flat-bottomed wok over high heat until a bead of water vaporizes within 1 to 2 seconds of contact. Swirl in the oil, carefully add the pork, and sear 1 minute on each side. Add the ginger, garlic, celery, onions, and chili and cook, stirring, for 15 seconds. Stir the marinade, swirl it into the wok, and bring to a boil. Cover, reduce the heat to low, and simmer 30 minutes or until fork tender, turning the pork over midway through cooking. Check the pork as it cooks, adding 2 to 3 tablespoons more water if the sauce is thick. *Serves 4 as part of a multicourse meal.*

Amy Tan *and the New Year's Dumplings*

譚家餃子聚會

I could hardly believe my good fortune when novelist Amy Tan invited me to join her and her three eldest sisters and their husbands for a *jiao-zi* party. I have always loved *jiao-zi*, the revered northern Chinese dumplings. Even though my family is Cantonese, *jiao-zi* is a favorite food, but we never prepared them at home. I had been to a *jiao-zi* party only once in my life—in Beijing, where such parties are famous. I don't know which prospect excited me more, learning how to make *jiao-zi* from experienced cooks or meeting Amy Tan and her family.

"I have to warn you that no one makes *jiao-zi* like my mother," Tan confides to me as we make our way down hectic Mott Street in New York's Chinatown, shopping for ingredients. Tan vividly remembers her mother's extraordinary *jiao-zi*, made for birthdays, Thanksgivings, Christmases, and, as is the tradition in northern China, for New Year's. Tan tells me that when her brother was in a coma her mother brought him *jiao-zi*. "It was his favorite food. If anything could tempt him into consciousness, surely it would be my mother's delicious dumplings. Even after he died, she brought *jiao-zi* as a spiritual food offering to his graveside."

Tan's family gathers in the eclectic kitchen of her New York apartment. I soon realize this gathering is not only a familial but a culinary reunion. "The art of making *jiao-zi* is achieving the right balance of filling to dough," explains Tan. "My mother's primary complaint about other people's *jiao-zi* was that the dough was either too thick or so thin that it developed holes and the filling leaked out. Likewise, the filling had to stay moist through cooking but not so moist that it caused the skins to fall apart."

Watching Tan's sisters form *jiao-zi*, it is evident the process is a seamless dance. Though the sisters are rarely able to meet (they live in China and America), their *jiao-zi* making has the appearance of an experienced assembly line production. Second-eldest sister Jin Do cuts a slender rope of dough into small rounds at precisely one-inch intervals. With seemingly one motion third sister Lijun transforms all of the baby cylinders into rounds, then pats them lightly into plump discs. Once they are dusted with flour they look like delicate confections. Using a doll-size rolling pin, eldest sister Yuhang makes quick back-and-forth rolling motions over the edges of each small round, using the slightest force of her palm while simultaneously rotating the round of dough with the other hand. She barely touches the tiny center of the dough so that it remains slightly thicker than the edges.

I marvel at the speed with which the family works, husbands and wives together. They are the *jiao-zi* magicians. Jin Do tells me she can make two hundred *jiao-zi* in an hour. With a round of dough in her left palm, she uses chopsticks in her right to expertly place a perfect dollop of the pork and cabbage filling in the dough's center. Then she folds the dough over the pork filling and presses in the center to seal. She applies a few tiny pleats to the left and right, presses both thumbs down to seal the dumplings, and finishes with hands folded, as if in prayer. The hands of all the sisters are so agile and quiet. Their chatter involves critiquing each other's wrapping technique and constant teasing over how *jiao-zi* should be correctly made. Tan says the family *jiao-zi* arguments are legendary.

Soon a large platter is filled with the delicate dumplings, lined in formation all facing the same direction, and equally spaced from each other, so orderly and serene. Before I can admire them an extra second, Tan's brother-in-law Yan Zheng whisks the platter away and begins cooking. He uses two woks—one filled with boiling water for the *jiao-zi*, the other for pan-frying them for *kuo tieh*, or

Amy Tan's sister Yuhang (left) instructs Amy on her favorite technique for folding jiao zi.

potstickers. He tells me that in China a large wok is essential for parties because each guest will easily eat twenty to thirty dumplings. For frying the *kuo tieh* he uses my flat-bottomed carbon-steel wok. In northern China a two-inch high flat-bottomed wok (like a sauté pan), called a *bing guo*, is used.

Within a short time, Yan Zheng proudly brings the first hot steaming bowls of dumplings and a platter of fried potstickers to the table. Everyone pauses to eat, dipping the dumplings into Jin Do's delicious tangy ginger sauce, while drinking chilled beer or wine. The combination is so satisfying. The dumplings are heavenly. The juicy, delectable filling, a balance of ground pork and cabbage encased in delicate dough, is perfectly cooked.

No sooner are the plates emptied than everyone returns to their dumpling tasks. And so it continues, weaving back and forth between wrapping dumplings, eating, and conversing. Through the course of the evening, the sisters reminisce about Lunar New Year's Eve parties where *jiao-zi*, a symbol of wealth because their crescent shape resembles ancient silver ingots, were eaten after the main meal from midnight until two A.M. "As the *jiao-zi* boiled it was important not to remove the lid too soon," says Lijun. "If you did, it could mean that you'd lose your fortune in the coming year. Sometimes we would put a coin inside one dumpling for luck. On New Year's morning, it was customary not to cook but we were always happy

to eat leftover warmed *jiao-zi*," recalls Lijun fondly.

The sisters remember another *jiao-zi* party during Tan's first visit to Beijing in 1987 with her husband, Lou, and her mother. The *jiao-zi* did not measure up to their mother's standards. "My mother felt my sisters' dough was too thick. The filling had too much cabbage or something that made it too watery—this is distinct from juicy. Oh, how I miss her commentary on making *jiao-zi*. It forever made me unable to even attempt to make one by myself," says Tan.

Tan candidly admits cooking is not her forte. She says that her mother would always allow the children to roll out a few *jiao-zi* but they were "never as perfect as our mother's dumplings," recalls Tan. "According to my mother, each *jiao-zi* should stand upright, a little like a miniature sofa, ever so slightly curved and, of course, look identical one to the other. She accused my dumplings of having the shape of a ghost," says Tan.

As the last scrumptious dumplings are eaten, everyone ladles the hot *jiao-zi* cooking liquid into their bowls. It is customary to drink the delicious broth, flavored by the dumplings, as a digestive. The next *jiao-zi* gathering, Tan tells me, will be on the anniversary of her mother's death. "The idea is to make *jiao-zi* and then complain as we eat them that they are not nearly as good as Mom would have made—thereby letting our mother know how much we miss her and that she is irreplaceable."

Far left: Yuhang uses chopsticks to place the pork filling on a dough round. Left: Lijun holds a platter of steaming jiao-zi. Opposite: Amy, Jin Do, and Lijun; the sisters form an assembly line, each performing a different task.

Boiling *and* Poaching

Amy Tan's Family's Jiao-zi

The key to making jiao-zi, *pork-filled dumplings, is to form a party like Amy Tan's family so that there are plenty of people to share the fun and work. The rounds of dough are easier to roll with a small 11-inch rolling pin. When stirring the pork mixture or adding the* jiao-zi *to the boiling water, many cooks believe you must stir in one direction only. If you are serving only* jiao-zi, *make two separate batches of this recipe.*

2 cups all-purpose flour, plus additional
    for kneading
8 ounces Napa cabbage (8 to 10 leaves)
3 teaspoons salt
1 teaspoon sugar
8 ounces ground pork (about 1 cup)
1 tablespoon minced ginger
2 teaspoons soy sauce
1 teaspoon Shao Hsing rice wine or dry sherry
1 teaspoon oyster sauce (optional)
Jin Do's Tangy Ginger Sauce (opposite)

1. Put the 2 cups flour in a medium bowl and make a well. Pour ¾ cup cold water into the well and stir until the mixture begins to pull away from the sides of the bowl. Turn onto a work surface lightly dusted with flour, and knead with lightly floured hands 5 minutes, adding more flour if necessary, until smooth. Cover with a slightly damp cloth and allow to rest 30 minutes.

2. Trim ¼ inch from the stem end of the cabbage leaves. Stack a few leaves at a time and cut crosswise into ¼-inch-wide shreds, then finely chop. In a medium bowl combine the cabbage, 1 teaspoon of the salt, and the sugar. In another medium bowl combine the pork, ginger, soy sauce, rice wine, and oyster sauce. Add the cabbage and stir until well combined. Cover and refrigerate.

3. After the dough has rested, knead it on a lightly floured surface until elastic and smooth, 2 minutes. Roll the dough into an even rope about 15 inches long. Cut the rope into ½-inch pieces to make 30 pieces. Roll each piece into a 1-inch ball. Pat the balls into plump 2-inch discs, lightly dusting them with flour. Cover all unused dough with a slightly damp cloth. Using a floured rolling pin, roll back and forth over the edges of each disc, making the center slightly thicker and the edges thinner. The rounds will be about 3½ inches in diameter.

4. Put 1 level tablespoon of the filling in the center of each round. Fold the round in half to form a half moon. Pinch one end of the half moon together. Starting at this end, use your thumb and index finger to make a pleat in the top piece of the dough, and press it firmly into the bottom piece of the dough. Continue making 3 or 4 more pleats until the dumpling is completely closed. Stand each dumpling with the rounded edge upright and put on a tray lightly dusted with flour.

Recipes to Celebrate the New Year

Only in northern China are *jiao-zi* served in the hours between the old and new year, portending the wish for a prosperous year. Throughout China, the Lunar New Year's Eve dinner is the most important meal of the year, symbolizing thanksgiving and family unity. The menu is carefully planned to include dishes that all augur good fortune: spring rolls to signify renewal; whole chicken to ensure the year will have a proper beginning and end; lettuce to represent growth (and because the Cantonese word for lettuce,

5. In a 14-inch flat-bottomed wok, bring 3 quarts of water to a boil, covered, over high heat. Once the water comes to a boil, add the remaining 2 teaspoons salt and half the *jiao-zi*, and return to a boil over high heat, stirring gently with a wooden spoon. Add 1 cup cold water and return to a boil. Boil about 5 minutes or until the pork is no longer pink and is cooked through. Remove the *jiao-zi* with a slotted spoon and divide among soup bowls. Cook the remaining *jiao-zi* in the same manner. Serve with Jin Do's Tangy Ginger Sauce. After the *jiao-zi* are eaten, ladle the hot *jiao-zi* liquid into the bowls. *Makes 30 dumplings; serves 4 as part of a multicourse meal.*

Jin Do's Tangy Ginger Sauce

Amy Tan's sister Jin Do has been known to make a gallon of this delicious sauce. Mincing the ginger releases more ginger flavor, but traditionally the ginger is finely shredded. At first the flavor of ginger is mild,

but it intensifies as it sits. I like to prepare the sauce a day before I plan to make jiao-zi.

3 tablespoons finely minced ginger
1/3 cup Chinkiang or balsamic vinegar
1/4 cup soy sauce
3 tablespoons sugar

In a small bowl combine the ginger, vinegar, soy sauce, and sugar. Keeps covered in the refrigerator up to 5 days. *Makes about 3/4 cup.*

Homemade Chicken Broth

This broth can be made in a well-seasoned 14-inch flat-bottomed wok with a tight-fitting lid. Otherwise, use a 4-quart pot. I am a firm believer that homemade chicken broth greatly enhances the flavor of dishes. I freeze my broth in 1-pint containers so that I always have some on hand.

One 4-pound chicken
2 teaspoons salt
Two 1/2-inch-thick slices ginger

Remove any fat pockets from the chicken and rub the chicken all over with salt. Remove as much skin as possible and rinse the chicken under cold water. Put the chicken in a 14-inch flat-bottomed wok or a 4-quart pot. Add 2½ quarts cold water, then turn on the heat to medium-high. As the water heats, skim the scum that rises to the surface, adjusting the heat so the broth never boils; skim until most of the scum has been removed. Add the ginger and bring to a boil over high heat. Cover, reduce the heat to low, and simmer 3 hours. Allow the broth to cool and then strain, discarding the chicken and ginger; cover the broth and refrigerate. The next day, using a spoon, remove the hardened fat on top. *Makes about 2 quarts.*

saang, sounds like "plentiful wealth"); shrimp to bring laughter and joy; oysters to bring good business; noodles to represent longevity; clams and scallops (which are shaped similarly to Chinese coins) to usher in good fortune; something sweet and sour to portend the wish for offspring (the Cantonese word for sour, *syun*, sounds like "grandchild"); and whole fish to signify abundance.

In the Essentials section there is a selection of New Year's menus (see page 218). Other appropriate dishes to eat for the New Year's dinner are in the Index listed under New Year's Celebrations.

Bernadette Chan's New Year's Poached Fish

Bernadette Chan's method for poaching fish is so simple. The fish is totally submerged in a wok with boiling water and cooks off heat. Poached fish is a popular dish to serve for the Lunar New Year.

One 1½- to 2-pound rock cod or carp, cleaned
        and gutted, with head and tail intact
1½ teaspoons salt
2 scallions plus ¼ cup finely shredded scallions
Two ½-inch-thick slices ginger, smashed,
        plus 1/4 cup finely shredded ginger
½ cup cilantro sprigs
2 tablespoons soy sauce
2 tablespoons vegetable oil

1. Thoroughly rinse the fish in cold water and drain. Gently rub the cavity and outside of the fish with the salt and rinse again. Bring a kettle of water to a boil.

2. Fill a 14-inch flat-bottomed wok halfway with water. Add the whole scallions and sliced ginger and bring to a boil over high heat. When the water is at a rolling boil, carefully add the fish. If the fish isn't entirely submerged, add additional boiling water. Cover and immediately turn off the heat. Allow to stand 15 minutes. Test the fish for doneness by poking the thickest part with a chopstick; the fish should flake. If not, return the water to a boil over high heat and cook, covered, 1 to 2 minutes more or until the fish just flakes. Carefully pour off the water from the wok. Gently slide the fish onto a warmed platter and pour off any water. Discard the scallions and ginger. Rinse the wok and dry it thoroughly.

3. Sprinkle the shredded ginger and scallions and the cilantro over the fish. Drizzle on the soy sauce. Heat the oil in the wok over high heat until hot but not smoking. Carefully pour the hot oil over the fish. The oil will make a crackling sound as it hits the fish. *Serves 4 as part of a multicourse meal.*

Walter Kei's Roasted Sesame Spinach

When Walter Kei taught me this recipe, he used a bunch of young spinach that he trimmed to a perfect 5-inch block. The presentation was spectacular. I have seldom found such small bunches. With bigger bunches, I cut the spinach into three 4-inch sections; and, if I am not serving guests, I trim only the stem end.

1 pound spinach
1 teaspoon white sesame seeds
1 tablespoon Shao Hsing rice wine or dry sherry
1 tablespoon soy sauce
1 tablespoon sesame oil

1. In a 14-inch flat-bottomed wok bring 1½ quarts water to a boil over high heat and add the spinach. Blanch until it is just limp, about 30 seconds. Drain in a colander and rinse under cold water. Rinse the wok and dry it thoroughly. Gather the spinach by the stem end. Squeeze or wring the spinach with both hands to remove excess water. The spinach should be quite dry. Put the spinach on a cutting board and cut off about ½ inch from the stem end. For a fancier presentation also cut off about ½ inch from the leaf end, leaving a block of spinach. Transfer to a platter.

2. Heat the wok over medium heat 5 to 10 seconds. Add the sesame seeds and roast in the dry wok, shaking the pan until the seeds start to pop and become light golden, about 30 to 40 seconds. Remove from the heat. In a small bowl combine the rice wine, soy sauce, and sesame oil. Drizzle over the spinach. Sprinkle on the roasted sesame seeds. *Serves 4 as part of a multicourse meal.*

Walter Kei's Roasted Sesame Spinach

Steaming

In China large woks are filled with water and fitted with round wooden covers. Stacks of covered bamboo steamers are positioned over openings to capture the escaping steam.

In ancient China, the wok was primarily used for steaming, boiling, poaching, braising, pan-frying, and even drying grains and tea leaves. Chinese scholars continue to debate whether stir-frying was developed as early as the Han dynasty (206 B.C.–A.D.220) or as late as the Ming dynasty (1368–A.D.1644). However, there is no doubt that steaming in a wok is an ancient Chinese cooking technique. The popularity of steaming is due in part to the invention of the wooden steamer and bamboo steamer insert prior to the Sung dynasty (960–A.D.1279). Today, steaming in a wok remains a vital and effective wok cooking technique.

Steaming in a Wok

• The best wok for steaming on any residential range is a well-seasoned 14-inch flat-bottomed carbon-steel wok. If you are using a round-bottomed wok, be sure that it is securely set on a wok ring or stand.

• If the wok is newly seasoned, do not use it for steaming, as the water will strip the seasoning. If you do not have a well-seasoned wok, either keep a wok just for steaming, or use a stainless-steel wok.

• There are two methods for setting up a wok for steaming (see below). Whichever you use, always bring the water in the wok to a boil first. Food should never be added to a steamer when the water is cold. Then carefully place the bamboo steamer in the wok or the plate of food to be steamed onto a steamer rack.

• Make sure the food to be steamed sits above the water. If the boiling water spills onto the food as it steams, there is too much water in the wok.

• Monitor the water level in the wok from time to time as you steam to ensure that the water does not evaporate. I keep a kettle of boiling water ready to replenish the wok as necessary.

• Turn off the heat before removing steamed food, and remove the lid with care, to prevent steam burns.

Method 1 The advantage of using a bamboo steamer set over a wok is that unlike a metal lid that drips condensed water back onto the food, the bamboo lid absorbs excess moisture. Be sure the lid is tight fitting. Bamboo steamers come in several sizes and can be stacked. The best all-purpose size is a 12-inch steamer for a 14-inch wok. Add water to the wok to a depth of ¾ inch, but do not allow the bamboo slats of the steamer to touch the water. Bring the water to a boil. Put the covered steamer containing the food to be steamed in the wok. When lined with Napa cabbage or cheesecloth, bamboo steamers are excellent for cooking dumplings directly on the slats. Soak new steamers in cold water for several hours before using. Wash bamboo steamers with hot water and a sponge, never using detergent. Air-dry before storing.

Method 2 This method is for steaming fish, poultry, meat, or vegetables on a plate as opposed to using a bamboo steamer. Use a heatproof plate or heatproof shallow bowl that is smaller than the wok so that there is room to grasp the dish with pot holders. There are also special plate-lifters for removing the dish from the wok. Add water to the wok to a depth of ¾ inch. Put a 1-inch-high steamer rack, cake rack, metal trivet, double-boiler disc, or an empty clean tuna fish can with both ends removed in the wok so it reaches above the water level. Bring the water to a boil. Carefully put the plate containing the food to be cooked on the rack and cover with a tight-fitting domed lid (see page 41).

Nevin Lim's Luffa with Gold and Silver Garlic

According to Nevin Lim, the Cantonese describe garlic that has been stir-fried as "gold," and when it has been steamed it becomes "silver." If luffa squash (see page 222) is not available, Lim uses cucumber, which requires a few more minutes of steaming.

10 ounces luffa or cucumber
¼ cup Homemade Chicken Broth (page 195)
¼ teaspoon salt
⅛ teaspoon sugar
Pinch of ground white pepper
2 tablespoons minced garlic
2 tablespoons corn oil

1. With a vegetable peeler, peel only the ridges on the luffa (or cucumber), leaving strips of green skin. If the skin appears to be tough, peel all the skin. Cut the luffa in half lengthwise. Cut on the diagonal into scant ½-inch-thick slices.

2. In a small saucepan bring the broth to a boil over high heat. Cook 2 to 3 minutes or until the broth is reduced to 2 tablespoons. Monitor the broth carefully so that it does not totally evaporate.

3. Put the luffa in a 9-inch shallow heatproof bowl. Sprinkle with the salt, sugar, and pepper. Stir in the reduced broth. Sprinkle with 1 tablespoon of the garlic. Put a 1-inch-high steamer rack in a 14-inch flat-bottomed wok. Add water to a depth of ¾ inch and bring to a boil over high heat. Carefully put the bowl on the rack, cover, and steam over high heat 5 to 7 minutes or until the luffa is just tender when pierced with a knife. Be sure to check the water level from time to time and replenish, if necessary, with boiling water. Carefully remove the bowl from the wok and set aside. Pour out the water from the wok and dry the pan.

4. Heat the wok over high heat until a bead of water vaporizes within 1 to 2 seconds of contact. Swirl in 1 tablespoon of the oil. Turn off the heat and add the remaining tablespoon of garlic. Stir-fry 1 minute off the heat. Add the remaining 1 tablespoon of oil and increase the heat to high. Stir-fry 30 seconds or until golden brown. Carefully drizzle the hot garlic and oil over the cooked luffa. The oil will make a crackling sound as it hits the vegetable. *Serves 4 as part of a multicourse meal.*

Winnie Hon's Silken Tofu with XO Sauce

I keep a jar of XO sauce as a staple so that I can make this recipe anytime. XO sauce is made by several Chinese condiment companies, but I prefer the version made by Winnie Hon, a gifted home cook.

One 1-pound block silken tofu, rinsed
3 tablespoons XO sauce (page 214)
    or store-bought
1 tablespoon soy sauce
3 tablespoons minced scallions
Pinch of sugar
2 tablespoons canola oil

1. Put the tofu block in a shallow heatproof bowl. Put a 1-inch-high steamer rack in a 14-inch flat-bottomed wok. Add water to a depth of ¾ inch and bring to a boil over high heat. Carefully put the bowl on the rack, cover, reduce the heat to medium, and steam 16 to 20 minutes or until the tofu is hot. Be sure to check the water level from time to time and replenish, if necessary, with boiling water. Carefully remove the bowl from the wok. Holding the bowl with pot holders, pour off any excess liquid, using a spatula to prevent the tofu from sliding out of the bowl. Pour out the water from the wok and dry the pan.

2. Top the tofu in the bowl with the XO sauce. Pour the soy sauce over the tofu and sprinkle with the scallions and sugar. Heat the wok over high heat with the oil until hot but not smoking. Carefully pour the hot oil over the tofu. The hot oil will make a crackling sound as it hits the tofu. *Serves 4 as part of a multicourse meal.*

Ray Lee's Cantonese Steamed Chicken

Ray Lee prepares this chicken by chopping through the bone, creating bite-sized pieces. I prefer to steam whole chicken legs, then bone the chicken before slicing it. When shopping for the two types of wet bean curd (see page 228), ask for them by their Cantonese names: baag fu yu and naam yu. Tangerine peel (see page 226) is available in Asian markets.

2 teaspoons minced garlic
1½ teaspoons minced ginger
1 teaspoon Shao Hsing rice wine or dry sherry
1 teaspoon black soy sauce
2 teaspoons vegetable oil
2 teaspoons cornstarch
2 whole chicken legs (about 1½ pounds)
One 1-inch-square piece dried tangerine peel
2 cubes white wet bean curd (about 1 tablespoon)
½ teaspoon red wet bean curd
¼ teaspoon salt

1. In a 9-inch shallow heatproof bowl combine the garlic, ginger, rice wine, soy sauce, oil, and cornstarch. Add the chicken to the marinade, coating both sides well and set aside. In a small bowl soak the tangerine peel in ¼ cup cold water 30 minutes. Drain and finely shred the peel to make about 1 teaspoon. Set aside. In a small bowl combine the white and red wet bean curd with 2 teaspoons cold water. Sprinkle the chicken with the salt. Spread the bean curd paste over the chicken. Sprinkle on the shredded peel.

2. Put a 1-inch-high steamer rack in a 14-inch flat-bottomed wok. Add water to a depth of ¾ inch and bring to a boil over high heat. Carefully put the bowl on the rack, cover, and steam over high heat 20 to 25 minutes or until a meat thermometer registers 170°F when inserted at the meatiest point of the thigh but not touching the bone. Be sure to check the water level from time to time and replenish, if necessary, with boiling water. Carefully remove the bowl from the steamer. *Serves 4 as part of a multicourse meal.*

Danny Chan's Steamed Salmon with Lemon

Chinese cooks traditionally steam fish with ginger and scallions, which are said to mollify the flavor of the fish. Chef Danny Chan's innovative twist is the addition of refreshing lemon. When Chef Chan steams shrimp, scallops, and lobster he uses the same method but omits the soy sauce.

One 1-pound salmon fillet
1 tablespoon soy sauce
¼ teaspoon salt
⅛ teaspoon ground white pepper
2 scallions, cut into 4-inch pieces
4 slices ginger
1 lemon
2 teaspoons sesame oil

1. Thoroughly rinse the fish in cold water and pat dry. Put the fillets in a 9-inch shallow heatproof bowl. Drizzle the soy sauce, salt, and pepper over the salmon. Sprinkle with the scallions and ginger. Cut the lemon in half crosswise. Cut half a lemon into 4 slices and put on the fish. Juice the remaining lemon and drizzle over the fish.

2. Put a 1-inch-high steamer rack in a 14-inch flat-bottomed wok. Add water to a depth of ¾ inch and bring to a boil over high heat. Carefully put the bowl on the rack, cover, and steam 8 to 10 minutes. Test the fish for doneness by poking the thickest part with a chopstick or fork; the fish should flake. If not, steam 1 to 2 minutes or until the fish just flakes. Be sure to check the water level from time to time and replenish, if necessary, with boiling water. Carefully remove the bowl from the wok. Drizzle the sesame oil over the fillets. *Serves 4 as part of a multicourse meal.*

A small serving of Ray Lee's Cantonese Steamed Chicken

The Dim Sum Academy

At The Peninsula Hong Kong I spent two days at its special Peninsula Academy Culinary Experience. Accompanied by Chef Paray Li, I visited Graham Street to see one of Hong Kong's traditional wet markets (fresh-food markets) and shopped at the Chan Chi Kee Cutlery Company, in Kowloon, known for its fine hand-hammered carbon-steel woks. The highlight of my visit was attending a private dim sum master class conducted by Chef Yip Wing Wah of the Spring Moon restaurant. Acknowledged as one of the great dim sum masters, Chef Yip is famous for his artistic and extensive repertoire.

Dim sum literally means "a dot on the heart," or the eating of little delicacies to touch the heart. A Cantonese teahouse tradition, it is an early morning or afternoon meal composed of steamed and fried dumplings along with a wondrous variety of bite-sized wrapped foods and pastries served with fine teas.

It was a rarified experience to learn the subtleties of Chef Yip's dim sum preparations. Ingredients are expertly cut into fine shreds or hand-chopped, lightly seasoned, then deftly wrapped into exquisite dumplings of every shape and variety. Beautiful to admire, the elaborate concoctions provide a taste of old-world Chinese elegance. Equally impressive is watching Chef Yip and his team of five dim sum cooks prepare their menu for the day. With astounding speed and precision, they produce on average twelve thousand delicate pieces of dim sum each day, all flawlessly wrapped by hand.

The following recipes, adapted for the home cook, are inspired by my session with Chef Yip: Shrimp Dumplings (page 206), Chive Dumplings (page 208), Scallop Siu Mai (page 208), and Scallop Crisp (page 210).

A basket of Scallop Crisp. Chef Yip uses two shapes for his crisps; part of the pleasure of dim sum is the creativity of the visual presentation.

Spring Moon restaurant maintains authentic traditions in the kitchen and the dining room. The tea ceremony harkens back to China in the 1920s.

Scallop Siu Mai

Opposite: Chef Yip Wing Wah kneads dumpling dough for his Shrimp Dumplings.

Shrimp Dumplings Spring Moon

Spring Moon restaurant in Hong Kong is known for its extraordinary shrimp dumplings. Chef Yip Wing Wah's light seasonings bring out the natural sweetness of the shrimp. Chef Yip says an essential step is to marinate the shrimp filling for 4 hours before forming the dumplings. (photo opposite)

¼ cup canned shredded bamboo shoots, rinsed
8 medium shrimp, peeled and deveined
     (about 7 ounces)
1 teaspoon sugar
½ teaspoon salt
1 teaspoon vegetable oil
Dumpling Dough (recipe follows)
2 large Napa cabbage leaves or cheesecloth

1. Cut the bamboo shreds into ½-inch lengths. Finely mince the shrimp to make 1 cup. In a medium bowl, combine the bamboo shoots, shrimp, sugar, salt, and oil. Cover with plastic wrap and refrigerate 4 hours.

2. Put 1 level tablespoon of the filling in the center of each dough round. Fold in half to form a half moon. Pinch one end of the half moon together. Starting at this end, use your thumb and index finger to make a pleat in the top piece of the dough, and press it firmly into the bottom piece of the dough. Continue making 3 or 4 more pleats until the dumpling is completely closed. Put the dumpling upright on a plate. Continue making dumplings.

3. Line a 12-inch bamboo steamer with the cabbage leaves or cheesecloth. Put half the dumplings on the leaves, ½ inch apart. Cover the steamer with its lid. Add water to a 14-inch flat-bottomed wok to a depth of ¾ inch and bring to a boil over high heat. Carefully put the covered steamer in the wok, and steam on high heat, 4 to 5 minutes or until the shrimp is just pink. Be sure to check the water level from time to time and replenish, if necessary, with boiling water. Carefully remove the steamer from the wok. The dumplings should be served immediately.

Continue steaming the remaining dumplings, replenishing the wok with more boiling water. *Makes 20 dumplings; serves 4 as an appetizer or part of a multicourse dim sum lunch.*

Dumpling Dough

Chef Yip Wing Wah makes perfect rounds of paper-thin dough by pressing the broad side of a lightly oiled cleaver against a tiny round of dumpling dough in a quick sweeping motion. This is a difficult technique to master. I find using parchment paper with a tortilla press or a flat pot lid produces uniformly thin rounds. Wheat starch (see page 228) and tapioca starch (see page 228) are both available in Asian markets.

1¼ cups wheat starch
¼ cup tapioca starch
½ teaspoon salt
2 teaspoons vegetable oil

1. In a large bowl combine the wheat starch, tapioca starch, and salt. Make a well and add the oil with 1 cup boiling water, immediately stirring with a wooden spoon as you add the water (the mixture will have a faint fragrance of wheat starch). Carefully begin kneading the mixture for a few seconds at a time by hand, as the mixture will be very hot. Add 1 to 2 tablespoons boiling water if the dough is dry. Or add 1 to 2 tablespoons of wheat starch if the dough is too wet. Knead an additional 2 to 3 minutes, or until smooth and still warm to the touch.

2. Divide the dough into 4 equal pieces. Roll each piece into a cylinder about 5 inches long. Put 3 rolls in a plastic bag so they will not get dry. Cut the remaining roll into 5 equal pieces. Put each piece of dough between 2 sheets of parchment paper in a tortilla press or under a flat lid and press into a thin round. Peel off the round of dough; it should be about 3½ inches in diameter and a scant ⅛ inch thick. Repeat with the remaining 3 rolls, covering the rounds with a damp cloth as you make them. *Makes twenty 3½-inch rounds.*

Shrimp Dumplings (above); Chive Dumplings (page 208)

Chive Dumplings Spring Moon

The Chinese love the pungent flavor of chive dumplings, and this version is ethereal. The dough is the same as the shrimp dumpling dough, except that chive water is added to make the dough a beautiful pale green color. (photo page 207)

3 dried shiitake mushrooms
6 medium shrimp, peeled and deveined
   (about 5 ounces)
1 cup minced Chinese chives
1½ teaspoons sesame oil
½ teaspoon salt
½ teaspoon sugar
Dumpling Dough Chive Variation (recipe follows)
2 large Napa cabbage leaves or cheesecloth

1. In a medium bowl, soak the mushrooms in ¼ cup cold water 30 minutes or until softened. Drain and squeeze dry. Cut off and discard the stems and mince the caps. Roughly chop the shrimp. In a medium bowl combine the mushrooms, shrimp, chives, sesame oil, salt, and sugar.

2. Put 1 level tablespoon of the filling in the center of each dough round. Fold in half to form a half moon. Pinch one end of the half moon together. Starting at this end, use your thumb and index finger to make a pleat in the top piece of the dough, and press it firmly into the bottom piece of the dough. Continue making 3 or 4 more pleats until the dumpling is completely closed. Put the dumpling upright on a plate. Continue making dumplings.

3. Line a 12-inch bamboo steamer with the cabbage leaves or cheesecloth. Put half the dumplings on the leaves, ½ inch apart. Cover the steamer with its lid. Add water to a 14-inch flat-bottomed wok to a depth of ¾ inch and bring to a boil over high heat. Carefully put the steamer in the wok, and steam on high heat 4 to 5 minutes or until the shrimp is just pink. Be sure to check the water level from time to time and replenish, if necessary, with boiling water. Carefully remove the steamer from

the wok. The dumplings should be served immediately. Continue steaming the remaining dumplings, replenishing the wok with more boiling water. *Makes 20 dumplings; serves 4 as an appetizer or part of a multicourse dim sum lunch.*

Dumpling Dough Chive Variation

1 cup chopped Chinese chives
Dumpling Dough (page 206)

In a blender or food processor combine the chives with 1¼ cups cold water on high speed until the water is green, about 1 minute. Squeeze the chives to extract 1 cup chive water; reserve the water and discard the chives. Bring the water to a boil in a small saucepan over high heat. Make the Dumpling Dough, replacing the boiling water in step 1 with the chive water, and complete the recipe.

Scallop Siu Mai Spring Moon

Chef Yip Wing Wah garnishes these exquisite dumplings with a dollop of crab roe, which can be substituted for the carrots. (photo page 204)

8 dried shiitake mushrooms
8 ounces fresh sea scallops
10 ounces ground pork (about 1⅓ cups)
1 teaspoon cornstarch
1 teaspoon sesame oil
1 teaspoon salt
½ teaspoon sugar
½ teaspoon ground white pepper
24 round won ton wrappers
¼ cup minced carrots
4 large Napa cabbage leaves or cheesecloth

1. In a small bowl soak the mushrooms in ½ cup cold water 30 minutes or until softened. Drain and squeeze dry, reserving the soaking liquid. Cut off and discard the stems and mince the caps. Divide the scallops in half, putting the thickest on a plate;

cover with plastic wrap and refrigerate. Mince the remaining thinner scallops. In a medium bowl combine the pork, mushrooms, minced scallops, cornstarch, sesame oil, salt, sugar, pepper, and 1 tablespoon plus 1 teaspoon of the reserved mushroom liquid.

2. Put the won ton wrappers on a work surface and lightly cover with a damp towel. Touch the tip of your left index finger to the tip of your thumb to form a small empty circle, or hole. Put one wrapper over the hole and put 1 tablespoon filling in the center of the wrapper. Let the filled wrapper drop halfway through the hole, and gently squeeze it closed with your fingers. Put on a work surface and carefully pleat the excess wrapper, pressing down the filling. Put the dumpling upright on a plate. Continue filling the rest of the wrappers. Cut the reserved scallops horizontally into 24 thin rounds. Put a slice of scallop on each dumpling. Put a pinch of carrot in the center.

3. Line a 12-inch bamboo steamer with the cabbage leaves, or cheesecloth. Put half the dumplings on the leaves, ½ inch apart. Cover the steamer with its lid. Add water to a 14-inch flat-bottomed wok to a depth of ¾ inch and bring to a boil over high heat. Carefully put the steamer in the wok, and steam on high heat 5 to 7 minutes or until the pork is no longer pink and just cooked. Be sure to check the water level from time to time and replenish, if necessary, with boiling water. Carefully remove the steamer from the wok. The dumplings should be served immediately. Continue steaming the remaining dumplings, replenishing the wok with more boiling water. *Makes 24 dumplings; serves 4 as an appetizer or part of a multicourse dim sum lunch.*

Classic Steamed Fish Spring Moon

Inspired by the clever way Chef Poon Chi Cheung of Spring Moon steams fish, I created this recipe for sea bass. He arranges scallions underneath the fish, which allows the steam to circulate.

One 1½-pound sea bass, cleaned and gutted, with head and tail intact
1½ teaspoons salt
3 scallions plus ¼ cup finely shredded scallions
3 thin slices ginger
1 ounce shredded smoked ham
⅓ cup Homemade Chicken Broth (page 195)
1 tablespoon soy sauce
¼ teaspoon sugar
2 teaspoons sesame oil
2 tablespoons vegetable oil

1. Thoroughly rinse the fish in cold water and drain. Gently rub the cavity and outside of the fish with the salt and rinse again. Trim the scallions to a length of 8 inches. Put the scallions across the center of a heatproof oval platter (be sure the platter fits into a 14-inch flat-bottomed wok without touching its sides). Trim the tail, if necessary, to fit the fish on the platter. Sprinkle the ginger slices and ham on the fish.

2. Put a 1-inch-high steamer rack in the wok. Add water to a depth of ¾ inch and bring to a boil over high heat. Carefully put the platter on the rack, cover, and steam on high heat 10 minutes or until the fish flakes when tested. Be sure to check the water level from time to time and replenish, if necessary, with boiling water. Test the fish for doneness by poking the thickest part with a chopstick or fork; the fish should flake. If not, steam 1 to 2 minutes or until the fish just flakes. Carefully remove the dish from the wok and discard the ginger and ham. Pour off any liquid in the platter. Pour out the water from the wok and dry the pan.

3. In a small saucepan heat the broth, soy sauce, and sugar over medium heat until just hot. Sprinkle the remaining shredded scallions over the fish and drizzle with the sesame oil. Heat the vegetable oil in the wok over high heat until hot but not smoking. Carefully pour the hot oil over the fish. The oil will make a crackling sound as it hits the fish. Pour the hot broth over the entire fish. *Serves 4 as part of a multicourse meal.*

炸 Deep-Frying

Scallop Crisp Spring Moon

The Spring Moon serves a heavenly scallop crisp for dim sum that Chef Yip wraps in two ways. This recipe is written for the triangle version. If you want to make the mini-rolls, use 16 spring roll wrappers and cut each down to a 7-inch square. Follow the wrapping directions for Vegetarian Spring Rolls, step 3, but use a rounded tablespoon of filling. (photo page 204)

4 fresh water chestnuts
12 medium fresh sea scallops (about 10 ounces)
½ cup minced Chinese chives
1 teaspoon sugar
¼ teaspoon salt
2 tablespoons all-purpose flour
8 spring roll wrappers (preferably 7½ inches square)
3 cups vegetable oil

1. Peel the water chestnuts with a paring knife and then mince. Mince the scallops to make about 1 cup. In a medium bowl combine the water chestnuts, scallops, chives, sugar, and salt. In a small bowl combine the flour with 2 tablespoons cold water.

2. Cut each wrapper in half to form 16 rectangles, 3¼ by 7½ inches. Put one cut wrapper on the cutting board with the shortest edge facing you. (Cover the remaining wrappers loosely with a damp cloth.) Spoon a slightly rounded tablespoon of the filling at the bottom left corner of the strip. Fold the bottom left corner over the filling to meet the right-hand edge, making a triangle. Continue to fold tightly, as if folding a flag; before you reach the end, lightly paint the far corner with the flour–water mixture. Set aside, seam side down. Repeat with the remaining filling and the 15 half wrappers.

3. Heat the oil in a 14-inch flat-bottomed wok over high heat until the oil registers 325°F on a deep-frying thermometer. Carefully add 4 to 5 triangles at a time and fry until golden brown, turning with tongs, about 2 minutes. Remove with a slotted spoon and place on a plate lined with sev-eral sheets of paper towels. Repeat with the remaining triangles. Let the hot oil cool before discarding. ***Makes 16 triangles; serves 4 as an appetizer or part of a multicourse dim sum lunch.***

Vegetarian Spring Rolls

This popular dim sum specialty is also an auspicious food to eat at Chinese New Year's celebrations, which officially begin the Spring Festival. As the rolls fry, they expand, so the Chinese believe if you eat spring rolls your fortunes will expand similarly. The rolls are ready as soon as they are browned, since the vegetable filling is already cooked.

6 dried shiitake mushrooms
1 tablespoon plus 3 cups vegetable oil
1½ teaspoons minced garlic
2 cups shredded Napa cabbage
2 cups julienned celery
1 cup julienned carrots
½ cup canned shredded bamboo shoots, rinsed
½ cup thinly sliced scallions
1 teaspoon salt
½ teaspoon sugar
¼ teaspoon ground white pepper
12 spring roll wrappers (preferably 7½ inches square)
1 tablespoon flour

1. In a medium bowl soak the mushrooms in ½ cup cold water 30 minutes or until softened. Drain and squeeze dry. Cut off and discard the mushroom stems and thinly slice the caps to make about ½ cup.

2. Heat a 14-inch flat-bottomed wok over high heat until a bead of water vaporizes within 1 to 2 seconds of contact. Swirl in the 1 tablespoon oil, add the garlic, and stir-fry 5 seconds or until the garlic is fragrant. Add the cabbage, celery, carrots, bamboo shoots, scallions, and mushrooms, and stir-fry 2 to 3 minutes or until the cabbage and celery are just limp. Stir in the salt, sugar, and pepper. Remove from the heat and allow to cool.

Deep-Frying in a Wok

- The advantage of using a wok for deep-frying is that much less oil is needed than with a deep-fryer. The well of the wok holds less oil, yet the wok's cooking surface remains spacious. Never fill more than half the wok with oil—3 to 6 cups is sufficient.

- The best wok for deep-frying on any residential range is a 14-inch flat-bottomed carbon-steel wok. Choose a wok that is at least 4 inches deep. Use pot holders when handling the wok if it has metal handles.

- Should you choose to use a round-bottomed wok on either an electric range or a gas range, the wok must be securely set on a wok ring or stand. Be aware that unlike a gas stove, where the heat can be immediately shut off, cool-down time on an electric range is slow.

- A deep-frying thermometer is the best way to judge the temperature of the oil. Experienced Chinese cooks place a bamboo chopstick in the hot oil to judge the temperature. Tiny bubbles appear around the chopstick when the oil temperature is about 325°F.

- Moisture causes oil to spatter; make sure the food to be deep-fried is as dry as possible.

- A slotted metal spoon or a Chinese mesh skimmer (available in several different sizes) is an essential utensil when deep-frying.

- Hot oil can be very dangerous; handle it with extreme care. Deep-frying requires your full attention; do not allow anything to distract you.

---

3. Put the spring roll wrappers on a work surface and loosely cover with a damp cloth. In a small bowl combine the flour with 1 tablespoon cold water. Put 1 wrapper on the cutting board with a corner facing you. Spread about 1/3 cup of the filling near the bottom corner into a 1½- by 4-inch rectangle. Fold the corner nearest you over the filling. Roll the wrapper over once, then fold in the sides. Continue rolling the wrapper up tightly; before you reach the end, lightly paint the far corner with the flour-water mixture. Continue rolling to seal into a tight cylinder. Set aside, seam side down.

Repeat with the remaining filling and wrappers.

4. Rinse the wok and dry it thoroughly. Heat the remaining 3 cups oil in the wok over high heat until the oil registers 325°F on a deep-frying thermometer. Carefully add 4 to 5 spring rolls at a time and fry until golden brown, turning with tongs, about 2 minutes. Remove with a slotted spoon and place on a plate lined with several sheets of paper towels. Repeat with the remaining spring rolls. Let the hot oil cool before discarding. *Makes 12 spring rolls; serves 4 as an appetizer or part of a multicourse dim sum lunch.*

Chef Hugh places ingredients into the fat, being careful not to splash. At home use tongs to keep hands clear of hot oil when deep-frying. Opposite: Nevin Lim's Traditional Oyster Chicken (page 214) served on a Ming/Qing dynasty plate.

Nevin Lim's Traditional Oyster Chicken

According to Nevin Lim, this is a forgotten traditional home-style Cantonese dish. The cooking technique is unusual. The chicken is deep-fried on medium heat for 3 to 4 minutes. For the last 15 seconds of frying the heat is raised to high, which Lim says "forces" the oil out of the chicken. The chicken is extremely tender and is served with a delicious sauce redolent of ginger. (photo page 212)

12 ounces skinless, boneless chicken breast, cut into 1-inch cubes
1 teaspoon plus ⅓ cup cornstarch
4 teaspoons plus 1 cup corn oil
2 teaspoons Shao Hsing rice wine or dry sherry
½ teaspoon soy sauce
¼ teaspoon ground white pepper
¾ teaspoon sesame oil
¼ cup Homemade Chicken Broth (page 195)
2 tablespoons oyster sauce
⅛ teaspoon black soy sauce
⅛ teaspoon sugar
2 scallions, cut into 2-inch pieces
1 small garlic clove, thinly sliced
3 tablespoons finely shredded ginger

1. In a bowl combine the chicken, the 1 teaspoon cornstarch, 1 teaspoon of the corn oil, 1 teaspoon of the rice wine, the soy sauce, ⅛ teaspoon of the pepper, and ½ teaspoon of the sesame oil. In a small bowl combine the broth, oyster sauce, black soy sauce, sugar, and remaining 1 teaspoon rice wine, ¼ teaspoon sesame oil, and ⅛ teaspoon pepper. Set aside.

Nevin Lim uses long bamboo chopsticks to keep his hands at a safe distance while deep-frying.

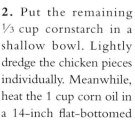

2. Put the remaining ⅓ cup cornstarch in a shallow bowl. Lightly dredge the chicken pieces individually. Meanwhile, heat the 1 cup corn oil in a 14-inch flat-bottomed wok over medium heat until the oil registers 325°F on a deep-frying thermometer. Carefully add the chicken, spreading it evenly in the wok. Cook 3 to 4 minutes or until light golden, turning with tongs. The last 15 seconds raise the heat to high. Remove the chicken with a slotted spoon and place on a plate lined with paper towels. Carefully remove the oil from the wok. Wash the wok and dry it thoroughly.

3. Heat the wok over high heat until a bead of water vaporizes within 1 to 2 seconds of contact. Swirl in the remaining 1 tablespoon corn oil, add the scallions, and stir-fry 10 seconds. Add the garlic and ginger, and stir-fry 10 seconds. Add the chicken. Stir the broth mixture, swirl it into the wok, and stir-fry 10 seconds until just combined and the chicken is cooked through. *Serves 4 as part of a multicourse meal.*

Winnie Hon's XO Sauce

Relatively new, XO sauce is a popular and sophisticated spicy condiment favored by Hong Kong chefs. Several companies make the sauce (see page 228), but nothing compares to Winnie Hon's homemade version using dried scallops (see page 225) and dried shrimp (see page 226). It is labor intensive, but the results are worth the effort. I once made this with a cast-iron wok. After I took the wok off the heat, the pan was so hot that it continued to cook the mixture, which made the chilies bitter. I recommend using a carbon-steel wok, which cools down much faster.

16 dried scallops (about 4 ounces)
5 shallots (about 5 ounces)
2 heads garlic (about 5 ounces)
16 fresh red Thai chilies, stems removed (about 1 ounce), cut crosswise into ¼-inch pieces
1 cup dried shrimp (about 3 ounces)
2½ cups canola oil
1½ teaspoons red pepper flakes
1 teaspoon salt
½ teaspoon sugar

1. In a 9-inch shallow heatproof bowl soak the dried scallops in about ⅓ cup cold water 30 minutes. Turn the pieces over and continue soaking an additional 30 minutes. Almost all the water will be soaked up and the scallops will fall apart when touched. Pour out any excess water.

2. Put a 1-inch-high steamer rack in a 14-inch flat-bottomed wok. Add water to a depth of ¾ inch and bring to a boil over high heat. Carefully put the bowl on the rack, cover, reduce the heat to medium, and steam 15 minutes. Be sure to check the water level from time to time and replenish, if necessary, with boiling water. Carefully remove the bowl from the wok. When cool enough to handle, remove the small hard muscle from the sides of the scallops. Finely shred the scallops. Pour out the water from the wok and dry the pan.

3. Peel the shallots, put them in a food processor, and pulse until minced, about 5 seconds. Transfer to a bowl. Peel the garlic, put it and the chilies in the food processor, and pulse until minced, about 5 seconds. Transfer to the bowl with the shallots. Rinse the shrimp in cold water and drain. Pat dry with paper towels. Put the shrimp in the food processor and pulse until minced, about 15 seconds. Transfer to a separate bowl.

4. Heat the oil in the wok over high heat until the oil registers 275°F on a deep-frying thermometer. Carefully add the shallot-garlic mixture and reduce the heat to low. Cook, stirring slowly, 8 to 9 minutes or until the mixture just begins to show a little color. The oil should have small bubbles and register about 210°F on the thermometer. Carefully add the shrimp and continue stirring on low heat 2 to 3 minutes or until the shrimp is fragrant. Carefully add the scallops, increasing the heat to medium, and continue stirring until the scallops are golden, 2 to 3 minutes. Remove from the heat. Stir in the pepper flakes, salt, and sugar. Cool. Divide into sterilized half-pint jars and refrigerate for up to 3 months. *Makes about 4 half-pints.*

Candied Walnuts

These walnuts garnish Susanna Foo's wonderful Mango Chicken (page 78), but they are also delicious served alone. Sometimes after frying, I sprinkle them lightly with a teaspoon of toasted sesame seeds. For the holidays I make a big batch for gifts.

1 pound shelled walnut halves
1 cup sugar
6 cups vegetable oil

1. Line the counter with about 2 feet of heavy-duty aluminum foil. In a 2½-quart saucepan bring 1 quart cold water to a boil over high heat. Add the walnuts and return to a boil. Drain the walnuts in a colander and immediately place them in a large bowl. Pour the sugar over the walnuts, and continually stir with a rubber spatula until the sugar is completely dissolved by the heat of the hot walnuts and no sugar granules are visible. The walnuts should be shiny and coated in liquid sugar.

2. Heat the oil in a 14-inch flat-bottomed wok over medium-high heat until the oil registers 375°F on a deep-frying thermometer. Carefully add the walnuts with a slotted metal spoon, spreading them in the wok. Cook undisturbed 2 minutes, letting the walnuts begin to brown. Then, using the slotted spoon, carefully stir the walnuts in the wok to make sure they brown evenly. Fry an additional 1 to 3 minutes, or until golden brown.

3. When the nuts are golden, immediately turn off the heat. Carefully and quickly begin removing them with the slotted spoon to the foil, leaving as much space between the walnuts as possible. Do not put the walnuts on the foil in clusters, as they will harden that way. To avoid severe burns, do not touch or taste the nuts until they have cooled. Carefully transfer them to a jellyroll pan lined with several sheets of paper towels. Towel-dry the nuts to remove as much oil as possible. When they have cooled completely, transfer to an airtight sterilized jar. Let the hot oil cool before discarding. *Makes about 4 cups.*

Essentials

Menus

New Year's Menus

Here is a selection of Lunar New Year's menus ranging in complexity. The first two menus are simpler (and serve a party of 6 to 8), while the last two are more complex (and serve 8 to 10). Each menu includes at least one dish that can be made ahead. Other auspicious dishes appropriate for New Year's Eve dinner can be found in the Index under New Year's Celebrations. The Chinese regard this as the most sumptuous meal of the entire year, and it should include your favorite dishes. Feel free to mix and match.

Preceding pages:
Dried, crushed chilies, also known as red pepper flakes,
in a market in Yangshuo, Guangxi province.

The Yao family. Auntie Linda, my mother's best school friend in Shanghai, and her family make a warm welcome for me with a carefully prepared family-style menu. Every dish was cooked in a northern-style wok.

Seasonal Family-Style Menus (serves a family of 4)

Spring

Auntie Yi's Stir-Fried Garlic Spinach
(page 138)

Julie Tay's Singapore–Style Squid
(page 111)

Kung Pao Chicken (page 74)

Classic Rice (page 120)

Summer

Susan Lin's Summer Long Beans
with Eggs (page 140)

Tina Yao Lu's Chicken with Spinach
(page 74)

Margaret Loo's Braised Tofu
and Mushrooms (page 182)

Aromatic Vegetarian Fried Rice (page 123)

Autumn

Liang Nian Xiu's Moon Hill Corn and Beans
(page 132)

Cousin Sylvia's Drumsticks with
Caramelized Onions (page 161)

Walter Kei's Shanghai–Style Pork
and Bean Sprouts (page 87)

Classic Rice (page 120)

Winter

Lee Wan Ching's Chinese Broccoli
with Ginger Sauce (page 140)

Cousin Zane's Sichuan Beef (page 95)

Uncle Lang's Three Teacup Chicken
(page 183)

Classic Rice (page 120)

Glossary

Bamboo shoots *(juk seun):* Available in cans whole, sliced, or shredded. Before using always rinse in cold water. The unused portion should be stored in the refrigerator in a plastic container, covered with cold water, for up to a week; change the water daily.

Bean curd: *See* Tofu.

Bean sauce *(meen si):* Also known as ground bean sauce, brown bean sauce, or yellow bean sauce, this condiment is sold in cans and jars. I prefer Koon Chun brand in the 13-ounce jar. It is made from soybeans, salt, wheat flour, sugar, sesame oil, and spices. Store in the refrigerator for several months. (photo page 224)

Bean spouts *(nga choy):* There are two varieties:

mung bean, which are more commonly available; and soybean. Mung bean sprout heads are the size of a grain of barley, about ¼ inch wide. Choose plump sprouts no more than 2½ inches long. Avoid long, stringy, brown, and limp sprouts, which are old. Store in a paper bag in the refrigerator's crisper bin for no more than a day.

Belacan shrimp paste *(ma laai zaan):* Also known as *blachan*, this is a Southeast Asian shrimp paste sold in 8-ounce bricks. Use a cleaver to shave off what you need. The brick should be wrapped tightly in foil, then put in a plastic bag and stored in the refrigerator for up to 1 year. (photo page 223)

Bok choy: This member of the cabbage family is

available in several varieties. The most common variety found in Chinatown is sold in bunches 8 to 11 inches long, with white stalks and unblemished dark green leaves. Premium bok choy is called **choy sum,** or heart of bok choy, and is more delicate. Other varieties available in Asian markets are **Shanghai bok choy,** *yul choy* (oilseed

rape vegetable), and *tatsoi*. Choose bok choy with tightly closed buds. Avoid any with open flowers, yellow leaves, or stems that are beginning to brown, all signs that the vegetable is old. Bok choy is available year-round but is best in the winter months. Store in the refrigerator's crisper bin for up to 3 days.

Chili bean sauce *(laat dao zeung):* Also known as chili bean paste, this is made with soybeans, chilies, and spices. Every brand differs slightly, so you must experiment to find the one you prefer. Store in the refrigerator. Chili garlic sauce may be used as a substitute, but it is less flavorful. (photo page 224)

Chilies, dried *(laat ziu gon):* These are 2 to 3 inches long, and should be fragrant, with a sheen. Peppers lose flavor and aroma as they age. (photo page 223)

Chilies, fresh *(laat ziu):* This book calls for three varieties. To reduce the heat, remove the seeds with gloves. They may be stored in a paper bag in the refrigerator's crisper bin for 1 to 2 weeks.

Anaheim: A slender pepper, 5 to 7 inches long. It is mild to moderately hot.

Jalapeño: This relatively plump pepper is tapered, 2 to 3 inches long, and fiery hot.

Thai or bird chili: This skinny pepper is 2 to 3 inches long and fiery hot.

Chili oil *(laat yao):* This reddish-orange oil is flavored with dried red chilies. Store in a cool, dark, dry cupboard for up to 6 months, or refrigerate. (photo page 224)

Chili sambal *(laat zeung):* An Indonesian spicy condiment sauce made of chilies, salt, vinegar, and sometimes tamarind. Store in the refrigerator for several months. (photo page 224)

Chinese bacon *(laab yuk):* Drier and harder than Western bacon, this dry-cured pork belly is available in Chinese butcher shops. It has an earthy, smoky flavor and comes in one slab, never in thin slices. You must ask for it by its Cantonese name, *laab yuk*; do not ask for "Chinese bacon." (photo page 227)

Chinese broccoli (gaai laan): Also known as Chinese

kale; the individual stalks are most commonly sold year-round in 2-pound bundles but are best in the winter months. The leaves are dark green, the stalks are 10 to 14 inches long and 1/2 to 3/4 inch in diameter. Tiny pale green buds are hidden in the leaves. Never choose broccoli stalks with dried ends, open flowers, or yellow leaves, all signs of age. Store in the refrigerator's crisper bin for up to 5 days.

Chinese eggplant (ke zee): The best eggplants are lavender, firm, and blemish free with a silky skin, 8 to 9 inches long and 2 inches wide. Because they are smaller than the Western variety, they are much more tender with almost no seeds and are less bitter. Select smooth, firm-skinned, and heavy eggplant. Store in the refrigerator's crisper bin for up to a week.

Chives: The Chinese have three different varieties, Chinese chives (see below), flowering garlic chives, and yellow chives, sold in Asian produce markets.

Chinese chives (gao choy): These look like hearty Western chives or very young scallions. About an

inch of the stem end is white; the remainder of the chive is dark green. Chives are sold in small to medium bunches ranging from 10 to 16 inches long. Store in the refrigerator's crisper bin for up to 5 days.

Cilantro (yin sai): Also known as fresh coriander or Chinese parsley, this herb has delicate leaves and a strong flavor and is best when sold with its roots. Select green, fresh leaves with thin stems, avoiding yellow, wilted leaves. Wash carefully in several changes of cold water to remove dirt before using. Put the cilantro roots in a glass of water, cover the

leaves with a plastic bag, and store in the refrigerator for up to 5 days.

Cloud ears (wan yi): Also known as tree ears, or black fungus, these dried fungi are gray-black. Cloud ears look like delicate, paper-thin, crinkled 1-inch leaves. They are sold in plastic bags and in bulk in Chinese grocery stores; they should be transferred to a jar and stored in a cool, dark, dry cupboard for up to a year. Do not confuse with wood ears which are much bigger and thicker. (photo page 223)

Coconut milk, canned, unsweetened (ye naai): My favorite brand is Chaokoh from Thailand. Shake the can before opening, as the thick cream always floats to the top. (photo page 224)

Curry paste and powder (ga lei): A blend of spices such as turmeric, ginger, peppercorns, cumin, coriander, cinnamon, and cloves. Curry pastes sold in jars have more rounded flavor than the powder. (photo page 224)

Edamame (mou dao): Although sometimes available fresh, shelled edamame are usually found in the frozen section of most Asian markets. They are also available in some health food stores.

Fermented black beans (dao si): Also known as Chinese dried black beans, or preserved beans. The small black beans, fermented with salt and spices, are a popular seasoning for meat, seafood, and poultry. The beans are sold in plastic bags or in small, round cardboard containers. Before using, the beans must always be rinsed in several changes of cold water. A favorite brand is Yang Jiang Preserved Beans, packaged in a cardboard box. The beans keep indefinitely in an airtight jar in a cool, dark, dry cupboard or in the refrigerator. (photo page 223)

Five-spice powder (m heung fan): This is a ground spice made up of Chinese cinnamon, cloves, fennel, Sichuan peppercorns, and star anise. It is sold in plastic bags or in a small jar. Store in an airtight jar in a cool, dark, dry cupboard.

Fuzzy melon *(zeet gwa):* This green squash with mild flavor ranges in length from 4 to 10 inches. Select fuzzy melon with very fine prickly hairs. The squash must be peeled before cooking. The best season for them is summer. Store in the refrigerator's vegetable crisper bin for up to a week.

Ginger, fresh *(geung):* This rhizome is available year-round. Select ginger that is heavy and firm, with rough but not wrinkled skin. Store in the refrigerator's crisper bin in a brown paper bag for up to 2 weeks. Dried or ground ginger is not a suitable substitute.

Gingko nut *(baag gwo):* Shelled and blanched fresh gingko nuts are available in 3.5-ounce Cryovac packages in some Chinese markets. You can also buy fresh gingko nuts and shell them yourself, but doing so is labor intensive. (photo page 227)

Hoisin sauce *(hoisin zeung):* This chocolate-colored sauce is mildly thick, sweet, and smoky. It is made from sugar, soybeans, garlic, sesame seeds, chilies, and spices. It is sold in cans or jars. I prefer Koon Chun brand sauce, which is available in a 13-ounce jar. Store in the refrigerator for several months. (photo page 224)

Long beans *(dao gok):* Also known as yard-long

beans, these beans are available as dark green beans and light green beans. They are available year-round but are best in the summer. The dark beans are crisper and the light less so. Both can be 18 to 30 inches long. Even when farm fresh, the beans are limp and have tiny brown blemishes. Store in the refrigerator's crisper bin for up to 5 days.

Lotus root *(leen ngao):* Lotus root is ivory colored, about 16 inches long, and has 3 sections (although some markets separate the sections) with little root hairs between each piece. Each section requires

careful washing to remove the mud in which it is grown. Lotus root season is September, October, and November, but it is available other times of the year. Never select lotus root that has been wrapped in cellophane; you must be able to smell the lotus root to make sure it has a clean smell. Select lotus root that is heavy, firm, and blemish free. Once the lotus root is cut, rinse it again to make sure all the mud has been removed. Cut off any dark spots. Store in the refrigerator's crisper bin for up to 5 days.

Luffa *(see gwa):* Also known as angled luffa, Chinese okra, or silk squash, luffa is dark green with thin ridges about ½ inch apart and is 10 to 20 inches long, 2 inches in diameter, with a slight curve. Choose squash that is firm but has soft skin and gives slightly

when squeezed. Rough, hard skin indicates the squash is old. Peel just the ridges if the squash is young, but if it is old, remove all the peel. Store in the refrigerator's crisper bin for 3 to 4 days.

Napa cabbage *(wong nga baag):* Choose cabbage with pale white to yellow crinkly leaves and creamy white stems year-round. Select cabbage that is blemish free, with no tiny brown or black spots. Store in the refrigerator's crisper bin for up to 10 days.

Noodles *(mein):* The following are a few of the more common fresh and dried noodles used in Chinese cooking and sold in Chinese markets.

  Broad rice noodles *(ho fan):* These are sold in long sheets folded to roughly the size of a folded kitchen towel. They are soft and flexible until refrigerated. Do not refrigerate them if you plan to use them the day of purchase. Broad rice noodles

1

2

3

4

5

6

8   **9**

7

12   **13**

10   **11**

14   **15**

19

16   **17**   **18**

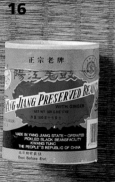

**Bottled and canned
Chinese staples**

1 Sesame oil
2 Chili oil
3 Coconut milk
4 Curry paste
5 Chili sambal
6 Chili bean sauce
7 XO sauce
8 Snow cabbage
9 Hoisin sauce
10 Bean sauce
11 Wet bean curd, white
12 Wet bean curd, red
13 Soy sauce
14 Black soy sauce
15 Oyster sauce
16 Chinkiang vinegar
17 Rice vinegar
18 Shao Hsing rice wine

are sold in Chinese bakeries, stores that sell fresh tofu, or at the checkout counters of some Chinese grocery stores. Store in plastic bags and refrigerate for 3 to 4 days. (photo page 227)

Cellophane noodles (*fan si*): These are also known as glass noodles, bean thread noodles, or green bean thread, and are available in a variety of package sizes, from 1.76 ounces to 17.6 ounces, in plastic bags in Chinese grocery markets. Store in a sealed plastic bag in a cool, dark, dry cupboard for up to a year. (photo page 223)

Flat rice noodles, dried (*gon ho fan*): Also known as rice sticks, these flat white noodles are about the size of linguine and are very brittle. The noodles come in a big rectangular block in a plastic bag. Store in a sealed plastic bag in a cool, dark, dry cupboard for up to a year. (photo page 223)

Fresh egg noodles (*san seen cyun daan mein*): These come in several varieties—**won ton** (photo page 227), chow mein, or **lo mein** (photo page 227) and have a golden egg color. Won ton and chow mein noodles are thin, lo mein are thick. They require only about 1 to 3 minutes of boiling. There are also **Hong Kong–style pan-fried noodles** (photo page 227), which are fresh pre-cooked noodles; they do not require boiling in water and can be immediately pan-fried. Lo mein noodles are available cooked and uncooked. All the noodles are available in the refrigerator section of most Chinese markets. Store in the refrigerator for 3 to 4 days.

Rice cakes (*nin gou*): These are Shanghainese noodles that look like white discs or ovals, about ¼ inch thick and 2 inches long. They are sold in plastic bags (about 24 ounces) in the refrigerator section of some Chinese markets. The noodles are quite firm, but after cooking they are soft and chewy. Store in the refrigerator. (photo page 227)

Oyster sauce (*hou yao*): A thick brown sauce sold in bottles and used in cooking and as a condiment. Oyster sauce varies greatly in quality. The brand I like is Lee Kum Kee; it has a woman and boy in a small boat pictured on the label. The sauce is made from oyster extracts, sugar, and salt. Store in the refrigerator for up to a year. Vegetarian oyster sauce, made from mushroom extracts rather than oysters, is also available in some Asian markets. (photo opposite)

Rice (*mai*): Two main varieties of rice are used in Chinese cooking, long-grain and sweet. Store all rice in a cool, dark, dry place.

> **Black rice** (*hag mai*): This is a glutinous rice with black and brown kernels. It is mainly used as a dessert ingredient. (photo page 223)

> **Long-grain rice** (*baag mai*): This is long and slender, about three times longer than it is wide. It is the most popular form of rice in the Chinese diet. The grains, when cooked, are light and fluffy. Some cooks prefer jasmine with its aromatic flavor and nuttier texture. (photo page 223)

Salted turnip (*teem choy pou*): There are a number of different types of salted turnip. The one I call for in this book is pronounced *teem choy pou* in Cantonese, but this does not appear on the package. The vegetable is khaki-colored and the pieces are 3 to 5 inches long and ½ inch wide. It is sold in 7-ounce packages in Chinese markets. (photo page 223)

Scallops, dried (*geung yiu cyu*): Dried scallops look like fresh scallops, except for their golden color. They are expensive and very flavorful. Dried scallops are sold in boxes or loose from large bins in grocery stores or herb shops. Broken scallops are less expensive and can be equally flavorful. Choose scallops that are fragrant, golden, and shiny. Store in an airtight jar in a cool, dark, dry cupboard. (photo page 223)

Sesame oil (*ma yao*): A seasoning oil made from roasted sesame seeds, it is golden brown and aromatic;

do not confuse with cold-pressed sesame oil. Choose pure sesame oil rather than one that has been blended with another oil. Store in the refrigerator for up to a year. Kadoya is a good brand. (photo page 224)

Shao Hsing (or Shaoxing) rice wine *(siu hing zao):* Made by fermenting glutinous rice, it is available in most Chinese grocery stores or in Chinese liquor stores and is inexpensive. Store at room temperature. (photo page 224)

Shiitake mushrooms: These mushrooms are available dried and fresh in Chinese markets.

> **Shiitake, dried** *(dung gwoo):* Also known as Chinese dried mushroom, or dried winter mushroom, as they are called in Japan, these dried fungi are brownish, gray-black mushrooms, and vary greatly in quality. They are sold in cellophane packages, boxes, and in bulk in Chinese grocery stores. Pale, thick mushroom caps with lots of cracks, the most prized, are called *fa gwoo*. The flavor of these mushrooms is robust and concentrated, with an almost meaty taste. The thinner, browner caps are less flavorful and less expensive. Store mushrooms in an airtight jar in a cool, dark, dry cupboard. (photo page 223)

> **Shiitake, fresh** *(seen gwoo):* Choose mushrooms that are firm, plump, and blemish free. They should have a clean, fresh smell. The hard stems must be removed before cooking. Place in a paper bag and store in the refrigerator's crisper bin for 1 to 2 days. (photo page 145)

Shrimp, dried *(ha mai):* These are ½ to 1 inch long and are very flavorful. They are sold loose in big bins or in plastic packages in Asian markets. Choose bright orange shrimp with a pleasant scent; avoid shrimp that look flaky. Store in an airtight jar in a cool, dry, dark cupboard for up to a year. (photo page 223)

Sichuan peppercorns *(fa ziu):* These are reddish brown and resemble peppercorns but are, in fact, berries. They are sold in plastic bags, with tiny twigs that must be picked out. The peppercorns can be difficult to find in the United States. Store in an airtight jar in a cool, dry, dark cupboard. (photo page 223)

Smithfield ham *(fo teui):* Also known as Virginia ham, Smithfield ham is a dried and salty ham that is used sparingly in recipes but adds great flavor. It is sold in Chinese butcher shops whole or sliced into 2- to 4-ounce steaks wrapped in Cryovac. Store it in the refrigerator. (photo opposite)

Snow cabbage *(syud lei hung):* Also known as red-in-snow, this is a famous cabbage preserved in salt. It is available in small cans. (photo page 224)

Soy sauce *(saang cao):* Also known as thin soy sauce, or superior soy sauce, this is the most common ingredient used in Chinese cooking. Soy sauce is saltier than black soy sauce and lighter in color. I prefer Kikkoman brand. (photo page 224)

> **Black soy sauce** *(lou cao):* Also known as dark soy sauce, this is blacker, thicker, and richer in color and slightly sweeter in taste than soy sauce because it has been aged longer. (photo page 224)

Spring roll wrappers *(ceun gyun pei):* These wrappers are found in the refrigerator section of Chinese grocery stores. Select wrappers that are paper-thin and translucent. Keep for a week refrigerated or freeze. (photo opposite)

Star anise *(baag gwo):* Each eight-pointed star is hard, reddish brown, and about the size of a quarter. Star anise is fragrant and has a distinct licorice flavor that is excellent in stews. Store in an airtight jar in a cool, dry, dark cupboard. (photo page 223)

Tangerine peel, dried *(gwo pei):* This is the sundried peel from the tangerine. It is quite hard and is dark brown on the outside and pale tan on the pith side. The peels are sold in plastic bags or loose in some Chinese markets or herb shops. Store in an airtight jar in a cool, dry, dark cupboard. (photo page 223)

1 Smithfield ham
2 Five-spice tofu
3 Gingko nuts
4 Chinese bacon
5 Chinese sausage
6 Won ton noodles
7 Lo mein noodles
8 Hong Kong–style pan-fried noodles
9 Spring roll wrappers
10 Rice cakes
11 Won ton wrappers
12 Broad rice noodles

Tapioca starch *(ling fan):* Also known as tapioca flour, this starch is available in 14-ounce packages. It looks like cornstarch. Store in an airtight jar in a cool, dry, dark cupboard. (photo page 223)

Tofu *(dao foo):* Also known as bean curd, tofu comes in many different varieties; these are only a few:

> **Firm tofu** *(dao foo):* This comes in 3-inch squares or in a rectangular block. One package can vary in weight from 14 to 19 ounces. Fresh tofu should have a clean smell. Refrigerate and change the water daily for up to 3 days.

> **Five-spice tofu** *(m heung dao foo gon):* Also known as spiced tofu, this is pressed tofu flavored with a soy sauce marinade. It has a dry, firm texture and is sold in 8-ounce packages in the refrigerator section. (photo page 227)

> **Silken tofu** *(waat dao foo):* This is custard-like and more delicate than firm tofu. It is sold in sealed packages in the refrigerator section.

Vinegar *(cou):* Chinese vinegar is primarily made from glutinous rice. Store vinegar at room temperature in a cool, dark, dry cupboard.

> **Chinkiang vinegar** *(zan gong cou):* This is a dark semisweet vinegar with a smoky flavor produced in eastern China, similar in taste to balsamic vinegar. (photo page 224)

> **Rice vinegar** *(baag mai cou):* This is a pale amber-colored vinegar, mild in flavor. (photo page 224)

Water chestnuts, fresh *(ma tai):* A dark brown bulb-like vegetable, lightly covered in dirt, water chestnuts are about $1\frac{1}{2}$ inches across and about 1 inch long. They are grown underwater in mud and have a thin skin. Choose water chestnuts that are heavy and firm. Put in a paper bag and store in the refrigerator's crisper bin for up to a week.

Wet bean curd *(fu yu):* Also known as fermented bean curd, this comes in two main varieties and, as with certain other ingredients, the English labeling will seldom help you. It is best to try to pronounce the ingredient by its Cantonese name. Once the jar is opened, wet bean curd must be refrigerated.

> **Wet bean curd, red** *(naam yu):* These are red-colored 1-inch cubes of fermented bean curd in a thick red flavorful sauce. (photo page 224)

> **Wet bean curd, white** *(baag fu yu):* These are beige-colored 1-inch cubes of fermented bean curd in a briny liquid. (photo page 224)

Wheat starch *(siu mak cing fan):* This looks like flour and is sold in plastic bags. A popular brand is Man Sang FTY. Store as you would flour. (photo page 223)

Wolfberries, dried *(gei zi):* Wolfberries look like oval, red raisins, about $\frac{1}{2}$ inch long and $\frac{1}{8}$ inch wide. They should be a bright red color and not deep burgundy, which shows age. Be sure to purchase pitted wolfberries, as they have a very hard, small pit that must be removed before cooking. Wolfberries are available in Chinese markets and herb shops. Store in an airtight jar in a cool, dark, dry cupboard for up to 1 year. (photo page 223)

Won ton wrappers *(wan tan pei):* These 14- to 16-ounce packages of paper-thin, silky dough are found in the refrigerator section of Chinese markets, available cut in squares or rounds. Always choose the thinnest dough. Refrigerate for up to 5 days or freeze for several months. (photo page 227)

XO sauce *(xo zeung):* This expensive condiment is sometimes called "the caviar of the Orient." The *XO* in the name pays homage to XO brandy, which is revered by the Chinese (there is no brandy in the sauce, however). This is made by several condiment companies (photo page 224), but homemade XO sauce (page 214) is far superior.

Metric Equivalencies

Liquid and Dry Measure Equivalencies

CUSTOMARY	METRIC
¼ teaspoon	1.25 milliliters
½ teaspoon	2.5 milliliters
1 teaspoon	5 milliliters
1 tablespoon	15 milliliters
1 fluid ounce	30 milliliters
¼ cup	60 milliliters
⅓ cup	80 milliliters
½ cup	120 milliliters
1 cup	240 milliliters
1 pint *(2 cups)*	480 milliliters
1 quart *(4 cups, 32 ounces)*	960 milliliters *(.96 liter)*
1 gallon *(4 quarts)*	3.84 liters
1 ounce *(by weight)*	28 grams
¼ pound *(4 ounces)*	114 grams
1 pound *(16 ounces)*	454 grams
2.2 pounds	1 kilogram *(1,000 grams)*

Sources

Wok Stores

Chan Chi Kee Cutlery Co.
G/F., 316–318 Shanghai Street
Kowloon, Hong Kong
852-2385-0317
Fax 852-2771-5186
www.chanchikee.com
In business since the 1920s, this extraordinary store specializes in hand-pounded woks for restaurants and home cooks. They are even more famous for their cutlery.

Eagle Kitchen Supply, Inc.
166 Lincoln Street
Boston, MA 02111
617-482-2188
This Chinese cookware store has one of the best selections of woks in the Boston area.

Hung Chong Imports Inc.
14 Bowery
New York, NY 10013
212-406-2715
Fax 212-385-0806
Owner Kenny Leung has a large selection of woks, cutlery, and utensils for restaurants and home cooks.

Ming Wo
23 East Pender Street
Vancouver, B.C. V6A 1S9
604-683-7268
www.mingwo.com
This general cookware store carries woks and accessories; the store has six different locations in Canada.

The Wok Shop
718 Grant Avenue
San Francisco, CA 94108
415-989-3797
888-780-7171
www.wokshop.com
Owner Tane Chan is passionate about woks and helping customers. This store offers every kind of wok and wok accessory. Chan also sells seasoned woks.

Woks 'n' things
2234 S. Wentworth Avenue
Chicago, IL 60616
312-842-0701
A favorite store in Chicago for woks, accessories, and cleavers.

Custom Wok Stoves

Flamtech Appliance, Inc.
114 Bowery
New York, NY 10013
212-274-8820
This impressive Asian kitchen showroom has an extensive selection of professional and residential wok stoves and exhaust hoods.

Robert Yick Company, Inc.
261 Bayshore Boulevard
San Francisco, CA 94124
415-282-9707
In business since 1910, this is probably the oldest fabricator of restaurant wok stoves in America. Owner Joe Yick has made custom wok stoves for Martin Yan, Ken Hom, Cecilia Chiang, and for countless Chinese restaurants and homes in the Bay Area.

Asian Herbs and Ingredients

Lin Sister Herb Shop Inc.
4 Bowery
New York, NY 10013
212-962-5417
Fax 212-587-8826
Herbalist Susan Lin offers a tremendous selection of herbs. Orders can be shipped via UPS.

Uwajimaya
600 Fifth Avenue South
Seattle, WA 98104
206-624-6248
800-889-1928
www.uwajimaya.com
This unique Asian supermarket has an impeccable selection of fresh produce and Asian dry goods available by mail order.

Cooking Schools

Chinese Cuisine Training Institute
6/F Pokfulam Training Centre Complex
145 Pokfulam Road
Hong Kong
852-2538-2200
www.ccti.vtc.edu.hk
Classes are available for professionals and the general public in Chinese regional cooking.

The Peninsula Hong Kong
Peninsula Academy Culinary Experience
Salisbury Road
Kowloon, Hong Kong
852-2920-2888
www.hongkong.peninsula.com
Classes in Cantonese cuisine are taught by the chefs of the Spring Moon restaurant and are open to hotel guests and Hong Kong residents.

Chinese Culture

Asia Society
725 Park Avenue
New York, NY 10021
212-288-6400
www.asiasociety.org

Asian/Pacific/American Studies Program & Institute
New York University
269 Mercer Street, Suite 609
New York, NY 10003
212-998-3700
www.apa.nyu.edu
The A/P/A Studies Institute sponsors events for the larger NYU and New York City communities, including conferences, seminars, book readings, exhibitions, film screenings, and musical performances.

China Institute
125 East 65th Street
New York, NY 10021
212-744-8181
www.chinainstitute.org

Museum of Chinese in the Americas
70 Mulberry Street
New York, NY 10013
212-619-4785
www.moca-nyc.org

Portland Classical Chinese Garden
239 Northwest Everett
Portland, OR 97209
503-228-8131
www.portlandchinesegarden.org
This authentic Suzhou–style garden offers programs and exhibits in Chinese art and culture.

Wossing Center for Chinese
243 Grand Street
New York, NY 10022
212-431-7373
www.wossing.com
Wossing offers courses on Chinese language and culture.

Chinese Antiquities

Abhaya Asian Art
www.trocadero.com/abhayaasianart
Owner David Camacho supplied many of the Chinese antiques photographed throughout this book.

Vintage Chinese Photographs
www.dennisgeorgecrow.com
Dennis George Crow specializes in images of China from the nineteenth to the early twentieth centuries.

Cookbooks

Bonnie Slotnick Cookbooks
163 West 10th Street
New York, NY 10014
212-989-8962
bonnieslotnickbooks@earthlink.net
An excellent source for out-of-print Chinese cookbooks.

The Breath of a Wok
www.graceyoung.com
Log on to our website for information on woks, recipes, upcoming exhibitions, and to tell us your wok story.

Selected Bibliography

Anderson, E. N. *The Food of China*. New Haven: Yale University Press, 1988.

Andrews, Colman. "Cast-Iron Man." *Saveur* 42 (April 2000).

Bartlett, Frances, and Ivan Lai. *Hong Kong on a Plate*. Hong Kong: Roadhouse Publications (Asia), 1997.

Chang Chao-liang, Qing-rong Cao, and Bao-zhen Li. *Vegetables as Medicine,* Kuranda, Australia: The Rams Skull Press, 1989.

Chang, K. C., ed. *Food in Chinese Culture*. New Haven: Yale University Press, 1977.

Cheng, F. T. *Musings of a Chinese Gourmet*. London: Hutchinson, 1954.

Chiang, Cecilia Sun Yun. *The Mandarin Way*. Boston: Little, Brown, 1974.

Chinn, Thomas W. *Bridging the Pacific: San Francisco Chinatown and Its People*. San Francisco: Chinese Historical Society of America, 1989.

Dahlen, Martha. *A Cook's Guide to Chinese Vegetables*. Hong Kong: The Guidebook Company, 1995.

Davidson, Alan. *The Penguin Companion to Food*. New York: Penguin Books, 1999.

Hom, Ken. *Chinese Technique*. New York: Simon & Schuster, 1981.

———. *The Taste of China*. London: Pavillion Books, 1996.

Hu, William C. *Chinese New Year: Fact & Folklore*. Ann Arbor, Michigan: Ars Ceramica, 1991.

Huang, H. T. *Fermentations and Food Science*. Pt. 5 of vol. 6, *Biology and Biological Technology,* in *Science and Civilisation in China*, by Joseph Needham. Cambridge: Cambridge University Press, 2000.

Lin, Florence. *Florence Lin's Chinese Regional Cookbook*. New York: Hawthorne Books, 1975.

———. *Florence Lin's Complete Book of Chinese Noodles, Dumplings and Breads*. New York: William Morrow, 1986.

McGee, Harold. *The Curious Cook*. New York: Farrar, Straus & Giroux, 1990.

———. *On Food and Cooking*. New York: Charles Scribner's Sons, 1984.

Newman, Jacqueline M. "Chopsticks and Woks." *Flavor & Fortune* 10, no. 2 (summer 2003): 11, 12, 14.

Spier, Robert F. G. "Food Habits of Nineteenth-Century California Chinese." *California History Quarterly* 37 (1958): 79–84.

Tropp, Barbara. *The Modern Art of Chinese Cooking*. New York: William Morrow, 1982.

Wegars, Priscilla. "The Ah Hee Diggings: Final Report of Archaeological Investigations at OR-GR-16, the Granite, Oregon 'Chinese Walls' site, 1992 through 1994." *University of Idaho Anthropological Reports,* no. 97. Moscow: University of Idaho, 1995.

Yan, Martin. *A Simple Guide to Chinese Ingredients*. Foster City, CA.: Yan Can Cook, 1994.

Young, Grace. *The Wisdom of the Chinese Kitchen*. New York: Simon & Schuster, 1999.

(Page references in *italics* refer to illustrations.)

Index

dried shrimp, 223, 226
    Cantonese Stuffed Tofu, Henry Hugh's, *177*, 178–79
    Winnie Hon's XO Sauce, 214–15
dried tangerine peel, *223*, 226
    Cantonese Steamed Chicken, Ray Lee's, 202, *203*
Drumettes, Ginger, with Oyster Sauce, Auntie Bertha's, 162, *171*
Drumsticks with Caramelized Onions, Cousin Sylvia's, 161
dry Chinese staples, 223
Dry-Fried Sichuan String Beans, Virginia Yee's, *158*, 160–61
drying:
    vegetables, 9, 63
    woks, 56
dry measure equivalencies, 229
dumpling(s):
    Chive, Spring Moon, *207*, 208
    Dough, 206
    Dough Chive Variation, 208
    Jiao-zi, Amy Tan's Family's (recipe), 194–95
    jioa-zi, 190–95, *191*, *193*
    Scallop Siu Mai Spring Moon, *204*, 208–9
    Shrimp, Spring Moon, 206, *207*

E
Eagle Kitchen Supply, Inc. (Boston, Mass.), 230
edamame, 221
    Shanghai-Style Snow Cabbage and, Mary Chau's, *134*, 135
egg(s):
    Chiu Chow–Style Pork Spring Moon, *80*, 81
    Farm-Style Omelets, Liang Nian Xiu's, 180, *180–81*
    Fried Rice with Ham, Scallions and, 120–21
    Long Beans with, Summer, Susan Lin's, 140
    Mandarin Fried Rice, Ming Tsai's, 121
    Smoked Chicken and, Florence Lin's, *154*, 156–57
    Water Chestnut and Pork Omelets, Che Chung Ng's, 164–65
egg noodles, fresh, 225
    see also lo mein
eggplant, Chinese or Asian, 221
    Spicy Garlic, 144
    Stir-Fried Fish and, Mrs. Miu's, *112*, 114–15
    Tofu, Mushrooms, and Sun-Dried Tomatoes, Susanna Foo's, 143
eight treasured tastes, 151–215
    boiling and poaching, 194–97
    braising, 172–89
    deep-frying, 210–15
    pan-frying, 160–65
    smoking, 156–57
    steaming, 198–209
electric ranges, cooking in wok on, 4, 36, 38–39, 40, 41, 64, 152–55, 211
electric woks, 39

F
family-style menus, seasonal, 219
family wok-a-thon, 166–71
Farm-Style Omelets, Liang Nian Xiu's, 180, *180–81*
fermented bean curd, *see* wet bean curd
fermented black beans, 221, 223
    Braised Spareribs and Asparagus, Cousin Doreen's, 174
    Crabs with Black Bean Sauce, Danny Chan's, *109*, 110

Pork and Cucumber, Helen Chen's, *82–83*, 83
    Stir-Fried Chicken and Shallots, 68–69
    Tofu with Black Bean Sauce, Cousin Judy's, *169*, 174–75
fire-iron woks, 24, 28
fire rings (wok rings), 39
fish and shellfish:
    Clams in Bean Sauce with Chilies, Stir-Fried, Lee Wan Ching's, *103*, 104
    Crabs, Ginger and Scallion, Danny Chan's, 184, *185*
    Crabs and Rice Cakes, Shanghai-Style, Tina Yao Lu's, *150*, 182
    Crabs with Black Bean Sauce, Danny Chan's, *109*, 110
    Fish, New Year's Poached, Bernadette Chan's, 196
    Fish, Steamed, Classic Spring Moon, 209
    Fish and Eggplant, Stir-Fried, Mrs. Miu's, *112*, 114–15
    Fish Slices with Chrysanthemum, Mandarin, CCTI, 110–11, *113*
    Oysters, Ginger and Scallion, Lichee Garden, 160
    Salmon with Lemon, Steamed, Danny Chan's, 202
    Scallop Crisp Spring Moon, 210
    Scallops, Stir-Fried Peppers with, Ken Hom's, 105
    Scallop Siu Mai Spring Moon, *204*, 208–9
    Scallops with Asparagus, Che Chung Ng's, 115
    Sea Bass, Pan-Fried, Uncle Lang's, 162
    Shrimp, Chili, Millie Chan's, 105
    Shrimp, Shanghai-Style, Jean Yueh's, 106, *107*
    Shrimp, Sizzling Pepper and Salt, Lee Wan Ching's, *102*, 104
    Shrimp and Pine Nuts Shang Palace, 114, *116*
    Shrimp Dumplings Spring Moon, 206, *207*
    Shrimp with Garlic Sauce, Stir-Fried, 106
    Squid, Singapore-Style, Julie Tay's, *108*, 111
    stir-frying, 102–15
    Striped Bass, Smoked, 157
Five-Flavored Boneless Pork Chops, Mandarin, Martin Yan's, 188
five-layer woks, 7, 39, *140*
five-spice powder, 221
    Mandarin Five-Flavored Boneless Pork Chops, Martin Yan's, 188
five-spice tofu (spiced tofu), 227, 228
    Shanghai-Style Snow Cabbage and Edamame, Mary Chau's, *134*, 135
Flamtech Appliance, Inc. (New York City), 230
flat-bottomed woks, 6, 36, 37, 38–39, 40, *40*, 50, 62, 64, 198, 211
flat dried rice noodles (rice sticks), 223, 225
    with Mushrooms and Ham, Mama's, *122*, 123
Foo, Susanna, 79
    Mango Chicken, 78, *79*
    Tofu, Eggplant, Mushrooms, and Sun-Dried Tomatoes, 143
Foshan, Guangdong province, China, *xiii*, 14–15, *15*
fried rice:
    Aromatic Vegetarian, 123
    with Ham, Egg, and Scallions, 120–21
    Mandarin, Ming Tsai's, 121
Fung, Sun Yui, *viii*
    see also Uncle Sam
fuzzy melon, 222, *222*
    with Dried Scallops, Mama's, *176*, 178

G
gao choy, see Chinese chive(s)
Gao Tian village, Guangxi province, China, *xii*, 5, 20–23, *22*, *23*
garlic:
    Chicken with Sugar Snaps and, 75
    Eggplant, Spicy, 144
    Gold and Silver, Luffa with, Nevin Lim's, *200*, 201
    Lettuce, Stir-Fried, 139
    Sauce, Stir-Fried Shrimp with, 106
gas ranges, stabilizing woks on, 39, 40, 41
Genghis Khan Beef, Martin Yan's, 91
ginger, 9
    Drumettes with Oyster Sauce, Auntie Bertha's, 162, *171*
    fresh, 222
    juice, making, 9
    Pickled, Chicken with Pineapple, Green Pepper and, Mrs. Miu's, 71
    Sauce, Chinese Broccoli with, Lee Wan Ching's, 140, *141*
    Sauce, Tangy, Jin Do's, 195
    and Scallion Crabs, Danny Chan's, 184, *185*
    and Scallion Lo Mein, 124–25
    and Scallion Oysters Lichee Garden, 160
    seasoning wok with, 46
gingko nuts, 222, 227
    Asparagus with Wolfberries and, Cecilia Chiang's, 146, *149*
glass noodles, *see* cellophane noodles
Graham Street outdoor market (Hong Kong), *72*, 204
grease buildup in kitchen, combating, 55
green beans, *see* beans
green bean thread, *see* cellophane noodles
Guangdong wok, 34, 36
    see also Cantonese–style wok
Guangxi province, China, *xii*, 5, 15–24, *16–25*
guo, 60

H
ham:
    Fried Rice with Egg, Scallions and, 120–21
    Fuzzy Melon with Dried Scallops, Mama's, *176*, 178
    Noodles with Mushrooms and, Mama's, *122*, 123
    Smithfield or Virginia, 226, *227*
hand-hammered woks, *2–3*, 6, 20–23, *22*, 24–28, *26*, *27*, *30–31*, *33*, *35*, 36, 38, *41*
Han dynasty, 24, 33, 34, 198
Hawaii, Chinese immigrants in, 126
hearth stoves, traditional, 7, 12, 20, *20*, 23–24, *25*, 28, 34–36, *58–59*, 152, 180
Hee, Dickson, *124*
    Oyster Lo Mein, 124, *127*
herbs:
    sources for, 230
    see also specific herbs
Hicks, Tom, 52
hoisin sauce, 222, *224*
    Chinese Barbecued Pork, 173
    Genghis Khan Beef, Martin Yan's, 91
    Sichuan Beef, Cousin Zane's, 95
Hom, Ken, 37, 52, 60, 63, 100
    Stir-Fried Peppers with Scallops, 105
Home-Style Chicken and Vegetables, Uncle Sherman's, 69, *69*
Hon, Winnie:
    Silken Tofu with XO Sauce, 201
    XO Sauce, 214–15
Hong Hop Noodle Company (New York), 124, *124*, *127*

Index